Footsore 4

Walks & Hikes Around Puget Sound

Second
Edition

By Harvey and Penny Manning/Photographs
by Vicky Spring
Maps by Gary Rands/The Mountaineers •
Seattle

*White River • Carbon River • Puyallup River •
Nisqually River • Southern Frontier • Whulge
Trail • Islands in the South Sound • Kitsap
Peninsula • South Olympic Peninsula*

THE MOUNTAINEERS

Organized 1906

To explore and study the mountains, forests, and watercourses of the
  Northwest;
To gather into permanent form the history and traditions of this region;
To preserve by the encouragement of protective legislation or otherwise the
  natural beauty of Northwest America;
To make explorations into these regions in fulfillment of the above purposes;
To encourage a spirit of good fellowship among all lovers of outdoor life.

4 3 2 1 0
5 4 3 2 1

Published by The Mountaineers
306 2nd Ave. West, Seattle WA 98119

First edition April 1979, revised September 1983
Second Edition 1990

Manufactured in the United States of America
Book design by Marge Mueller
Book layout by Nick Gregoric

Cover photo: *A small estuary off Hood Canal. Olympic Mountains in the distance*

Title photo: *The author, Harvey Manning, after 3,000 miles of walking for the*
Footsore *series*

All photos by Kirkendall/Spring except for the following: pages 8, 11, 17, 25, 34, 59,
83, 146, 205 by Bob and Ira Spring; pages 21 and 31 by John Spring

Library of Congress Cataloging-in-Publication Data
(Revised for volume 4)

Manning, Harvey.
  Footsore : walks & hikes around Puget Sound.

  Includes indexes.
  1. Hiking—Washington (State—Puget Sound Region) —Guidebooks. 2. Puget
Sound Region (Wash.) —Description and travel—Guide-books. I. Title.
GV199.42.W22P835 1982   917.97'79   82-2100
ISBN 0-89886-156-X (v. 1)
ISBN 0-89886-167-5 (v. 4)

INTRODUCTION 4

Footsore is a single book in four volumes and it would be wasteful of the publisher's space and the reader's time to repeat all the introductory information in each book.

Introduction 3 to *Footsore 3* presents a tidy little manual on how beaches come to be where and what they are and on tricks of the tides and waves a beachwalker should know. These apply in the South Sound as well as in the North Sound and the rest of Whulge.

Introduction 2 to *Footsore 2* describes the operation of a commercial tree farm and explains how to be a reasonably contented walker there. The information for the Weyerhaeuser lands on the White and Mashel and Nisqually is the same as for the Weyerhaeuser lands on the Snoqualmie: Heaven help us.

Introduction 1 to *Footsore 1* is basic and indispensable to all the volumes. The data-coding system is explained, the Two-Hour Rule, and the Ten Essentials. Another matter it treats is fundamental to *Footsore* walking: the rules for getting along peaceably on those private lands (notably tree farms) where the owners have a "pass-through" policy, otherwise known as "tolerated trespassing." Other fundamentals, found in *Footsore 1*'s introduction to the Whulge Trail, are the Trespasser's Code and a treatise on the law of the beach. The treatise explains why it is that owners of beachfront who have bought the adjoining tidelands are convinced they own the beaches, and why they are wrong. *However*, the treatise commands the reader not to argue the point of law on the beaches, to go away if told to do so. The courts will be years adjudicating the point—when at last it comes to court—and meanwhile it is these here guidebook writers who are going to get all the threatening letters on legal letterhead.

To expand: please, dear reader, never ever confront a ruffled property owner with the statement, "The book says we can walk here!" This book always insists that even if the beaches are not really and fully "private," the walker must not go upon them unless the "owners" fail to object. Please read *Footsore 1*'s introductions and take them to heart and keep both yourself and us out of trouble.

A final time the reminder: much *Footsore* country is in such flux that a guidebook cannot give a moneyback guarantee. This volume was fully surveyed—every route described was *walked*—in 1977-1978. A front-to-back revision in the fall and early winter of 1987 checked every trailhead, threw out trips that had been trashed beyond easy redemption, walked all the new routes and all the old that needed it, and embodied current information supplied by trustworthy native guides. The text is candid when for any reason, such as the Drought of 1987 and the resulting fire closure up to the start of snow closure, an area was not walked or rewalked. (Another reason sometimes was sheer lack of financial ability. The older surveyor longed to walk, again, the shore of Hood Canal from the Great Bend to Bangor but couldn't afford the luxury. Not to disillusion walkers chained to desks and longing for a wilder freer life with no loss of material riches, guidebook writers do it less for the money than the love.)

Should you find a situation not as we describe, check the date on the copyright page. If it says 1989 and you are there in 1999—shame on *you*. If we expend all this love on new editions, the least you can do is buy them all. (But please *do* complain, anyhow—your cards and letters are a welcome help.)

Maps

What Introduction 4 will do that the others don't is bring you up to date on maps.

For civilized terrain the sketch maps in these pages suffice. In primitive regions they should be supplemented by U.S. Geological Survey maps, obtainable locally from map and hiking shops or by mail (write for a free state index map) from:

INTRODUCTION

Branch of Distribution, Central Region
U.S. Geological Survey
Box 25286, Denver Federal Center
Denver, Colorado 80225

The maps noted in the chapter introductions are in the 1:24,000 (7-$\frac{1}{2}$-minute) and 1:62,500 (15-minute) series that between them cover all *Footsore* country.

The new 1:100,000 sheets encompass larger areas and are useful for overview, yet have a surprising amount of fine detail. The Bellingham, Port Townsend, Seattle, Tacoma, Skykomish, and Snoqualmie Pass quadrangles are published. Also at this scale are the county maps.

The old 1:250,000 series covers even larger areas for even broader overviews but with minimal detail. The *Footsore* sheets are Victoria, Wenatchee, Seattle, Yakima, and Hoquiam.

Valuable variants of the USGS 15-minute sheets are published privately in the Green Trails series. Some GS information is deleted to improve clarity, other information is added. A hiker does well to carry both: the Green Trails for current status of roads and trails (updated every 2 years), the GS original for certain excised information (such as old logging roads) crucial to some *Footsore* routes.

Essential to the contentment of a *Footsore* pilgrim is a map of his entire world permitting ready identification of all visible works of God and man. *Puget Sound Country: A View From the Northwest*, a pictorial overview map drawn and published by Richard Pargeter and sold at map and hiking shops and many bookstores (as are the others), confines itself to the vicinity of the true and veritable Puget Sound, and thus is comprehensive for *Footsore 4* and *1* and some of *2*.

Puget Sound Region: Washington, a pictorial landform map by Dee Molenaar, covers all lands from the Cascades to the Olympics, Canada to Chehalis—precisely the *Footsore* world. In fact, it was produced specifically because the older author here nagged the cartographer-artist there for about ten years.

The Pic-Tour maps by Robert Kinzebach, aerial photos with roads and trails and routes overprinted, are the equivalent of a guidebook.

Finally, a hiker can do a lot to keep up on changes in terrain and trails by subscribing to *Signpost*, which in the past 20 years has become recognized as *the* journal about trail conditions and trail politics. It is now the official journal of the Washington Trails Association, leader in the campaign to win justice for the pedestrian in a wheel-crazy world. For information on joining and subscribing, write Washington Trails Association, 1305 Fourth Avenue, Suite 518, Seattle, WA 98101.

Harvey and Penny Manning
Cougar Mountain

CONTENTS 4

CONTENTS

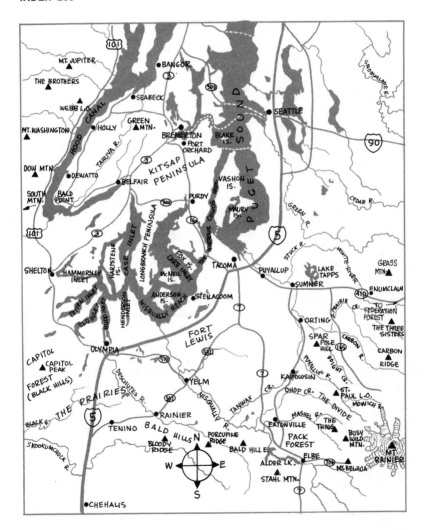

WHITE RIVER

Something scary here. Arriving on the lower White utterly ignorant of the region, a perceptive visitor quickly—and nervously—would note the difference between this river and those to the north. The black sands, the black and red boulders. That's lava rock. There's a volcano upstream. And the murky water, the wide gravel bed with an interweaving of channels old and new. That's rock milk and channel-braiding. There's a glacier upstream. A dangerous combination, a glacier and a volcano.

Indeed. Tell it to The People who were peacefully going about their business 5800 years ago when the steam bomb exploded 30 miles away on The Mountain, melting thousands of tons of snow and ice, sending down the valley to Puget Sound a roaring slurry of muck, perhaps 2.5 billion cubic yards of it. The Osceola Mudflow. Leaving in the lowlands a deposit up to 70 feet thick. A once-in-a-dozen-millennia rarity? No. Rainier has spewed countless such "lahars"; just 600 years ago the Electron Mudflow rumbled down the Puyallup to saltwater. Come the next big show and real estate in Enumclaw, Buckley, Kent, Auburn, Sumner, and Puyallup—all of whose sites were buried by the Osceola—won't be worth a nickel.

If man has performed no single so dramatic a stunt of river manipulation, he's puttered for decades, tinkering this way and that with the White. Long ago the farmers got sick of the river's habit of periodically swapping outlets, sometimes flowing north in the Big Valley to join the Green and empty into Seattle's Elliott Bay, sometimes south in the Big Valley to the Puyallup and Tacoma's Commencement Bay. After it switched from the Green to the Puyallup during a winter flood in 1906, they called in the engineers to build dikes to fix it in a southward course. At the point of diversion, where it exits from the narrower (true) White Valley into the Big Valley, the river changes name, golly knows why, to the Stuck.

After a disastrous flood of the 1930s wreaked havoc in the Big Valley and demonstrated the shortcomings of Commencement Bay for industrial development, the Mud Mountain Dam was built above Enumclaw; the river is no longer permitted to flood and on occasion is reservoirized upstream from the dam, whose fate in the next Osceola is a subject of amused speculation by Luddites.

Last, in 1911 Puget Power devised a scheme to put the White to work, at Buckley diverting water through a flume to a reservoir, Lake Tapps, thence into turbines at Deiringer and a return to the White (Stuck) in the Big Valley. As a consequence, when everybody is cooking supper and taking a shower and watching TV and making aluminum all at once, the White-Stuck between Buckley and Deiringer dwindles to the minimum legally required for the comfort and convenience of fish.

The White thus is a tame and useful river—until the next Osceola. But it doesn't feel tame. None of these tinkerings diminish its excitement for the hiker. Expecially the one who keeps an ear cocked, alert for dull distant booms up that-a-way.

The lowest segment of the province, the Stuck River in the Big Valley, was but cursorily surveyed for this book. Miles and miles of gravel mining and boxes in a row were disheartening. Yet the dikes, open all winter, close to the city, are popular with locals and ought not be ignored.

The detailed survey began at Pacific (south Auburn), on the edge of the Big Valley at the mouth of the White Valley—and discovered a wonder. Here at virtual sea level, hikable all year, on Metro bus lines in southern neighborhoods of Puget Sound City, is wildness. For 15-odd miles upstream the plain elevated above the river canyon is thoroughly civilized; down in the canyon, on alluvial terraces and gravel bars beneath steep bluffs, are river and woods and solitude, a finger of wilderness thrusting far out from The Mountain into the city.

As the northernmost of Rainier's great rivers, the White is the shortest route for the most people to the national park. But the park is full-up all summer with folks from

White River Valley from Snoquera Palisades Trail

Iowa and Japan and mucked-up by snow the rest of the year. Moreover, it's a long drive for a day hike. Outside the park, along the White, are many nice walks closer to home, lonesomer, and in many cases open all year.

A majority of the trips in this chapter are on the White River Tree Farm (and Tree Mine) of the Weyerhaeuser Company. On the north side of the valley is a continuous ridge which as it moves east is successively called Boise Ridge, Grass Mountain, Huckleberry Mountain, and Dalles Ridge. On the south side are outer buttresses of Rainier and the tributary valleys of the Clearwater, West Fork White, and Huckleberry Creek. In this intensively exploited country, where plantations range in date from the 1930s to a few minutes ago and the clearcutting is proceeding now to elevations above 4000 feet, are hundreds of miles of superb, little-driven footroads. Down low, hikable except in dead winter, are green tunnels in tall second-growth forests. Higher are excellent snowline-probers in younger trees. Highest are top-of-the-world, freshly scalped ridges with views from here to forever, always dominated by the immense white heap.

Walking along logging roads has a special appeal. When the gates are closed to the public, as is mainly the case for the hikes described here, the roads are quiet (no motorcycles allowed) and lonesome, because—to be frank—the appeal is lost on the average hiker, who can't look at a stump without mourning the tree. The introduction to *Footsore 2* discusses in detail "How to Learn to Stop Worrying and Love Clearcuts." Once a person has done so, he can be very peaceful and happy on the ridges above the White. Buy the appropriate USGS, Green Trails, and Kinzebach maps. Write Weyerhaeuser, Box W, Snoqualmie, WA 98065, for a free map of the hundreds of miles of roads on the White River Tree Farm, and there you go.

The firmest fan of the big sky, the naked hills, the panoramas, now and then hungers to see what trees older than 20-40 years look like. For that, there are Federation Forest State Park and the Mather Memorial Strip, truly religious experiences.

USGS maps: Lake Tapps, Auburn, Sumner, Buckley, Enumclaw, Cumberland, Greenwater, Lester

White River State Park (map—page 13)

The abrupt contrast is flabbergasting. This way, downstream, the "Stuck" River, flowing south through the Big Valley in a neatly diked channel, between rows of houses and fields of cows. The other way, upstream, the White River, issuing from a wildland where braided channels migrate back and forth across a floodplain confined between tanglewood cliffs. Here, several minutes' walk from houses of Auburn and from a Metro bus stop, a person might be in Mt. Rainier National Park. In fact, the White River wildland corridor extends with scarcely a break from Auburn to the glaciers.

Land for the White River State Park has been acquired. Development began in 1988. The opening is scheduled for 1989. A campground will be provided. A ¼-mile trail will be built along the river. Beyond that, details are sketchy at this writing. One thing is clear: in the previous edition of this book the area was classified as "never on Sunday" and described as "garbage-scabby." State Parks will be cleaning up the garbage and clearing out the wheels. This is to be *foot country*. State Parks be praised.

From Auburn drive south on Auburn Way toward Buckley. Exit onto R Street and continue about 1 mile to the bridge over the Stuck-White River. Turn left on the road signed for the state park (signs will go up in 1989; in 1988 it was not signed except for "Feature Farms Inc."). The park entrance will be at some point along this road, elevation 100 feet. The in-park road will go an unknown distance to the trailhead. You won't be able to miss it. You won't be able to miss the river, and that's your route.

The White River above White River State Park

The river is diked for a considerable distance; in the era of the motorcycle hell the older surveyor walked 3 miles from the bridge on the dike-road one afternoon and found it good. Then the local hoodlums were let out of the daytime detention center and he fled. The dike itself has a volcanic interest, being composed of columnar basalt. The river, of course, is the best route, on bars of black sand and boulders of black andesite and red andesite. Exactly as in the national park, one feels the close presence of volcano and glaciers, one remembers the Osceola Mudflow. The volume of water in the river at any given time is determined partly by rainfall and snowmelt, but also by how much water Puget Power is diverting into Lake (Reservoir) Tapps to serve the Deiringer powerhouse. Often the river has barely enough water to float the fish, as the state Department of Fisheries is wont to complain. But one sunny day in 1976 the river was "turned on" without notice and two children were drowned in their front yard. Puget Power is very very careful about this, but human error happens; watch out for unannounced "walls of water."

The walker soon leaves the wide-open spaces of the Big Valley, passes the portal bluffs, and enters the more cloistered and much-jungled true White Valley. Ducks swim, fish jump, kingfishers dive. There is no real end to the walk. In low water (when the glaciers aren't melting and all the TV sets are turned on) the river is a safe and easy wade from side to side, back and forth. Follow a bar until it pinches out, wade a channel to another bar. Above the Puget Power diversion intake you'll have to cut that out, of course, but by then you're almost to Mud Mountain Dam. (See White River Bottom.)

Round trip 2-8 miles or more, allow 1-5 hours or more
High point 200 feet, elevation gain 100 feet
All year
Bus: Metro 150 south from Auburn on R Street to 29 Street, walk 8 blocks to
**   the bridge**

Game Farm Park (map—page 13)

Across the river from White River State Park is another park, another entry to the wild White Valley. State Parks had a hand in this one, too, purchasing a game farm where the state Wildlife (formerly Game) Department used to raise Chinese pheasants and the like to be turned out in the fields to try a diet of birdshot. The area was turned over to Auburn Parks Department, which is developing a complex of bawfields. But there will be paths, too. The one that matters leads to the banks of the river.

From Auburn drive south on Auburn Way toward Buckley. Exit onto R Street and between 29 and 31 Streets turn into the park. (Gates open from sunrise to sunset.) Drive to the far end of the parking area, between the amphitheater on the left and restrooms on the right. Elevation, 100 feet.

Walk straight ahead the short way to the river and the closed-to-public-vehicles dike-road. Turn upstream. Try to figure out where the White used to turn north up the Big Valley to join the Green River. In 1/4 mile reach the bluff and enter the true White Valley. In another 1/4 mile the dike ends and so do the wheels and the fun begins. From here the way is strictly on river bars, along the toe of the wildwood bluff, and where it is vertical cliffs of clay, gravel, and till, perhaps up to the knees in the river. Some problems may not be soluble by conservative hikers—or in high water by any sane hikers. How far to go? The way was surveyed a dozen miles upstream (see White River Bottom)—some of it doubtless too strenuous for most tastes. About 1-2 miles probably are sufficient entertainment for a Sunday afternoon.

Round trip 1-4 miles or more, allow 1-4 hours or more
High point 200 feet, elevation gain 100 feet
All year
Bus: Metro 150 south from Auburn on R Street to 29 Street, walk 8 blocks to the bridge

White River Bottom (map—page 13)

One would never guess, driving through farms on the Osceola Mudflow plain, that a stone's throw distant, down the 125-250-foot bluffs at the edge of the plain is a river bottom where the human presence is virtually unfelt. Old and very old woods roads wander this way and that, and fishermen's paths seek riverbanks, and gypos cut alder and river-rafted cedar logs, and here and there are small pastures and glimpses of houses on the brink of the bluff. But most of the time, down there in the broad bottom up to 1 mile wide, amid braided, shifting channels, marshy sloughs, tanglewoods, and beaver ponds, one could imagine the year to be 1850—or 1650.

Getting down to the river through the belt of residential land along the rim of the bluff may require a bit of poking about. For the access used on the surveys of 1977, 1981, and 1987, drive Highway 164, the Auburn-Enumclaw Road, to 4 miles west of Enumclaw and turn south on 196 Avenue SE to the bluff edge, where the road bends east and is signed SE 456 Way. In a scant 2 miles from Highway 164 spot a mucky road (signed "No Dumping") that drops abruptly westward from the rim. (If you hit 212 Avenue SE, you've gone a bit too far east; back up.) In a street machine, park here, elevation 640 feet.

Otherwise (that is, in a beetle), drive carefully down the bluff to the bottom, to a Y. The left fork, upstream, was surveyed only a short distance but seemed to promise all manner of interesting explorations. The right fork proceeds downstream, goes out to the river and eventually leaves motorcycles behind and becomes trail, brush, gravel, and etcetera.

The route beyond here cannot be described usefully; the maze of paths would only be made the more confusing and the river keeps changing all the time so that gravel bars are now dry, now underwater. However, even an inexperienced hiker can find

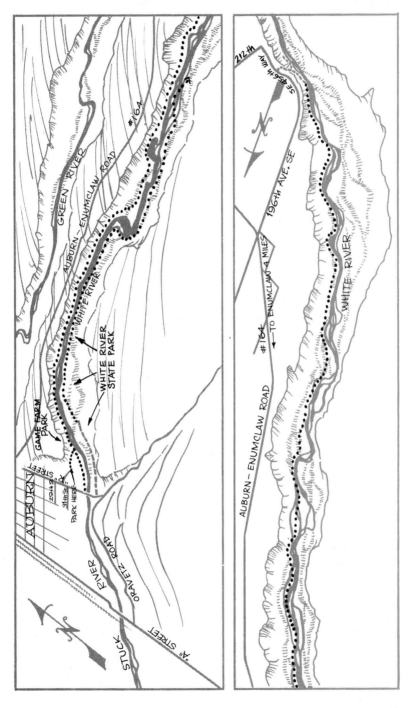

machine-free solitude by carefully picking a way on woods roads, paths, and gravel, now near the bluff, now near the river, now far from both. A fine encounter with the river comes in 1 long mile from the star. In another 4 or so miles (not streamflow or crowfly but footplod) the river cuts the base of a gravel-clay bluff, possible to skirt at low water but one of many logical turnabouts for a hike. The survey continued downstream to Game Farm Park (which see), constantly rewarding but complicated by brush and barb wire.

Round trip 2-10 miles, allow 2-8 hours
High point 640 feet, elevation gain 400 feet
All year

Mount Pete County Park (map—page 15)

What accounts for the "Enumclaw Blobs," the miniature mountains pimpling the pastured plain? The Canadian glacier and its Big River explain their existence. Hearts of hard basalt explain their steepness. The Osceola Mudflow provided the surrounding flatness. What accounts for the survival on the biggest of the blobs, Mount Pete, of a grand stand of virgin forest, a veritable wildland arboretum? Well, in 1979 the state DNR proposed to log it, and one would have thought from the instant uproar the proposal was to install Golden Arches in the Garden of Eden. Somebody loves ol' Pete. Lots of bodies. And they know how to yell. By 1988 they were heard in the King County Courthouse; the County Council was proceeding with plans to trade lands with the DNR, Weyerhaeuser, and a smaller owner and create Mt. Pete County Park.

Aha! Will it be "Pete"? The tin ears of local folks have introduced a variation, "Peak." "Mount Peak"—*indeed*. Further, some stolid geographer has persuaded the official maps to call it "Pinnacle Peak." What have all these people got against the fellow the blob was named for—Pete? Of the formerly famous Pete's Pool? In 1986 another name was put forth by the Washington State Senate—"Mt. Frances"—to honor former Representative Frances C. North. Golly knows her labors to create the Mt. Si Conservation Area and protect other natural habitats richly deserve commemoration. But again, what about poor old Pete?

Drive Highway 410 to the eastern outskirts of Enumclaw and at the Enumclaw Park swimming pool (formerly Pete's Pool) turn south on 284 Avenue SE. Follow it 1.5 miles and turn west (right) on SE 472. In 0.5 mile, at a sharp bend right, park on the shoulder by the obvious trailhead, elevation 770 feet.

The trail is very steep and can be slippery but is wide and well beaten. At Christmas of 1983 the Great Enumclaw Hurricane destroyed a portion of the trail with a mudslide 75 feet wide and 450 feet long. However, the Outdoor Bound class of Enumclaw High School has built a detour and regularly maintains the entire trail. Beginning in lush undergrowth of a moist, mixed, second-growth forest with at least four varieties of ferns and lots of frogs, the way quickly ascends to startling big Douglas firs, up to 4 feet thick, plus a full assortment of other good green things suitable for a virgin forest. In 3/4 mile the path joins the old road built to serve the lookout tower, removed in the mid-1960s. Now narrowed to a trail, in 1/4 mile the road, after passing the finest of many displays of columnar basalt, curves around to an end close under the summit, 1801 feet.

With the tower gone and the trees a-growing, the panorama ain't the 360-degree circle of yore nor even the 200 degrees of this book's previous edition. Essentially there is—in 1988—no view. King County Parks may be expected to open windows to provide looks at beautiful downtown Enumclaw and other points west, and vistas from the Issaquah Alps to McDonald, Boise Ridge, Grass—and Rainier, with the Clearwater River valley and Three Sisters prominent. And a voyeur's view down to cows and chickens at the foot of the peak. In mind's eye one can see the Osceola Mudflow surging down the White River valley, dividing to sweep around both sides of

Baldy and Pete and overwhelm camps of The People. (Is the racial memory responsible for the name, "Enumclaw," which means "place of the evil spirits"?)

Round trip 2 miles, allow 3 hours
High point 1801 feet, elevation gain 1030 feet
All year

Baldy Hill (map—page 15)

Baldy Hill didn't make the previous edition of this book and may not make the next, but until King County Parks rips some of the excess greenery off the summit of Mt. Pete, it will be the place to go for views of Osceola Mudflow country.

Drive Highway 410 east from Enumclaw to the Weyerhaeuser millpond. Just before the log-haul bridge crossing the highway, look right for a road marked by a rusty yellow rail-car water tank. Park here or on the wide shoulder beside the millpond, elevation 1020 feet.

Walk from the water tank on the gated road that bends acutely northeast between the highway and a clearcut. Shortly the road enters woods for a very nice and flat 1/2 mile to a powerline crossing. Just beyond is a fork. Switchback left, returning to the powerline and ascend steeply, near a small creek, into views straight down to the mill. In a scant 1/4 mile from the start of the steepness is an intersection. Go left in the clearcut, the views growing, a scant 1/2 mile to a prominent rocky point just below the summit of the clearcut knob of Baldy Hill's east summit, 1580 feet. (As of 1988 the higher west summit, 1664 feet, has thick trees and no road-trail; that, of course, will change in time.)

A brief scramble up logging slash leads to a grassy knob, lovely for picnicking but with minimally better views. From the rocky point or the meadow, these extend over the Enumclaw Plain to Whulge and Olympics and the other way to Boise Ridge, Grass Mountain, Three Sisters.

Round trip 2 1/2 miles, allow 1 1/2 hours
High Point 1500 feet, elevation gain 500 feet
All year

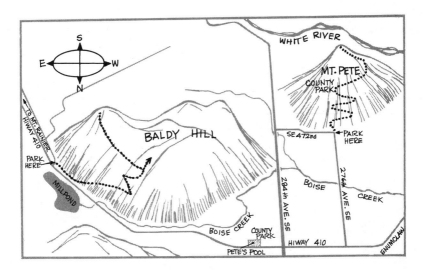

Boise Ridge (map—page 18)

Atop the abrupt—indeed, cliff-topped—scarp of Boise Ridge are airplane-wing looks down to Enumclaw and farms around, naught but Tacoma murk to block views over the plain to Puget Sound and the Olympics.

That's the good news. The bad news is that since the previous edition of this book the virgin forest of the summit trail has been logged and the sole route lies in clearcut on road. It is a popular road, and thus the trip can be recommended for walking only in the off-season, such as the wheel-stopping snowbanks of early spring and the misery weather of late fall. However, the last part of the road will freak out many cars and drivers, and that's why it rates description as a walk.

The middling news is that this is Weyerhaeuser land, subject to the company's policy on road closures. As of 1988 the policy is this: Many gates are permanently closed to the public. Most are open to the public *weekends only*, and only from the start of the lowland lakes fishing season to the end of the hunting season. (In fire season the gates may not open to the public for weeks or even—as in 1987—months.) Now, pay special attention: A person driving here on weekdays will see many gates open. But they are open for log-hauling, not public driving. To go through an open gate on a working day is to risk being strewn all over the landscape by one of the new generation of super-long, super-wide log trucks, or being arrested for trespassing by a company patrolman, or being locked in overnight, in which case you will be arrested in the morning. If in doubt about a gate, call (206) 825-8110 during business hours.

Drive to Cumberland by any of several routes. One simple way is to take Highway 169 to 4 miles south of Black Diamond and turn east on the Enumclaw-Franklin Road, following it under various names to Cumberland, there intersecting the Enumclaw-Cumberland-Kanaskat Road. On the latter road at the north edge of Cumberland turn east on SE Kuzak Road. Twisting and turning through the fascinating glacier-complicated drainages of Deep and Coal Creeks, the road goes 2.2 miles to a T with the big wide Green River Mainline. Turn right on this major log-haul road (the Weyerhaeuser mill) and proceed (going by a gate that bars the mainline to the public on weekdays *even if it is open*) 4.8 miles. Turn off left on road No. 5307. With the leisurely elevation-gaining rate of the 1902 logging railroad whose grade it follows, the broad road runs south through a young plantation to the steep scarp and its basalt walls. In 1 mile from the mainline, take care lest you plunge over the brink while gawking. Better to stop at a viewpoint and fill your eyes with hundreds of square miles from the Weyerhaeuser mill to Enumclaw to Tacoma to Seattle.

These views are lost as the road swings around the end of Boise Ridge into the valley of Boise Creek, entering the universal clearcut that soon will finish denuding the whole of Boise Ridge and, across the valley, Grass Mountain's West Peak. In wide views of naked hills and giant Rainier, the way leaves the old railroad grade behind. Sideroads go off left up the ridge and down right to the valley bottom. Continue sidehilling straight ahead, the road still good, though steeper and rougher. At 4.7 miles from the mainline is a Y, elevation 2600 feet. The mild-mannered car and driver will wish to park here. (It is not compulsory to drive even this far.)

Afoot, ascend the steep, narrow, rough, and airy road, which switchbacks left to attain the summit ridge at 2950 feet, 1/3 mile from the mild-mannered car. Look down to basalt-hearted hillocks dotting the green plain of the Osceola Mudflow, to houses and barns, cars and cows, and into the dimness where lies Tacoma, the Invisible City. On a crystalline winter day, look out to Bald Hills and Black Hills and Olympics, Lake Tapps and Vashon Island, and downtown Seattle.

The 3080-foot summit of Boise Ridge, 1/2 mile south, was still forested and viewless in late 1987. The could change any minute.

Round trip 2/3 mile, allow 1 hour
High point 2950 feet, elevation gain 350 feet
April-November weekends

Grass Mountain in a cloud

Grass Mountain—West Peak (map—page 18)

Little lower than the Main Peak (which see), the West Peak of Grass Mountain is far enough removed to be a whole different thing. It shares Rainier, of course, the monster heap of snow across the White River valley. With this it combines a broad panorama of the Puget Sound lowlands which commence just a couple miles away, below the abrupt Cascade scarp.

In the previous edition of this book, a down-low gate was usually open and the walking began up-high. That gate now is permanently closed to the public and the

WHITE RIVER

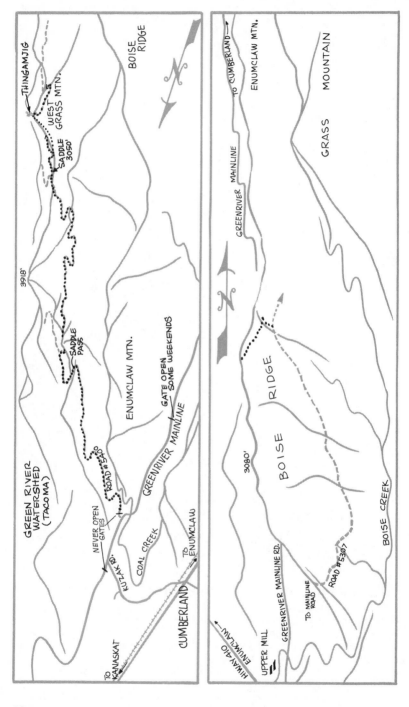

walking starts very low and a long way from the farthermost destination. However, a person need go only partway to enjoy splendid views. Further, unlike many other hikes on the Weyerhaeuser White River Tree Farm, this doesn't rely on gates being open to gain access to the "trailhead" and thus can be done any time of the week, any time of the year (except during fire closures). The closed gate means no motorcycles, no 4x4s, just hikers. Not even many logging trucks, now that the area is nearing a condition of bottom-to-top, horizon-to-horizon clearcut. Hike it blithely on a sunny Sunday. On a lonesome Tuesday. Hike it in winter on a snowline-probing walk to teach the kids how to throw snowballs. In spring to climb out of greening spring into white winter.

Drive to Cumberland and the Green River Mainline (see Boise Ridge). Turn right on the mainline, which is not gated at this point. In a few yards cross Coal Creek and park, elevation 1180 feet.

Turn left on road No. 5400, pass the gate, and steeply ascend above South Fork Coal Creek, switchbacking, avoiding lesser sideroads. At 3 miles from the mainline the road crosses a ridgecrest saddle, 2550 feet. From here it proceeds upsy-downsy in plantations of various dates from the 1960s to the 1980s and, perhaps, lingering bits of cool virgin forest with nice creeks. Views begin before the 2500-foot saddle and continue with scarcely an interruption; any number of vista points may be declared The Destination, the spot to get out the camera, the thermos jug of iced orange juice, and the Butterfingers.

However, some will feel compelled to go on. Because the Thingamajig is there. A short way from the saddle is a Y; go right, uphill, in clearcut views across the East Fork Coal Creek to the northernmost peak of Grass, 3521 feet. At a 2800-foot saddle the road crosses over to the South Fork Coal Creek side of the mountain and traverses slopes of Peak 3921, a superb bald viewpoint. As lesser roads go left and right stay straight.

At 3200 feet, just past a big view west to Enumclaw Mountain and Boise Ridge and out to Enumclaw, a shoulder of a divide spur is crossed from Coal Creek to Boise Creek drainage. Passing more sideroads, the main road now descends moderately to a long wide saddle in the main crest of Grass, bottoming at 3050 feet, 3½ miles from Saddle 2550. Charley Creek is below to the left, Boise Creek to the right, and straight ahead rises the West Peak in all its naked glory topped by an enormous Thingamajig.

Go directly across the saddle, avoiding sideroads left and right, to the foot of Grass and a Y; go right. In a few yards a sideroad switchbacks right; go straight. Dodging deadend spurs, switchback to a 3550-foot saddle in a spur ridge, the view now extending to the Main Peak.

From this saddle the service road to the summit Thingamijig takes a roundabout route. Instead, turn right up lesser roads and cat tracks that ascend the crest to the summit, a tad under 4000 feet, at 1½ miles from Saddle 3050.

Goggle at the Enormous Thingamijig; it appears to be the Bell System relay to Mars. Then look down Scatter Creek to the White River and across to the White-Clearwater-Prairie-Carbon sector of Rainier. And, of course, The Mountain. Look along the bald ridge to the Main Peak of Grass and north down Charley Creek to the Green River and out to McDonald Mountain and Cascades as distant as Baker. And look west past Boise Ridge to Enumclaw and farms and cities and smog and saltwater and Olympics.

Round trip 6 or 16 miles, allow 4 or 10 hours
High point 2550 or 4000 feet, elevation gain 1400 or 3300 feet
May-November

Mud Mountain Dam (map—page 22)

The previous edition of this book praised the U.S. Army Corps of Engineers for building, in 1976, the White River Rim Trail, described in these pages as "one of the longest and finest low-elevation walks close to Puget Sound." What we didn't know then was that the Corps had built the trail on Weyerhaeuser land with no guarantees. The rim has been logged. The trail may, or may not, be restored the full 4 miles to Scatter Creek. Being of little faith, we will not speculate on the joys to be provided by the new trail. Not for half a century will it have the forests of the old. And then it will be clearcut again. However, a bit of walking may be salvaged in the dam vicinity.

Drive Highway 410 east from Enumclaw to the sign announcing Mud Mountain Dam and turn right 2 miles. Park in the first lot, signed "Rim Trail," with a map showing what used to be. Elevation, 1300 feet.

The Rim Trail, partly on old woods roads and service roads, mainly on built path, goes along nicely a mile or so, and then runs into 1984-86 clearcut and is obliterated, destroyed, gone.

The trip, therefore, is on the rim only at the start. What you do to have a nice day is descend right on one of the two service roads, near the trail beginning and at the start of the clearcut. Go to the river—go, that is, in the non-flood season when there is a river and not a brown-water flood-control reservoir. Left to itself, the river cleans the mud from the black and red lava boulders, builds bars of black sand. A person can poke along any desired distance—in fact, to Scatter Creek and the vicinity of Mt. Philip. Carrying a pack. Camping anywhere. Freely building great big "John Muir fires," no permit required.

Round trip to river 3 miles or more, allow 2 hours or more
High point 1300 feet, elevation gain (on return) 200 feet
All year

A second little walk is worth doing while at the dam. Beyond the farthest parking area, at the sign "Vista Point," do the $1/3$-mile trail. At the top is a staggering view of the dam that was begun in 1939 and completed in 1953. It rises 425 feet above bedrock, one of the world's highest earth-core-and-rockfill dams. Built to control floods, the dam has a reservoir that, when filled, is a lake $5^{1}/2$ miles long, covering 1200 acres. But the upper portions of the reservoir area are normally not filled and most of most years there is no reservoir at all; except for a stretch above the dam the White River usually appears wild and free. At the bottom of the Vista Trail is a view that in flood time can send a person reeling.

Look across the dam to the far rim. The Corps once drew up plans for a trail over the dam and up the other side of the river, and even for a route to the top of Three Sisters 3 (which see). Someday.

Round trip to Vista $2/3$ mile, allow 1 hour

Mount Philip (map—page 24)

A company forester named this little peak for John Philip Weyerhaeuser, former president of the firm. The nice little trail the forester built was ideal for short walks and short-legged walkers, offering a sizeable reward for a small effort: a rock garden on a surprising cliff, views down to braided channels of the White River (at the upper end of the Army Engineers' ephemeral "White River Park"), the tributary valley of the Clearwater, and footings of Rainier—though The Mountain itself is hidden.

But the forester went away and no successor cared. Pieces of the sign that once pointed to the trail can be seen rotting in the forest floor. Blowdowns have obliterated much of the tread. No short legs are going to want to tackle this journey. A group of volunteers easily could reopen the trail in a day; a sturdy forester, in a morning.

Mud Mountain Dam

Drive Highway 410 east 3.4 miles from the turnoff to Mud Mountain Dam. Watch carefully for an obscure woods road making a reverse turn downvalley on the left (north) side of the highway. Park here, elevation 1450 feet.

Cross the highway and a bit upvalley look for red flagging at the forest edge and a very obscure aluminum sign, "Mt. Philip." Passing big old stumps in an alder bottom, in a short bit the path reaches a Y; go right, as suggested by a post with an arrow. Beyond here a choked forest dating from the logging in 1931 is thinning itself and in the process dropping trees over the trail. Crawl over and under. Where the trail can't be found at all, follow red-yellow flagging. Nearly to the top, find a switchback, pass a wide cat track on the right, and break out in the open atop the cliff, a dandy spot for the trail-restorers to hold their celebration picnic.

Round trip 1 mile, allow 1 hour
High point 1700 feet, elevation gain 300 feet
February-December

Stink Lake and Goodwater Railroad (map—page 24)

Two trips, one a moody walk, much of the way claustrophobic in dense young forest, the other a lazy stroll along an abandoned railroad grade, with old trestles to

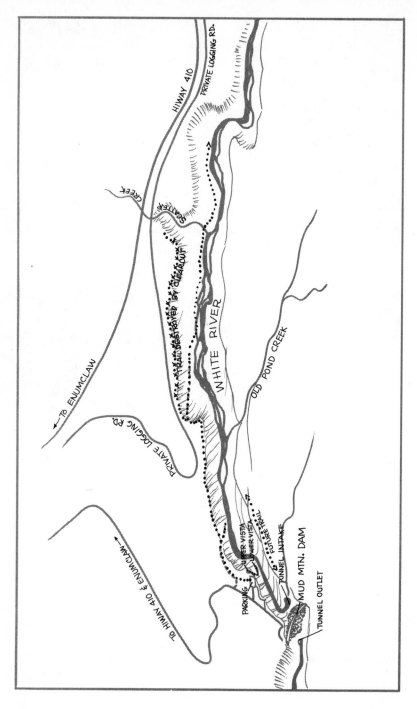

admire, waterfalls to refresh the eyes and brow, and the famous Goodwater Spring. Or make it all one trip, a loop, though the connecting link does not come with a moneyback guarantee.

Drive Highway 410 to the Mt. Philip (which see) parking area, elevation 1450 feet.

The gate on the road making the reverse turn downvalley is never open to the public, nor are any of the roads to which this connects. Thus, never a legal wheel to disturb the reverie. Also, never any worry about the Weyerhaeuser gate policy. The trailhead is freely open the week and the year around.

Stink Lake

The woods road gradually veers from the highway, passing an old railroad trestle whose stringers serve as out-in-the-middle-of-the-air nurse-logs for hemlocks. In $1/2$ mile hit a more-used road from the west; turn right (east) on it, ascending upvalley. Pass obviously lesser spurs and in another $1 1/4$ miles, after a switchback left, come to a Y; turn right on the little-used less-good road which drops to a mudhole, then ascends to cross a leftward-flowing headwater branch of Scatter Creek. The way is now up, in $1/4$ mile hitting another poor road; turn right. A bit later, at a Y, again go right, soon crossing a rightward-flowing creek and now, on the flat, following an old railroad grade northeasterly. In 1 mile from the Y, 3 miles from the highway, the "goal" is attained. Sort of. The road passes first a marshy pond littered with debris of beaver logging and then a window out to debris of human logging. By poking around in the woods one can get near—but not to—shores of the "lake," really a collection of marshy potholes in a little basin, 2300 feet. The stink apparently is from gasses of decomposing vegetation—nostrils occasionally catch a whiff of rotten eggs.

Now, for the loop link that comes and goes from year to year, depending on whether it is used or not used. Back at the beaver pond look for a boot-beaten path downhill. The way descends near the Stink Lake headwater of Clay Creek, then trends away from it, drops off a scarp into the creek valley, sidehills on an old roadbed, and at $3/4$ mile from the beaver pond hits a logging-railroad grade abandoned in 1950—one of the last such lines to operate in the state.

Round trip to Stink Lake 6 miles, allow 4 hours
High point 2300 feet, elevation gain 850 feet
March-November

Goodwater Railroad

At the parking area find an unsigned trail just before the gate, going right into the nice, cool woods and dropping a bit to the railroad grade. Watch for famed Goodwater Spring gushing from the forest floor beside the grade; even in the 1987 Drought it trickled. Locals claim the water has the best flavor in the country; but, of course, since the Great Big Giardiasis Epidemic nobody drinks water anymore.

The next big attraction is a nearly intact and splendid trestle on which the railroad bypassed an imposingly vertical lava cliff. A waterfall showers off the overhang; compare the flavor with the spring. More trestles. Then, at $2 1/4$ miles, the grade-trail comes to a clearcut of the early 1970s; until the plantation growth closes them off, there will be views of big white Rainier and the White River valley.

(Note: This is Weyerhaeuser country and the forest could be clearcut and railroad converted to a log-haul road overnight.)

Round trip 4$1/2$ miles, allow 1 hour
High point 1700 feet, elevation gain 300 feet
February-December

Loop trip 6 miles, allow 4 hours
High point 2300 feet, elevation gain 850 feet
March-November

WHITE RIVER

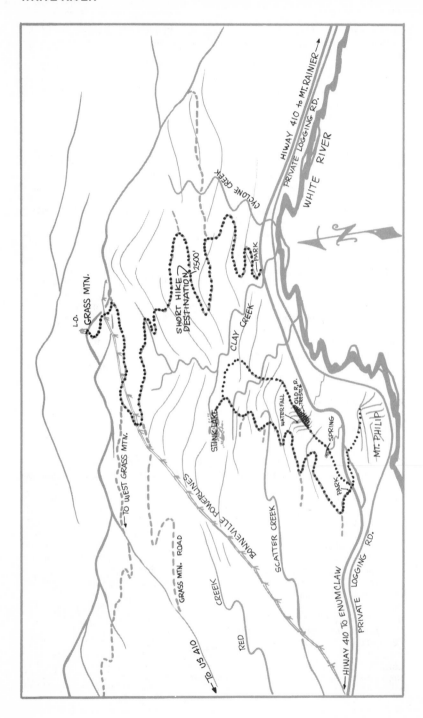

Grass Mountain—Main Peak (map—page 24)

Grass Mountain is some 15 miles long, rising from the Green River at the Cascade front and extending far into the range, for most of its length forming the north side of the White River valley. The only reason it's not longer is that a certain point, for no apparent reason, the map gets tired of Grass and starts calling the ridge Huckleberry Mountain. This much mountain obviously provides material for any number of hikes, mostly in the stark landscapes of recent clearcutting, the views beginning early and growing and growing as elevation is gained. As representative examples on the highest or Main Peak, two hikes on the same route, one low, the other high, will be described. (For another summit see Grass Mountain—West Peak.)

Drive Highway 410 east 5.9 miles from the turnoff to Mud Mountain Dam. Just after crossing Clay Creek (unsigned), espy on the left a logging road making a reverse turn and climbing to a power transformer. The gate here is always closed to the public so don't worry about the Weyerhaeuser gate policy (see Boise Ridge). Just park, elevation 1500 feet.

Because the way is open to feet at any time of week or year, it can be done when you please. A snowline-prober unmarred by snowplaying 4x4s is a splendid notion, climbing until the kids have thrown all the snowballs they want and the dogs have filled up on white candy and the snow becomes more nuisance than pleasure. Choose a delicious meltwater torrent or an especially big viewpoint and call it a lunch.

The narrow, rough, steep road ascends Clay Creek valley, at $3/4$ mile, 1900 feet, swinging under a basalt cliff to splendid views down to the highway, Stink Lake, Philip, and Rainier. Now on a flat railroad grade in second-growth from the 1930s, the road contours east 1 mile to the edge of Cyclone Creek valley. Bending left, in $1/2$ mile it comes to a Y, the right fork dropping to the creek; go left, climbing to a railroad grade that contours west at 2300 feet a scant 1 mile, then switchbacks east onto another flat grade for $1/2$ mile to a series of view windows. Here, at 2500 feet, $3^3/4$ miles from the highway, is a satisfying turnaround.

Grass Mountain after first snowfall

For a time the views get no better—rather, worse, as the slope lays back. But the top of the world awaits the long legs. Proceed from the windows across a cutbank of rotten lava rubble on a steep sidehill. The road switchbacks west and ascends to a T at 2650 feet. The right fork drops to Cyclone Creek; turn left on another railroad grade that goes on and on—and on—swinging into a number of creeklets feeding Clay Creek, each with its ghosts of old trestles. Windows open on Rainier. And now from nice young forest begin views to the scalped ridges of Grass.

Approaching a Bonneville powerline which crosses Grass from the Green to the White, out in a flat of late-1970s alder-logging on state land, pass a sideroad right to the powerline. Now climbing, pass a gravel pit and at 6½ miles, 3100 feet, meet the Grass Mountain road (see below) at a point some 10 miles from Highway 410.

Turn right on the wider road and settle down to grind out altitude. During the first ½ mile keep right at two Ys; from then on simply forge ahead, passing many obviously deadending spurs. The road starts up across the steep final slopes of the mountain, clearcut in the 1960s, the new plantation a sprinkling of shrubs, Views become continuous and overwhelming. At 4000 feet is a saddle; now there are views down to the basin in Lynn Lake and north to the Green River. The road ascends the ridgecrest, on top of the stripped-naked world, to the summit at 4382 feet, 8½ miles.

What a world! Out the White River to Enumclaw, Puget Sound, Seattle, the Olympics. Across the Forbidden Valley of the Green River to McDonald, Issaquah Alps, Si, Baker, Glacier, and beyond the Cascade Crest to Stuart. Let's see, there must be something else. Oh yes, The Mountain.

The summit is decorated by the usual batch of over-communication towers.

Why not, you ask, simply drive the Grass Mountain road, which takes off from Highway 410 at 0.4 mile from Mud Mountain Dam turnoff? Because heavy logging is in progress and the road will be firmly gated to the public until perhaps 1991. Very good.

Round trip 7½ or 17 miles, allow 5 or 11 hours
High point 2500 or 4382 feet, elevation gain 1000 or 2900 feet
February-December or May-November

Three Sisters (map—page 27)

Hikers driving toward the virgin forests and flower meadows and dazzling glaciers of Mt. Rainier may not notice, just as they leave the lowlands, a huge bulk of landscape lofting steeply above the White River. If they do, they may wish it weren't there, so they could see The Mountain. What they don't realize is that this *is* The Mountain, the outermost thrust. Another distinction is that its summit provides the most stupendous panorama anywhere of Puget Sound country and the northern hinterland of The Mountain.

The key to the trip—and to this whole enormous area of The Naked Mountain, skinned clean by loggers—is the Bridge Camp Gate. For the applicable Weyerhaeuser gate policy, see Boise Ridge. This gate is open to the public, weekends only, from fishing season start to hunting season end. But Three Sisters rise so high that the upper road is snowed in almost to summer. Spring, therefore, is the ideal time. Drive as high as practical, park, and quickly leave behind the most indefatigable of 4x4 snowplayers, not to mention the motorcycles. The creeks are large and loud, the early flowers are a yellow-and-white riot, and by the time you attain the summit you'll feel you've climbed a mountain. (You have.)

Drive Highway 410 east 5.4 miles from the turnoff to Mud Mountain Dam. Turn right on the White River Tree Farm road signed (or not) "Bridge Camp Gate." Cross the Mainline and the White River bridge to the broad flat of "Camp Junction" and at the maze of smaller roads bend right on big, wide road No. 6000. At 4 miles from the

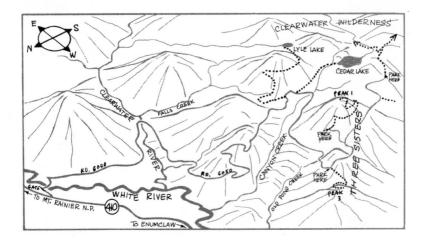

highway turn right on road No. 6050, immediately crossing the Clearwater River, elevation 1400 feet.

One of the last major railroad-logging operations in the Cascades was conducted here, ending atop the Three Sisters ridge in the 1950s. The road follows the old rail grade almost exactly; the way passes many photographable trestles. It also passes any number of superb viewpoints. Creeks. Down low, second-growth forests dating from the 1930s. Up high, clearcuts of the 1970s, only beginning (or not yet) to grow shrubs. It will occur to a person driving the road in summer and fall that any spot would be a dandy spring "trailhead," and any of the many vista points would be a splendid spring destination.

Ascending at railroad-easy grade, the road swings out around the major ridge between the Clearwater and Canyon Creek, goes endlessly upvalley along the latter, and at 8.5 miles from the Clearwater bridge crosses the Canyon Creek bridge, 3400 feet. Along the way there are great views over the White River to Grass Mountain and Enumclaw, and sideroads to Lyle and Cedar Lakes trails (not surveyed for this book—just follow the fishermen). From Canyon Creek the ridge turns downvalley and climbs to a saddle in the crest of Three Sisters ridge and a broad landing flat, 3608 feet, 11.5 miles from the Clearwater bridge.

Three Sisters 3

From the landing turn off on a narrow service road 0.3 mile to a gate and turnaround, 3680 feet. Park.

The razzer-free service road leaves the contouring railroad spur and turns up to the crest in shrubby silver firs and grassy meadows, delightfully pseudo-alpine. In 1½ miles is the summit, 3969 feet—and the obligatory radio tower. Views have been constant the whole way. For the denouement, though, push a couple hundred feet through a fringe of scrub to the bald brink of a cliff.

It's one long step down to Enumclaw. Buckley, too. And bug-infested Highway 410. The Weyerhaeuser mill. The reservoirized White River. All around is the immense second-growth wilderness of South Prairie and Canyon Creeks. And out there beyond the mountain front are the Osceola Mudflow, Lake Tapps, Big Valley, cities and towns and farms, Issaquah Alps, Whulge.

Round trip 3 miles, allow 2 hours
High point 3969 feet, elevation gain 300 feet
May-November

Mt. Rainier from Three Sisters 1

Three Sisters 1

Continue walking or driving 1 mile upward from the saddle; the steepening, roughening road rounds scrub-covered, viewless Three Sisters 2 to a second saddle, 3950 feet, and a major Y.

If the snow is deep above or the energy in the legs low, go uphill right on road No. 6050 for 1.1 miles and turn off (driving or walking) 0.4 mile downhill and flattish to a spur-end promontory, 4200 feet, a satisfying destination with a stunning view only excelled by that from the peak.

(Road No. 6050 leads to the trail to Celery Meadows and the Clearwater Wilderness. See *100 Hikes in the South Cascades and Olympics*.)

To bag the peak, go left from the 3950-foot saddle on road No. 6065 for 0.3 mile to a Y, 4100 feet. If you haven't already done so, park.

Walk the right fork, steep and rough and rarely molested by sports except in elk season (the entire ridge smells like an elk barn). In ½ mile is a Y directly under the summit; go right, crossing the south face of the peak to the far ridge, recrossing, and again, and at 1½ miles attaining the summit, 4980 feet. The familiar name, "Snagtop," comes from a fringe of charred snags; the truck-loggers who picked up where the railroad-loggers quit left a smidgeon of hard-to-get-at trees on the summit cliff and then their slash fire killed them.

The vista from Three Sisters 1 is a five-star goshamighty whambam zowie. Slashfire-blackened stumps spatter the brownish 1970s clearcuts, a vivid contrast to virgin green of Carbon Ridge, dazzling white of Rainier. Winthrop Glacier and Little Tahoma, Curtis and Liberty Ridges and Willis Wall, Ptarmigan Ridge and Echo and Observation, Mowich Face and Sunset Ridge. South over Carbon and Puyallup and Nisqually valleys, Spar Pole Hill and The Divide and Bald Hills and Black Hills. North over the White valley, Boise Ridge-Grass Mountain-Huckleberry Mountain-Dalles Ridge and high Cascades beyond, from Stuart to Chimney to Glacier to Baker. West, Tacoma and Seattle, Puget Sound and Olympics. The circuits overload. The brain explodes.

(Note: The clearcuts you see are mostly Weyerhaeuser, partly Mt. Baker-Snoqualmie National Forest. The virgin green you see is largely Clearwater Wilderness, partly Mt. Rainier National Park. You know what the white is.)

Round trip from 4100 Y 3 miles, allow 2 hours
High point 4980 feet, elevation gain 900 feet
May-November

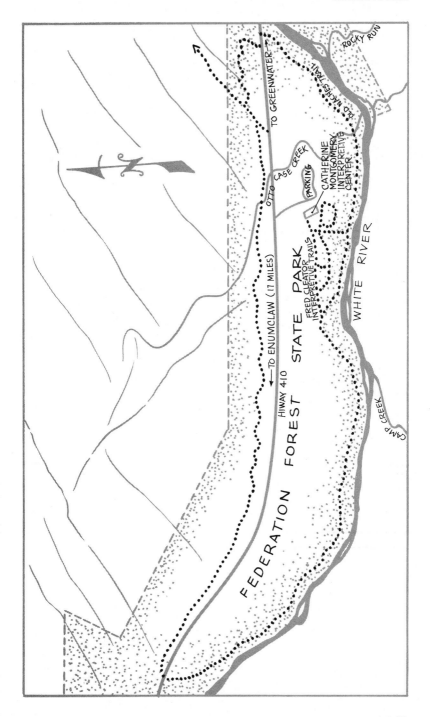

Federation Forest State Park (map—page 29)

A half-century ago leaders of the Washington State Federation of Women's Clubs realized there soon would be no low-elevation virgin forests of big trees except those protected in parks. Their efforts led to acquisition of this 612-acre preserve, part of it aptly called "Land of Giants." Plantings by the Interpretive Center, plus identifying signs of the nature trails, provide a fine classroom in which to learn the native shrubs and trees, including centuries-old Douglas fir, western red cedar, western hemlock, grand fir, Sitka spruce (uncommon this far from the ocean), yew, and more.

Drive Highway 410 east from Enumclaw 17 miles to the Interpretive Center and parking area, elevation 1650 feet. Here begin the two Fred Cleator Interpretive Trails, both loops, the West Trail just short of 1 mile, the East under $1/2$ mile. Together they introduce five distinct forest communities on a broad river terrace perched some 30 feet above the present level of the White River. Also preserved is a section of the Naches Wagon Road, or Naches Trail, over which the Longmire party came from the east in 1853.

Begin with a tour of the Center, if open; if not, study the plantings around it, all identified with tags, a living textbook. Then walk the interpretive trails, totalling some 2 miles. Then the river trail, 1 mile long, to the gravel bars of the White.

Now properly warmed up, take the loop trail (Hobbit Trail), 5 miles in length, that tours the whole park from one end to the other on both sides of the highway. Start at the Interpretive Center and follow the path as it winds along the bench with views of the White River, dips into tall trees, passes Bilbo Baggins' house (a hollow stump with windows and a door), crosses springs and marshes to the far west end of the park. Then cross to the north side of Highway 410 and loop back to the Interpretive Center.

Finally, the broad gravel swath of the glacier-fed White River is close at hand; hikers weary of ogling and gasping at forest giants and ghostly saprophytes can burst free from green twilight into bright day and wander the braided channels for miles.

Round trip 1-12 miles, allow 1-10 hours
High point 2000 feet, minor elevation gain
February-December

Snoquera Falls (map—page 33)

Along the Chinook Pass Highway on the approach to Mt. Rainier lies the Mather Memorial Strip, dedicated to the first director of the National Park Service. In the portion outside the park, in Mt. Baker-Snoqualmie National Forest, the Forest Service is pledged to preserving the visual integrity of the White River valley as seen from the highway. Thus the valley floor and walls will remain forested—and beautifully so.

In this strip, on a flat alluvial terrace, during early New Deal days was located a camp of the ERA, older-folks version of the CCC, occupying a former campsite of the 1890s trail to the Starbo Mine on slopes of Rainier. From Snoqualmie minus almie plus ERA came the names, Snoquera Creek, Falls, Palisades, Flats, and Camp Snoquera, later renamed Camp Sheppard.

The site is now leased to the Chief Seattle Council of the Scouts of America. Under direction of former Camp Ranger Max Eckenburg and support Ranger Ivan Kay, Scouts based at the camp built some 30 miles of trail, with another 20 or so miles on the master plan for their successors to complete. The system ties into both the Pacific Crest Trail and the Wonderland Trail so the camp is a base for hikes in all directions. However, coverage in this book is restricted to trails in the immediate vicinity of camp, on or near Snoquera Flats.

Drive Highway 410 east 11 miles from the hamlet of Greenwater to the sign, "Camp Sheppard," and turn left into the large, marked parking area and picnic ground, elevation 2400 feet. When closed, park on the broad highway shoulder.

Federation Forest State Park

The Snoquera Falls trip is a favorite. Big-tree virgin forests. Intimidating looks up-up-up lava precipices of The Palisades of Dalles Ridge. Views down to the White River, whose greenery completely hides the highway. May is the best time to see the falls—in that season the meltwater-swollen torrent plunges into a 30-foot-deep heap of avalanche snow, and spray clouds drench hikers. The display of icicles hundreds of feet high is worth an early-winter visit. Formerly the hike could be done as a loop but a monster slide has made the downvalley leg dangerous from both rockfall and falling hikers. So please throw away previous editions of this book.

From the east end of the parking lot the Moss Lake Nature Trail takes off toward the valley wall. In a short way it crosses an old road and in a scant ¼ mile comes to Campfire Circle in a stunning grove of forest giants. Here is the start-end of the ¾-mile nature trail loop, circling the marsh bottom of the "lake," whose amazing display of many varieties of moss usually climaxes in July.

Now, look up to the Palisades and admire your destination—up on that 500-foot near-overhang of a cliff see the thin ribbon of Snoquera Falls pluming down—or in spring see a Niagara flooding down—or at the right hour of a fall day see the mists windblown in a wavering rainbow. You must go there. Just beyond the Campfire Circle intersect a road-wide trail. Go right, signed, "Snoquera Falls Loop Trail No. 1167—Snoquera Falls 1½ miles." In ½ mile is a junction; go left, signed "Snoquera Falls 1 mile." The path ascends in glorious old forest, joy enough in its own right. But hark. What is that sound? Why does the earth tremble? What is the source of these clouds drifting through the trees? Even in season when the falls aren't falling, well may one cower, gazing up the beetling black walls. They do not have a permanent look. One imagines more substantial and fearsome falls than mere water. Such as the one that took out the other segment of the loop trail.

Round trip 3¹/₂ miles, allow 2 hours
High point 3100 feet, elevation gain 700 feet
May-November

Snoquera Palisades (map—page 33)

Having looked up-up-up the Palisades from the bottom, ascend a spooky little gorge on a giggle of a trail and look down-down-down from the top.

Drive Highway 410 east 10 miles from the hamlet of Greenwater to 1 mile short of Camp Sheppard (see Snoquera Falls). If you come to the camp entry, go back. Spot a turnout, unsigned. As one is headed toward Sheppard, the turnout is located just beyond a point where the basalt cliffs squeeze the highway to the river. The advantages of this starting point over the one in the camp are less confusion and a shorter distance. Elevation, 2350 feet.

Walk the path into the woods to the powerline and follow the line right a short way to a junction signed "White River Trail No. 1199. Dalles Creek Trail junction ³/₈ mile." Go left, into woods, ¹/₄ mile to a junction. Go left on Dalles Creek trail No. 1198, which turns uphill and parallels the dark, lush, big-tree depths of Dalles Creek ravine.

When Max and Ivan declared the Scouts were going to build a trail up this gorge, Forest Service engineers burst into hysterical laughter. And truly, it's such a place as no trail has a right to be. Under drippy black-and-green-mossy Palisades walls, by pillars and clefts in the lava, amid big cedars anchored to rock, the trail switchbacks by a short spur to Lower Dalles Falls. Now, trapped in its idiot resolve to ascend this dank dark slot, the path writhes and wiggles between fern-garden cliffs and solemn great trees, trying to escape. The route is never dangerous, though looking up and down the switchbacks may give hikers the vertigo. After some 30 switchbacks in ¹/₂ mile the trail passes the Upper Falls, most of the year a small trickle, and incredibly breaks free of the gorge onto a forest shelf above the Palisades.

Now on gentle slopes, the trail turns southerly, traverses into a nice valley of a more relaxed Dalles Creek just below another falls hiding upstream in a little canyon. One has the suspicion that vast amounts of air are close by—and at 3350 feet the way emerges from trees onto the bald brink of a promontory. Be careful! Don't run to the edge! Cautiously step out on the viewpoint, look to nearby higher Palisades in stark profile, look down to forests of the valley, up to the 5270-foot summit of Sun Top.

Continue on, leaving the brink for more forest, ascend to the edge of the little Dalles Creek canyon just passed, then switchback out near the edge of the Palisades. At the turn of another switchback take the short sidepath to Point of Springs, a thrilling viewpoint with the added embellishment of ice-cold springs. Return to the main trail and continue into a pole forest of an old burn and break out on the bald brink of North Snoquera Point, 4000 feet, 3 miles from the highway. This brink is not so giddy and invites cautious poking around in the rock garden of herbs and shrubs. Look down to Camp Sheppard, 1600 feet directly below; to leap off would seemingly risk being skewered by the camp flagpole. To previous views now are added Rainier.

Continue if you wish to a bridge over Snoquera Creek or onward to South Snoquera Point, 4800 feet.

Round trip 6 miles, allow 4 hours
High point 4000 feet, elevation gain 1650 feet
June-November

Skookum Flats (map—page 33)

Machines speed along the highway on one side of the White River. On the other side, in big old trees of Mather Memorial Strip, between the lava cliffs and river gravels, hikers can forget there are machines in the world.

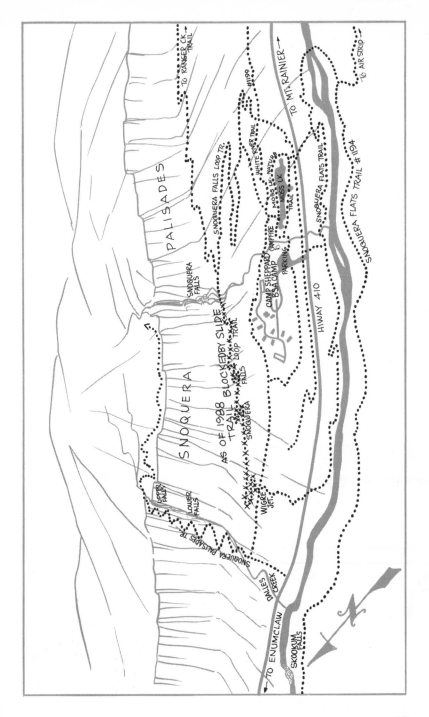

WHITE RIVER

From the 2400-foot parking lot at Camp Sheppard (see Snoquera Falls) walk toward the highway on the entry road, find a trail paralleling the highway, and follow it upvalley a scant ¼ mile. At a sign pointing right to Skookum Flat Trail and Buck Creek Trail, cross the highway, jog left a hundred feet, and take the Buck Creek trail dropping into woods to the White River trail. Follow this upstream ½ mile to a footbridge, perfectly safe but likely to give acrophobes a thrill. On the far side, 1 mile from Sheppard, is a junction with the Skookum Flat Trail.

The trail upstream makes a pleasant 1¼-mile walk to the emergency airstrip. Downstream is the choice trip, however. Except at the very end, the 4½ miles to the Huckleberry Creek road are a constant delight, now on alluvial terraces, now beside the water, always in giant forest, here and there with looks across the valley to the Snoquera Palisades. At 2¼ miles from the junction is Skookum Falls, a satisfying turnaround. But just a bit farther are Skookum Springs Seeps, from whose 300 vertical feet of mossy basalt wall water droplets fall free. In any event, to avoid breaking the spell don't go all the way to the road; at 4 miles, when Dalles Campground is spotted across the river, turn back, thus avoiding the sight of logging, of which any user of this book can see a plenty on other trips.

The constant little ups and downs hardly raise a sweat. A bit of snow is a minor obstacle on the easy route—indeed, snow adds interest, since this unmachined side of the river is an animal highway and a hiker is likely to see tracks of coyote, bobcat, deer, rabbit, and a variety of little critters, raccoon-size, mouse-size, bird-size.

Round trip to Skookum Falls 6½ miles, allow 4 hours
High point 2500 feet, elevation gain 500 feet
March-December

Hiker's bridge across the White River

CARBON RIVER

In 1881 Bailey Willis opened a tourists' horse trail to the Carbon River from the new coal-mining town of Wilkeson, and next year cut a way over the ridge to Mowich, where (or perhaps on the North Fork Puyallup) he erected the cluster of log cabins grandly called Palace Camp. Prospectors later built a spur to Mowich Lake and Spray Park; a grindstone they left at the spur junction gave it the name of Grindstone Trail. When the railroad was extended to new mines farther up the Carbon, the Bailey Willis Trail became known as the Fairfax Trail, ultimately extended through Puyallup country to the Nisqually River.

Except for bits in the national park, the old trail system—here and throughout the Carbon province—has been obliterated by logging. Hikers long ago gave it up as a lost cause and herded into the park. However, the short hiking season there, the driving distance from cities, and the boots-boots-boots marching up and down, are reviving interest in the hinterland. Its time is coming—again.

If there's any smartness left in the world, the first of the Carbon subprovinces, the river itself, is sure to become not just locally but nationally famous. From saltwater of Puget Sound to glaciers of Rainier, the proposed Carbon River Parkway, a branch of the proposed Tacoma-to-Tahoma Trail, would go from city streets to valley pastures to forested gorges to icefields. Better yet, let the Parkway be subsumed under the Foothills Trail that is highly likely to become a reality by 1993.

In the angle between the Carbon River and the White River (with its tributaries, the Clearwater River and Canyon Creek), is an enormous realm little known to walkers but immensely rich in low-to-high delights. At Wilkeson begins a long and roundabout but veritable buttress of Rainier, running from Gleason Hill to Carbon Ridge to Independence Ridge to Sluiskin Peaks to Old Desolate to Curtis Ridge to the summit icecap. The Clearwater Wilderness in Mt. Baker-Snoqualmie National Forest preserves the pristine integrity of a portion of this buttress. A Carbon Ridge Trail has been proposed to extend its full length.

On the other side of the Carbon is "Ptarmigan Ridge," so called here because it indeed is an extension of that ice-and-lava cleaver out through Tolmie and "Park Boundary Peaks" and down to Spar Pole and Microwave Hills—a continuous buttress of Rainier from summit icecap to lowland plain. The outermost segment is in the Kapowsin Tree Farm. Because the access is from the Puyallup side, that cornucopia of walking routes will be treated in the next chapter.

The opportunities hereabouts for establishing major and unusual trails are exciting. There used to be others. In 1978 the older surveyor proposed to the U.S. Forest Service that it exchange some lands and acquire some easements for a trail corridor running from a Metro bus stop in Buckley up the canyons of South Prairie Creek to what has become the Clearwater Wilderness. These slot canyons, their jungled cliffs and rapids and cataracts, were literally wilder than the interior of the North Cascades and Olympics. Forest Service officials were enthusiastic. To what end? Scenes that were praised in the previous edition of this book have been clearcut and dropped from this edition, laid upon the consciences of Forest Service and timber companies.

Look from Seattle/Tacoma to Mt. Rainier. The footings of The Mountain itself are hidden by Carbon Ridge, whose peaks are, west to east, Burnt Mountain, Old Baldy, "Old Nameless," and—highest and most prominent—the half-horn of 5933-foot Pitcher Mountain, which everybody sees and nobody has ever heard of. Much of Carbon Ridge has been put in the Clearwater Wilderness. Draining its north slopes is a stream nobody has ever heard of—South Prairie Creek. Too bad.

USGS maps: Lake Tapps, Enumclaw, Wilkeson, Buckley, Orting, Sumner

Hiking along the Carbon River

Foothills Trail (map—page 38)

Walk the Tacoma-to-Tahoma Trail from Commencement Bay up the Puyallup River to its confluence with the Carbon River. Then turn off to do the Foothills Trail along abandoned Burlington Northern (nee Northern Pacific) railroad grade from McMillin to Orting to South Prairie to Wilkeson to Carbonado, a 21-mile walking, bicycling, and horsing route. As of 1988 the Citizens Against the Trail are so vocal that the Pierce County Parks and Recreation Department is proceeding with diplomatic caution, seeking to convince residents that the trail poses no threat to the peace, quiet, and privacy of the Orting valley. The Foothill Rails to Trails Coalition, vigorously supporting the Parks Department proposal, numbers among its members virtually the complete roster of regional hiking, bicycling, and horse-riding groups, the Pierce County Council, Tahoma Audubon and the Washington Native Plants Society, Boy Scouts, and the 6000 citizens who signed petitions to the County Council. Prospects thus appear excellent. Time must pass, of course, before the trail is official; 1993 is an estimate. Please, *do not* try to open it prematurely with your feet. Parts of the route were freely walkable at the time of survey in late 1987. Others were barricaded. Others may be by the time you arrive.

The potential of the open-all-year Foothills Trail brings tears of joy to the eye of the imagination. Backpack the whole distance and then some, on a bay-to-glacier expedition. Stroll a short bit in the evening. Fish the river. Canoe or kayak. Watch the birds. Study the flowers and ferns. Poke about in the coal seams and the exposures of gorgeous Wilkeson sandstone. Enjoy the century-and-odd-decades history of coal mining, coking, quarrying, railroading. Or just have a picnic.

Pierce County Parks has not completed its plans as of this writing. The following descriptions do not reflect the official position but only the pokings-about of the surveyors as 1987 was ending.

McMillin to Orting to Crocker

The rail grade, now a gravel road, runs close by the highway from McMillin, elevation 110 feet, then veers away toward the river and remains there, in controversy country, to Crocker, 290 feet. For a partly alternative route, see Carbon River Parkway Trail.

One way 6 miles
High point 290 feet, elevation gain 180 feet
All year

Crocker to South Prairie to Cascade Junction

From Crocker the rail grade crosses the Carbon River and leaves it to ascend a sizable tributary, South Prairie Creek. (Parkway Trail sticks with the Carbon River.) For a bit the grade is beside the highway, but when that crosses the river, the trail is near and often beside the creek a while, until the highway recrosses to parallel the grade into South Prairie. In another mile is Cascade Junction, 480 feet. At a Y of rail grades, the line to Wilkeson turns right to ascend Wilkeson Creek.

At survey time the bridge over South Prairie Creek just northeast of South Prairie had partly rotted out. A bit farther along, short of Cascade Junction, the grade was barricaded by large stumps thoughtfully snarled with barb wire and signed "Private Property—Keep Out." As of 1988 it doesn't appear to be a place to have a nice day.

One way 6 miles
High point 480 feet, elevation gain 190 feet

Cascade Junction to Wilkeson

At Cascade Junction, where the main line proceeded north to Buckley, the Wilkeson-Carbonado-Fairfax branch went off right, up Wilkeson Creek. On the survey at the end of the 1970s, the branch line plunged into a daunting thicket but quickly opened out to a bridge crossing South Prairie Creek a bit above its confluence with Wilkeson Creek. Local Folks obviously came here in season to swim in the cool pool.

At 1/2 mile from the junction the line touched the bank (riprapped with—what else?— Wilkeson sandstone) of Wilkeson Creek. Here at a bend in the stream, secure from civilization in a splendid forest starring enormous cottonwoods, was a fitting spot to sit and watch spawning salmon, dippers, or whatever other traffic was on the water avenue.

The survey assault thrust some distance farther but ultimately was hurled back by nettles-salmonberries-burdock. However, the grade was intact—in fact, ties and rails were in place—and it was plain that an armed band rather easily could slash a path the 3 miles from the Fitting Spot to Johns Road, on the outskirts of Wilkeson, 780 feet.

However, due to the ticklish diplomatic situation, in 1987, the younger surveyor let this stretch alone. Especially since she couldn't get as far as Cascade Junction.

One way 5 miles
High point 780 feet, elevation gain 300 feet

CARBON RIVER

Wilkeson

In 1869, inventorying the booty heisted five years earlier in the Northern Pacific Land Grant, railroad surveyors found sandstone and coal on a tributary of the Carbon River. From the company treasurer the resulting town took its name, Wilkeson. The place reeks of history, a century and more of artifacts lurking in the bushes. And it's pretty, too. The better to enjoy the town and its surroundings, read *Carbon River Coal Country*, by Nancy Irene Hall.

Drive Highway 410 to a complicated, confusing junction at the southwest edge of Buckley. Turn south on Highway 162-165 for 1.5 miles and then follow Highway 165 as it swings left, proceeding to Wilkeson. For the full tour park near the timber arch welcoming you to town, elevation 780 feet.

Muse through the cemetery; there's another off the highway on Johns Road. Poke into sidestreets for the 19th century architecture, including the handsome building signed "Holy Trinity Orthodox Church in America 1900." At the far edge of town turn left onto Railroad Avenue, past the striking Wilkeson-sandstone school.

Where Railroad Avenue turns left over rusty tracks a sideroad goes right; park here for an alternative start. The sideroad forks; do both. The low road, left, goes by the coke ovens, beehive-like mounds of brick, their age shown by the size of the trees atop them. The high road, right, climbs a black-soiled hill one abruptly realizes was not erected by nature but rather is a 100-foot heap of waste rock; look down to Wilkeson Creek, which long ago was pushed to the side of its wide valley floor to make room for mine, railroad, and town.

The main attraction of the town nowadays is the region's largest quarry, off-limits to visitors unless prior arrangements are made. However, there is no objection to

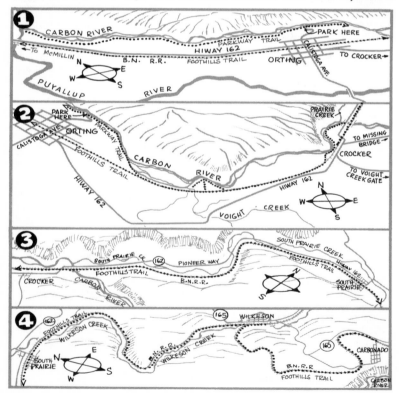

The Holy Trinity Orthodox Church in Wilkeson

walkers politely following the road of Wilkeson Cut Stone Company ¼ mile from Railroad Avenue to the fringe of the stone-cutting works. The quarry can be glimpsed, far up the hill. Overhead cables (used to) bring monster slabs down to the shed where gangsaws patiently cut into the stone at the rate of 4 inches an hour. The first use of the stone was by the railroad, for fill and riprap, widely distributed around the region. In 1883-84 the first stone was taken out for construction—of St. Luke's Episcopal Church in Tacoma. A man named Walker quarried blocks from 1911 on, taking them to Tacoma by rail for splitting. In 1915 the present plant was built, the machinery pretty much devised on the spot by self-taught engineers; with minor modifications it remains, a time-warp trip to early days of the Industrial Revolution. Until the 1920s most Seattle streets were paved with Wilkeson cobblestones. In 1982 the company went bankrupt and the quarry was closed, whether permanently or not remains to be seen.

Across Railroad Avenue from the quarry entrance a sideroad switchbacks off the main road, up the hillside, into the canyon of Wilkeson Creek; the black slope on the far side was the location of one of the several coal mines in town.

Round trip 4 miles, allow 3 hours
High point 950 feet, elevation gain 170 feet

Wilkeson to Carbonado

From Wilkeson tthe rail grade winds deviously over a minor height of land to Carbonado, 1200 feet. It was not surveyed for this guide.

For the route onward to the Carbon Glacier, see Carbon River Parkway Trail.

One way 4 miles
High point 1200 feet, elevation gain 250 feet

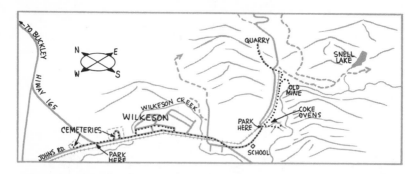

Carbon River Parkway Trail (map—page 41)

The Carbon River Parkway Trail is not a competitor of the Foothills Trail, but rather a predecessor, proposed by the first edition of this book, in 1979. The surveyors are happy to yield. However, the old idea is rather more comprehensive than the new and has features worth considering for inclusion.

The old notion was this: Here is a green-jungle, white-water lane of lonesome wildness reaching out from Mt. Rainier National Park nearly to the lowlands. The gorgeous gorge and splendid forest, the colorful rocks, both sedimentary and volcanic, the foaming cataracts, the old coal mines and coke ovens and vanished villages are at such elevation as to be open to walking the year around. What to do with them? How about a Parkway Trail? Connected to the Tacoma-to-Tahoma Trail? A continuous route from saltwater to volcano icefields, The Whulge to The Mountain?

Though the general line is the same as the Foothills Trail, the exact route is somewhat different, as well as longer.

Carbon Mouth to Orting

Pent between gravel-forest precipice and dike, the Carbon wends its final miles to the confluence with the Puyallup in green lonesomeness, the walker scarcely aware Orting is near.

Drive Highway 162 to Orting and turn north on paved Calistoga Avenue, which becomes gravel River Street. Park at the blockade, elevation 180 feet.

Walk downstream on the dike or, when available, on bars of gravel and black volcanic sand tracked by deer and ducks and raccoons. The dike is hedged by forest now and then broken by pastures. On the far side the river cuts the foot of a cliff of gravels and jungle rising as tall as 400 feet. A waterfall plumes down. On a log in the middle of the river sits a heron.

In 2³/₄ miles the dike ends and a gravel bar thrusts out to a tip between the Puyallup and Carbon Rivers, the former often yellow-green murky with rock milk while the latter is crystal clear—or, sometimes, brown with glacier mud. The presence of The Mountain is closely felt. A dandy spot for lunch.

Round trip 5¹/₂ miles, allow 2 hours
High point 180 feet, elevation gain minor
All year

Orting to Crocker

The Trail follows gravel bars, dike, and railroad grade as the route leaves the Big Valley of the Puyallup River (or, actually, of the Really Big River of Pleistocene times) for the Carbon's own cozier valley.

Park as before and walk upstream, admiring river and birds, wildwood wall, columnar basalt of the dike, and bullet-pocked concrete piers of some old mystery.

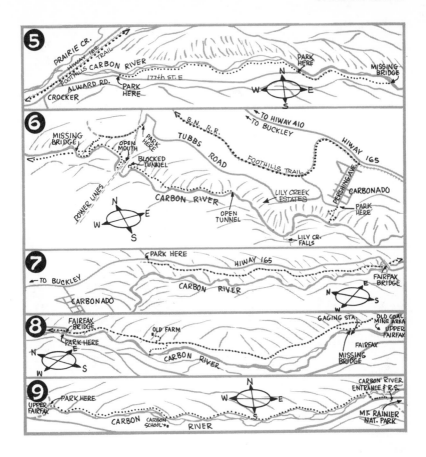

Ahead rise Microwave and Spar Pole Hills and, farther along, the Park Boundary Peaks and Rainier itself.

In ³/₄ mile an easy-around stock fence halts razzers; footpath continues ¹/₄ mile to the railroad. The river is joined by the alder-arched birdlane of Voight Creek.

The best part of the trip is a sidetrip. Dive off the tracks on a path through woods to river gravels. First walk the wild "island" downstream ¹/₄ mile to the junction of Voight and Carbon, then upstream ¹/₄ mile to a point where the tracks can be retained at 1¹/₂ miles from the start.

In the next 1 mile the walker is forced by river-near houses to stick to the tracks, which cut inland. But gravel bars and dikes resume for a final ¹/₂ mile to South Prairie Creek. The walk also can start here, parking by the Highway 162 and rail bridges.

Round trip 6 miles, allow 4 hours
High point 300 feet, elevation gain 120 feet

Crocker to Missing Bridge

Now begins the heart of the matter—the wild river, the solemn gorge. A little green Eden amid the clearcuts. Elf and fairy country.

From Orting drive Highway 162 south 1 mile to Crocker Grange Y and then east (left) 2 miles. Just before the railroad underpass turn east (right) on Alward Road (177

Riverside treasures of Wilkeson sandstone along the Carbon River

Street E), past a row of coke ovens. In 0.5 mile, where the road touches the river, park on the shoulder, elevation 330 feet.

In the forests live people who don't mind being occasionally wiped out; their floodplain habitations are hidden from a person walking gravels of the braided channels. The splendid stream brawls through the most exciting collection of boulders in any *Footsore* river: black and red Rainier andesite, iron-yellow Wilkeson sandstone, white granite, black coal, gray lignite chunks of petrified trees, gaudy clinkers from coke ovens, plus rusty artifacts from old towns. A scant 2 miles of ecstasy for a pretty-rocks fan leads to another contact with the road, where it ends. For a shorter walk park here, elevation 440 feet.

No houses now, because 300-foot walls of lush forest and outcropping sandstone press close to the river. And no wheels because boulders at road's end block them off. Only feet continue into the utter wildness, following the ancient railroad grade cut in the jungle slopes. Fern-hung rock ribs jut into green pools. Black-sand beaches invite children to build castles and everybody to take off shoes and wade.

All too soon it's over, sob. In a scant 1 mile the rail grade runs out in the air; on the far side is the causeway-abutment of the missing bridge. So, turn back. But first descend to the abutment of quarried Wilkeson sandstone resting on an outcrop of the same rock to the large black-sand beach overhung by maples. Except for the river, quiet. Having walked the grade upstream for the sake of trees and ferns and flowers, walk the gravels downstream for the sake of boulders and dippers.

Round trip (long version) 6 miles, allow 4 hours
High point 520 feet, elevation gain 200 feet

Missing Bridge to Blocked Tunnel

Gentlefolk will want to wait until the bridge is no longer missing, the Parkway Trail is built, before doing this short stretch. But brush beasts will find beauty here, now. And solitude. And the open end of the blocked tunnel.

Drive Highway 165 to Carbonado and turn right, into and through town, on Pershing Avenue. Just past Carbonado Tavern the road (now Tubbs Road, though unsigned) bends sharp right along the canyon rim, joins another road from the right, and passes the sewage-treatment plant, swinging left and becoming narrow and gravel. At 2 miles from the tavern, where Tubbs Road crosses a wide powerline swath, turn left on the service-and-logging road to the gate. Park here, elevation 837 feet.

Or, if the gate is open, perhaps drive on. Follow the logging road as it veers rightward from the powerline and in a scant 1/2 mile reaches the canyon rim. The rail grade is 300 steep feet below. You can't miss it. No way down is dangerous if care is taken. Most, though, are mean and nasty medleys of thorns and logs and muck. The single neat way is the crest of an indistinct ridge, easily found from below (making the return a cinch) but requiring luck to find from above. The recommended procedure is to continue a couple hundred feet from where the logging road hits the rim, plunge over the brink, and look for the best. If fortune smiles, in several minutes you'll reach the grade precisely where it leaves the valley wall and strikes out across the floor on a causeway.

First walk downstream, out on the causeway to its end in rotting trestlework. Game traces lead easily to a wonderful wide gravel bar. Ah, solitude! Ah, pretty rocks and pools! Ah, dippers dipping, sandpipers peeping! Ah, salmon spawning! Ah, picnicking, wading, napping! Ah, wilderness!

Now, upstream, resolutely cheerful as a gap in the grade puts you on game paths through a creek's brambles and slop; if only the deer were taller their routes would be more satisfactory. But soon the pain is rewarded by the open end of the blocked tunnel, the interior heaped with old rail ties. By clambering over the dry-rotting jackstraw a person might explore the Stygian depths. A happier tour is along the foot of the sandstone cliff to the river and upstream on a bar. The cliff overhangs 20-odd feet at the bottom, sheltering an alcove garden of maidenhair fern and dangling shrubs. Ah, charmingness!

When the river is very low, or the walker totally insane, the cliff corner can be rounded. To what purpose? Around the corner the rail grade resumes and in 1 mile (don't expect a rose garden, but plenty of thorns) is an open tunnel 90 feet long with a 30-foot-high ceiling. On the way are lovely gravel bars that invite picnics, and edged cliffs of Wilkeson sandstone stupendously overhanging the grade. Then, Lily Creek Estates. See below. Bah, humbug.

Round trip 2¹/₂ miles, allow 3 hours
High point 837 feet, elevation gain 400 feet

Blocked Tunnel to Carbonado

The following description was written in 1978. Read it and weep:

Here is the canyon climax—the narrowest chasm, the steepest walls. And here is the busiest walking, not only trees and flowers and rocks, loud waters of the river and white ribbon of Lily Creek Falls, but coke ovens, an old mine, and railroad tunnels ....

Enough. In 1980 the canyon climax was carved into Lily Creek Estates and hikers were repulsed. Then the road slid out and hikers returned. Then, in late 1987, the surveyor found the gorge forest logged, the coke ovens and other artifacts of "Carbonado in the Canyon" expunged, and earthmoving monsters standing poised to do golly knows what awfuls.

The significance of this dead-end rail spur from Crocker is that it terminated in an entirely different coal-mining operation from that of "Carbonado on the Canyon Rim." The question now is, can anything be salvaged? Can a connector trail climb from the Blocked Tunnel to the Foothills Trail?

Abandoned railroad tunnel below Carbonado

Carbonado to Fairfax

Walk with ghosts along a wild river in a glory of a second-growth wilderness. Follow a long-abandoned railroad by a long-deserted farm in the middle of nowhere to a coal mine long swallowed by forest.

Drive Highway 165 past Carbonado 0.7 mile. Look sharp just at the far end of a wide shoulder, just before a sign, "Speed Zone Ahead, 35 mph," and spot a gated road leading to a log-haul road that utilizes the old rail grade. Park on the shoulder, elevation 1209 feet.

Walk the clearcut, then forest, on the railroad grade sliced in canyon cliffs; far below in lush forest is the river. At 2 miles the grade passes under the Fairfax Bridge (Highway 165). The walk thus far is a pleasant, peaceful stroll on a weekday.

For the shorter version, drive over the Fairfax Bridge to parking on the west side, elevation 1324 feet. Walk back across the bridge and skid down to the railroad.

The highway is across the valley, unseen and rarely heard; this is the wild side. In a few yards look to the left for a dark hole that goes down, down, down to the coal. At ¹/₄ mile is a ghost—sandstone foundations of some unguessable structure; old maps show a mine downhill here. At 1 mile the ghosts throng—above the tracks, and also below, are fields of an abandoned homestead. Ascend the hill to concrete foundations of the house. Descend to pastures on a wide alluvial terrace. Beyond lichen-hung fruit trees find a rude path dropping to the river in an enchanted spot, canyon walls plunging to pools of glacier limeade. What went wrong in Shangri La? Aside from the train quitting and the house burning down?

The farm marks the onset of perfect peace. Grassy-overgrown and often log-blocked, the rail grade goes on, but no wheels intrude the forest of big firs and spruces and maples. A few boots—yet the walking is easy enough, if slow.

The missing bridge over Carbon River

CARBON RIVER

At 2 miles from the farm, 3 from Fairfax Bridge, the grade touches the river and the route leaves the grade, here blocked by slides and washouts. Game paths on flats beside the river lead in a short bit to the trip end.

Talk about ghosts! Wander the woods and ponder the "unnatural" look of the terrain. Suddenly, from the black earth of a mountain-beaver excavation, from clinkers enwrapped in tree roots, deduce these are the outlines of coal operation. In mind's eye strip away the half-century-old forest and see rail spurs and bunkers and buildings and machinery and waste-rock dumps of the Fairfax Mine.

Follow the main rail grade to pilings and concrete and sandstone blocks pushing into the river—another missing bridge. On the other side is a stream-gaging station. And, unseen, the hamlet of Fairfax, where in olden days tourists got off the Northern Pacific train and were conducted by pack train to The Mountain.

Round trip from near Carbonado 11 miles, allow 8 hours
High point 1350 feet, elevation gain 300 feet

Round trip from Fairfax Bridge 7 miles, allow 5 hours

Fairfax to National Park

The final segment is noted mainly for completeness, since it'll not be a popular walk until the Parkway Trail is built. The ultimate route should stay on the wild side of the river, not crossing to Fairfax; at present, however, the brush is too much.

Drive Highway 165 a long 0.5 mile past the Fairfax Bridge to the Y and go left, toward the Carbon River entrance to Rainier National Park. In 3 miles, shortly after passing a couple roadside homes and the clearing where the school stood until a decade or so ago, and just after crossing Evans Creek, in a Y with no signs; go left, switchbacking downhill 0.7 mile to a valley-bottom T. The cluster of houses here is the center of Upper Fairfax. Unfortunately, the inhabitants don't take kindly to prowling strangers, even if they are harmless history nuts, so drive on, right, past a two-storey brown house that was the railroad station, and shortly cross the Carbon River. Park out of the way on a shoulder, elevation 1400 feet.

Proceed upstream from the bridge, partly on woodland paths, partly on river gravels; just here the riverbed widens out to a "valley train" of braided channels that continues to the Carbon Glacier. In 4 miles the river can be crossed on the road No. 1811 bridge to the park boundary. In some 8 more miles on park roads and trails is the terminus of the Carbon River Parkway Trail, the snout of the Carbon Glacier.

History is thick hereabouts. The railroad continued 2 miles past Upper Fairfax to the hamlet of Carbon, which then had a school and a ranger station. From there the "incline" of a logging railroad went 1500 vertical feet up the south valley wall to a logging camp. On the north valley wall, 150 feet above the river, was the enigmatic Cliff House. At various times there were several logging railroads, on both sides of the valley, and three lumber mills. Before that were the coal mines and coke ovens, still to be seen, as are the old cemetery and remains of logging camps moldering in second-growth forests. And in just about the beginning there were Bailey Willis and his trail.

Round trip to road No. 1811 bridge 8 miles, allow 7 hours
High point 1700 feet, elevation gain 300 feet
All year

South Prairie Ridge (map—page 47)

See four of Rainier's great valleys—White, Carbon, Puyallup, and Nisqually. See four large cities—Bremerton, Olympia, Tacoma, and Seattle. And glaciers and buttresses of The Mountain, and towns and farms, lakes and Puget Sound, all from a marvelous clearcut desolation.

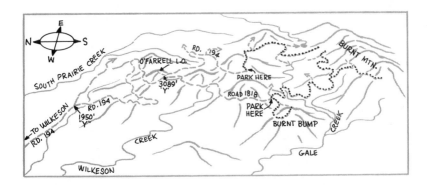

Drive from Wilkeson (which see) to the far end of town and turn left on Railroad Avenue (probably unsigned, but readily identifiable by the rusty railroad tracks) past school and quarry. Stick with the obvious main road switchbacking up from the valley to a broad plateau ridge. At 5.2 miles from Highway 165 is a Y at 1950 feet; go right on road No. 194. The road resumes climbing, making a giant switchback onto the end of South Prairie Ridge. At 4 miles from the Y pass a narrow, rough road climbing left to the now-towerless, now-viewless site of O'Farrell Lookout; a few yards beyond are a quarry and a Y at 3089 feet.

This trip comes in a whole mess of versions, including a swell snowline-prober. For that, maybe park at the 1950-foot Y and walk the 4 miles of splendid narrow footroad in 30-foot second-growth, many little creeks in season, and windows out to lowlands. Or, park at the 3089-foot Y and walk either of the forks, in steadily shorter trees, by constantly more windows.

Beyond this Y are two basic trips, left and right.

South Prairie Ridge
Go left at the Y on road No. 194, swinging around ridges and valleys, up and up, 1.5 miles to a Y at 3534 feet. Go right on 194 for 1 mile to a 3840-foot saddle in a spur ridge. Park here, if not before, because shortly the way emerges from early 1950s second-growth into a mid-1960s skinning and views become continuous.

Walk 194 as it ascends 1 scant mile to a 4050-foot saddle in the main crest of South Prairie Ridge. Off left, at 4144 feet, was Carbon Ridge Lookout, now towerless but still big-view. However, views are everywhere on the embarrassingly naked ridge, so at the Y in the saddle go right, contouring around the head of a little valley past Peak 4679 to a pass at 1 mile from the saddle. At the Y just beyond, stay left, continuing to ascend the nose of a spur. At 1/2 mile from the pass, upon rounding the nose, leave the road and turn left up the spur crest on a cat track. In a scant 1/2 mile, about 3 miles from the 3840-foot saddle, is the ridge summit, 4640 feet.

From amid the stumps of the timber-mining operation (centuries will pass before another forest regrows here) look down to ponds at the head of South Prairie Creek, over to Three Sisters, out to the White valley. To the south, hiding behind virgin-timbered Burnt Mountain, is Rainier. The big picture is in the other direction, out over the lowlands—for that, see the ravings below.

An interesting extension of the trip is onward and upward to the top of Burnt. Bits of old trail are found in the forest—and the potential can be seen of the trail once proposed to run the length of Carbon Ridge from Gleason Hill to the national park.

Round trip 6 miles, allow 4 hours
High point 4640 feet, elevation gain 800 feet
June-November

From Prairie Creek Ridge to the Osceola Mudflow (Enumclaw) plain

Burnt Bump and Gale Grandstand

Go right at the 3089-foot Y on road No. 1818 for 2.5 miles to a triple fork in a saddle at 3125 feet. Park here, if not before. Two choices.

First, take the right fork and ascend a steep, rough track, going right at a Y, and in a long ½ mile attain the scalped summit of Burnt Bump, 3360 feet. Zounds! This bump on a spur thrusting out in headwater valleys of Gale Creek is positively the best bump, the finest viewpoint, around. Rotate and see: naked brown barrens of South Prairie Ridge, virgin greens of Burnt Mountain, great white glaciers of Rainier, Gleason Hill, Carbon valley, Ptarmigan Ridge from Park Boundary Peaks to Spar Pole Hill, Puyallup valley and Ohop valley and The Divide, Mashel and Nisqually valleys, Bald Hills and Olympia and Black Hills, the full length of the Big Valley from Orting to Renton, Tacoma and Puget Sound, Olympics and Bremerton, Lake Tapps and Enumclaw and Buckley, Issaquah Alps and Seattle, Lake Washington and Elliott Bay, Three Fingers and Index.

Second, take the middle fork, rough and narrow, driven only by rare sports. Views don't get better but provide endless variations on the theme from big-sky clearcuts of the 1950s to 1970s, and there's a gaggle of lovely streams. At 2 miles is one of these; just beyond, on a shoulder at 3500 feet, is a Y. Two choices. Do both.

First, the right, which swings on around a valley ½ mile to a lovely-rushing branch of Gale Creek. Of the many spurs in this small-shrub terrain, the main one climbs past an odd marsh-bowl cirquelet and in ¾ mile from the creek ends at 3800 feet on the very end of Burnt Mountain, directly above Gleason Hill and the Carbon valley.

Second, the left, a rude track which climbs and traverses left over the creek to end on a shoulder at 3800 feet. Turn right, steeply uphill, and follow cat tracks to a higher road at 4100 feet. Turn right ¼ mile and at 4120 feet, where the road continues ahead, switchback left up to the spur crest. At the Y there, go right, to the road-end atop the spur at 4400 feet, about 1¾ miles from the triple fork. This viewpoint is just a spit below the crest of South Prairie Ridge.

Various round trips 1-11 miles, allow 1-7 hours
High points 3360 to 4440 feet, elevation gains 250 to 2000 feet
May-November

PUYALLUP RIVER

As the Puyallup is Tacoma's river, Tacoma is the Puyallup's city, and it is therefore fitting to place them together in a chapter. A second reason is that the structure of this book makes it appear Tacoma has little good walking. That is not so. But it is true that much of the city's best is in another chapter, the Whulge Trail—Commencement Bay, Bayside Trails, and Point Defiance Park.

To address the river: The White River issuing from Emmons and Winthrop Glaciers, the Carbon River from Carbon Glacier, the Mowich River from Mowich Glacier, and the Puyallup from Tahoma and Puyallup Glaciers, all flow as one into Commencement Bay, the sum of the rock-milky melt, snowfed trickles and rainfed springs, from the entire northeast and north and most of the west slopes of The Mountain. Some stream. Rainier's biggest. One wants to be respectfully humble when discussing this mighty river. Down it from the White 5800 years ago rumbled or squished the Osceola Mudflow. And down the Puyallup proper a mere 600 years ago the Electron Mudflow buried Orting under 15 feet of boulders and muck; floods devastated the rest of the valley, dumping 5 feet of mud at Sumner. Another bad day for the Indians.

The proposition presented in these pages is that there should be a Tacoma-to-Tahoma Trail, open the whole year, mostly within minutes of major neighborhoods of Puget Sound City. Extending from The Whulge to The Mountain. Of more than local or regional significance—a national trail.

Until September 1, 1987, the Trail was not practically walkable very far beyond the mountain front. Though the Kapowsin Tree Farm freely permitted hikers on its road system, the distance to Mt. Rainier National Park was too great for day hikes and camping was not allowed. However, Champion International now has taken the bold step other timber companies have pondered for years but never dared—it has expanded the product output of Kapowsin Tree Farm to encompass recreation. Champion hopes recreationists will participate in the experiment by using the land and then writing letters of criticism and suggestion.

The eastern part of the tree farm should have been put in the national park in the first place. Now would be the ideal moment to correct the mistake. The land is completely scalped, the next crop of trees is far in the future, the cost per acre never will be lower.

However, even in the present semi-nude condition and under private ownership the area has a rich potential for family camping, driving view roads, and quiet hiking in the Foot-Only Zones. To be sure, there is a fee. Other tree farms merely tolerate recreation, which is free but in the main ranges from low-grade to grim. Champion's intention is to use fee income to provide quality recreation. One way or another, the experiment must succeed. Hikers must do what they can to help.

USGS maps: Tacoma North, Tacoma South, Puyallup, Sumner, Orting, Kapowsin, Golden Lakes, Mt. Wow
Walkable all year

Tacoma and South

Most of the best Tacoma walking is on shores of the Whulge and banks of the Puyallup River. However, several trips of smaller compass have the capacity to stretch the dimensions of a pedestrian afternoon well along toward eternity.

West Hylebos Wetlands State Park Natural Area (map—page 50)

Northernmost of the eight fingers of Commencement Bay pushing into the Puyallup River delta is the Hylebos Waterway, which in fact is the dredged-out lower extremity of Hylebos Creek, a stream whose three forks and five tributaries drain the glaciated highlands between Federal Way and Milton and west Auburn. The wetlands at the headwaters of the West Fork stretch credibility just about to the limit. Not that they should have been left behind by the Pleistocene glacier, but that they should still *be here*, not industrialized, urbanized, highwayized and generally drained and paved. Various fortuitous accidents preserved them into our time. Then came Francis and Ilene Marckx to make life so uncomfortable for public officials that in the end they established—starting in 1981 with a gift of land by the Marckxes—a state park. Not that the Marckxes are content. The West Hylebos Wetlands are insufficiently protected by the 100-acre park, King County Wetland edge, and 100-foot buffer. And the East Hylebos Wetlands, on the other side of Highway 99, are twisting slowly in the wind. But the Marckx case has been abundantly made: this is a most remarkable and fascinating urban wildland, virtually untouched by human development, containing examples of virtually every sort of underwater structure, from lakes and streams and springs to marshes, floating bogs, deep sinks, and sand boils.

Drive I-5 to Exit 142B, signed "Federal Way," and go off on 348 Street. Pass three stoplights, the last at 9 Avenue S. In a long block from there turn left on 4 Avenue S, past a couple houses, to a "Parking" sign just beyond the Marlake houses on the right. Elevation, 220 feet. This is the temporary entrance, until the State Parks interpretive center is built. In the interim, please check in with the Marlakes or the people in the little house below them.

Walk down the road by the little house and orchard to the start of the 1½-mile loop trail. Do not omit the sidepath, the Trail of the Giants, featuring huge old Sitka spruce (one of the smaller trees was cored and found to date to 1662) and a sand boil, active from November to June, the dance of the grains of sand so mesmerizing that susceptible people might well go into a trance.

Look for quaking bogs with Labrador tea and kalmia and also swamp birch; big western red cedar and hemlock (only one corner of the park was logged, in the 19th century) and a recently fallen Pacific yew (an estimated 500-1000 years old), Oregon

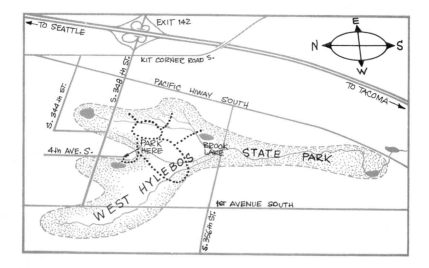

Textured bark on the "old spruce"

ash, and cottonwood; the deep sinks, supplied with a pole to let you measure the depth (17 feet!) for yourself, and giving an air to the scene by bubbling up fumes of sulphur gas. The tally of birds is 114 species, of mammals in the dozens, flowers (uncounted), shrubs (18), mosses (25), liverworts (6), lichens (18), fungi, and "unidentified aquatic forms" (is the Loch Ness Monster one of those?). All this (and more) is explained by self-guiding leaflets and hand-lettered signs.

Returned from the loop, visit the display, "Beginning Growth of Fossil-Related Trees," including the Gingko and dawn redwood formerly native to Washington; Man Lake, to see Canada geese, ringnecks, golden eyes, buffleheads, wood ducks, and nearly all local waterfowl; and the arboretum containing three of every conifer found in the state (23 in all) and a variety of rhododendrons.

Loop trip 1¹/₂ miles, allow many hours
High point 220 feet, minor elevation gain

Swan Creek Canyon (map—page 52)

A wildland's value varies inversely with the square of the distance from home. What would be merely nice in the heart of a national park is beyond price in your backyard. Thus is magnified the preciousness of Swan Creek Canyon, a refuge of green wild peace on the exact city limits of Tacoma.

Drive I-5 to Exit 135 and go off to Highway 410, following "Puyallup" signs. Well out of the interchange, 410 bends left; diverge right, past Puyallup Tribal Smoke Shop, on Pioneer Way. In 0.7 mile, just before Waller Road, note an old farm on the right and a chain-closed lane, signed "Swan Creek Trail," entry to a Tacoma-Pierce County park of 200-plus acres. Park on the wide shoulder near the gate, elevation 20 feet.

Follow the lane through pastures and orchard into woods. As the canyon is entered the roars and growls and belches and sneezes of civilization are muted, freeing the auditory scene for creek chatter and bird babble. In a scant ¹/₄ mile the way touches the creek, here flowing over a fish-ladder weir. Though the road-trail continues, cross

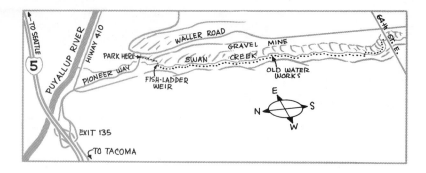

the weir to a new trail, nicely graded but defensively built to exclude the razzers who snarl and spin around the uplands but are no problem down here. (Legally that is—the park is off-limits to machines, guns, and horses. But the scofflaws are always with us.)

And so, enjoy. Now beside the gravel-rattling creek, now contouring high on the sidehill, the upsy-downsy path ascends the valley in the snug isolation of a spacious wild living room, a green grotto under arching maples and alders. The way burrows through vine maple, passes giant cedar stumps, trickling tributaries. The forest floor and understory are an arboretum—skunk cabbage and maidenhair fern, youth-on-age and ginger, devils club and elderberry—and escaped exotics to knit the brows of wildflower watchers. Historical interest is added by relics of an ancient waterworks—wire-wrapped wooden pipes, mossy concrete cisterns and a springhouse. Above the latter, Swan Creek diminishes sharply. (Additional historic interest: under an older name, "Bummer Gulch," the canyon sheltered one of the area's largest hobo jungles.)

Waterskates in Swan Creek

Early morning in Swan Creek Canyon

The creek dwindles, the canyon narrows. The forest changes from fern-hung maples to Douglas fir and hemlock and salal. At a long 2 miles the trail ends, where an old road (for pioneers' wagons?) once dipped into the canyon to cross. Hippety-hop over the creek and proceed on lesser trail a final scant ½ mile to trail's practical end where the creek flows in a culvert under 64 Street.

Despite sidetrails constantly branching off to residential neighborhoods and schools and grownover gravel mines, in all this distance not a house is to be seen and the rantings and ravings of civilization are far away.

Round trip 5 miles, allow 3 hours
High point 320 feet, elevation gain 600 feet

Chambers Creek (map—page 54)

Hard to believe, when deep within it, that Chambers Creek canyon is in the midst of a metropolis. Were it not for the sounds of traffic on the canyon wall, a person could be in pristine wilderness. "Creek" is too small a word; the stream once was called "Steilacoom River" and it supports four runs of salmon (king, coho, chum, and pink) as well as steelhead and cutthroat trout. Wildlife finds refuge—otter, muskrat, mink, raccoon, coyote, deer, bobcat, porcupine, aplodontia, and miscellaneous critters. Birds, too—136 species have been identified. Salamander, rubber boa, western fence lizard. Dragonflies and water beetles.

Primevally the river-creek emptied into the estuary of saltwater Chambers Bay; a railroad, a lumber mill, and other industry impact this lower portion of the canyon. A dam and tidegate have converted the upper portion of the bay to freshwater Chambers Lake, and though there is an arterial on the north side, the south side is a spacious, wheelfree haven. For how long? Though Pierce County Parks and Recreation, County Planning, and the state Departments of Fisheries and Game have given various sorts of statutory protection, the modern Midases who at a touch convert wildland to gold are itching to get their fingers in; the Friends of Chambers Creek, formed in 1981, is manning the barricades.

Drive I-5 to Exit 30 and go off onto 56 Street, which becomes Cirque Drive. In 3.5 miles turn left onto Bridgeport Way. In 0.7 mile turn right on Chambers Lane, which becomes Chambers Creek Road. In 1.5 miles 64 Street goes straight ahead right; turn left on Chambers Creek Road, down to the canyon bottom, across the narrow bridge over Chambers Bay-Lake. Park on the right just beyond a building signed "Chambers Creek Fish Trap." Elevation, 40 feet.

Walk back toward the bridge, a cyclone fence on your right. Go around the fence, through a gate frequently busted by razzers and midnight garbage-dumpers and as often repaired by the county or a Friend. Turn upvalley on an old logging road 400 feet to a three-way junction. The right fork climbs to homes. The middle fork is the main canyon trail. Take the left fork, the bay-lake trail, into cedar and maple forest, by huge

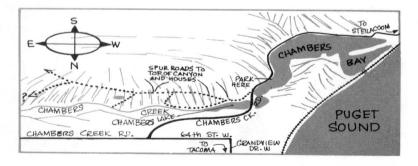

Autumn leaves carpet the Chambers Creek trail

old stumps with excellent examples of loggers' springboard notches. Go slow and quiet, binoculars at the ready for the waterfowl. Beyond the head of the lake-bay are cattail marshes. More birds.

At least two paths split off to climb to the main canyon road-trail. The second gets there in a single switchback and some brush. Proceed upvalley on the road-trail a short bit to a junction. The right climbs to homes. Stay left, passing a profusion of springs seeping from the canyon wall. Views down to the creek.

In ¼ mile from that junction is another. Take both forks, one at a time. First, sidetrip down to the creek, passing spring-fed Pontiac Pond (named for the derelict automobile on the shore) to the magnificent creek. Sit on the bank and look, and listen.

Returned to the main trail, continue up the valley in big cedars and big maples robed in fern and moss. In a scant ¼ mile the road-trail climbs to a house and an old gravel pit. Where the road-trail diverges in that direction, look down left to an overgrown path to the creek. Overgrown. But good!

Round trip 3 miles, allow 2 hours
High point 150 feet, elevation gain 110 feet

Snake Lake Nature Center (map—page 56)

Snake Lake is interesting on several counts. For one, it is not notable for snakes—the name is for the shape. Second, it is fed by a 1200-acre watershed to the north—the streets of Tacoma! Water that once filtered through swamps and marshes over weeks and months now flushes through the pipes in hours. As a consequence the lake is changing in character from open to closed—to marshes and swamps. The city uses it as a detention basin to regulate flow down Flett Creek to Chambers Creek. Third (and hurrah!), the 54-acre reserve of the Metropolitan Park District of Tacoma has been set aside as an ecological study area. "The park is not a playground. The visitor is reminded that the park belongs to the plants and animals. People are visitors in *their* space." Some 20 species of mammals, from red fox to flying squirrel to voles and shrews. Birds—more than 100 species. The surveyor's favorites were the ten pairs of wood ducks nesting at the lake.

Go off I-5 on Exit 132 to Highway 16. In 2.7 miles turn right on 19 Avenue. At Tyler Street turn right and then immediately left into Snake Lake Nature Center, elevation 300 feet.

The three self-guiding nature trails total 2 miles.

The short loop is from the parking lot to the Heron (1st) Bridge, loop trip ½ mile.

The medium loop goes down the west side of the lake to Blackbird (2nd) Bridge, crosses, and returns on the east side of the lake-swamp along the old grade of the Tacoma-Lake City Railway, built in 1890 from Old Tacoma to a resort on American Lake, way way out in the country. The route returns to Heron Bridge, where the wood ducks were hanging out, and to the parking lot. Loop trip, 1 mile.

The longest loop is the bestest, incorporating just about the whole show. It sets out down the west side of the swamp-lake, passing shelters for birders, and goes under the freeway bridge to Mallard (3rd) Bridge and Cottonwood Shelter. Next, back to Blackbird Bridge, and across and up switchbacks from wetlands habitat to forest

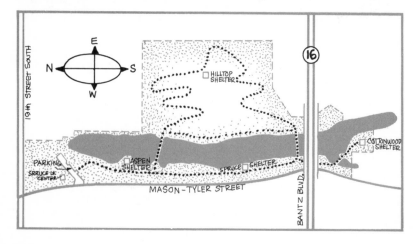

habitats, through Douglas fir, madrona, and a few Pacific dogwood (check to see how they are coping with the current Dogwood Plague). The trail tops out at 423 feet, soon after passing a kettle left behind by the glacier some 12,000 years ago. The descent passes a few Oregon white oak on the way back to Heron Bridge and the parking. Loop trip, 1³/₄ miles.

The self-guiding pamphlet explains many sites, including a bee tree, black cottonwood, cascara buckthorn, bitter cherry, poison hemlock, Goose Prairie (mowed for the Canada geese), filberts, green heron, open water in scoops dug out by peat-mining, an ancient ant hill, and the greater yellowlegs. Fun and instruction for the whole family. (But be *quiet*, children.)

Round trip, long loop, 1³/₄ miles, allow 1¹/₂ hours
High point 423 feet, elevation gain 130 feet

Tacoma-to-Tahoma Trail (map—page 61)

This was the way taken by Tolmie on his botanizing trip in 1833, the first European to walk the slopes of Rainier—or Tahoma as some think it is better called. It's a way that walkers of today can take as well, following banks of the Puyallup River from Commencement Bay by industrial plants to pastoral floodplain to forests of the mountain front, and thence via several alternatives to wilderness of the national park. Close to where people live, open the whole year, the Tacoma-to-Tahoma Trail is an idea whose time should come. But a pedestrian needn't wait—the trips described here sample the river's moods and suggest the potential. They also provide, right now, a lot of nice days.

Commencement Bay to Fife

The best grimy-industrial tour in the book, this walk over the Puyallup delta—the Port of Tacoma—is most exciting on a work day when all the satanic contraptions are bumping and grinding and honking and bellowing, infernally fascinating. Yet serenely sliding through the bustle is the quiet river, green-brown from pollution by glaciers and farms, afloat with ducks and gulls and fishermen, but not with ships because the river—or Puyallup Waterway as the final stretch is called—is rarely used for docking; this activity is confined to the half-dozen other waterways dredged in delta silt.

Drive Highway 410 to about halfway between I-5 and Puyallup. Between Mileposts 3 and 4, at 48 Street, turn north over the river on a narrow old bridge. Turn west on North Levee Road 3 miles to its end at a railroad bridge. Park here, elevation 20 feet.

Cross the railroad tracks, drop to the dike, and away you go downstream. The levee is unobstructed, the gravel road little used. In all of *Footsore* this is the premier walk for bridges, some old, some new, some supported by piers of wood or concrete, others on concrete pillars. In sequence there are: a railroad bridge, I-5 monster bridge, another railroad bridge, old Highway 99 bridge, a third rail bridge (there's a lot of good train-watching), Lincoln Avenue Bridge, a fourth rail bridge, this a swing-opener to let ships through, and finally the classic 11 Street Bridge with a tower-lift center section.

Along the way are views to downtown Tacoma on the hill above the delta. At the end are views over the bay to ships coming and going and sitting at anchor, and to the ASARCO smelter stack, Point Defiance, Vashon and Maury Islands, and the Olympics. Also at the end is the special treat, the chief entertainment—the Katzenjammer Castle of the Simpson Tacoma Kraft Company pulpmill, hissing, squealing, humming, and roaring, pouring clouds of steam from a dozen stacks and a hundred cracks in the walls—the greatest plume north of the Chehalis Steam Plant.

Round trip 5 miles, allow 3 hours
Practically no elevation gain, this and all following trips

11th Street Bridge over the Puyallup River

Fife to Puyallup

Waterway narrows to River, sedately but powerfully flowing between dikes. Industry ends and farms begin. Birds flit in riverbank brush, fowl fly and dive, fish swim. The view of Tahoma is famous.

To do the complete route, drive as before to the west end of North Levee Road. Walk back east on it, passing the first farm, and in a short bit drop to the waterside footroad, where just about any day of the year fishermen are parked, quiet and friendly. The beer cans mainly are dropped by squirrelers at night; razzers are rare in daytime.

An old tradition among Puyallup High School students was to decorate the concrete walls of the levee. The gaudy artwork was diverting; due to weathering and moss, none lasted long. However, the wall now has been architecturally modernized by the addition of a rock facing.

There's time for pondering, looking across the foreground of murky stream to the far glaciers. This is one of only three outlets of The Mountain's waters, the others being the Nisqually and Cowlitz Rivers. Here, contained in the Puyallup, are also the White, the Carbon, the Mowich, and all their tributaries.

At 5½ miles is the Highway 161 bridge, the proper turnaround. But first visit the historical marker noting the construction here by U.S. soldiers in February 1856 of Fort Maloney to protect the John Carson ferry, thought necessary after Indian attacks of the previous October. Here the Military Road from Steilacoom to Bellingham crossed the river. For more history, enter Puyallup and in ½ mile from the bridge turn left to Pioneer Park and the restored 17-room mansion of Ezra Meeker, who arrived in Puget Sound by wagon train in 1852 and platted the town in 1877.

Round trip 11 miles, allow 7 hours

Puyallup to Sumner and the White-Stuck River

The junkiest section of the route. Even when the Trail is established this part will be walked (or more likely, jogged) mainly by local folks and fanatics. However, a truly Momentous Event—a Major Confluence—is not to be missed. The downstream access originally used by the older surveyor has been totally fouled up and made essentially footproof. The upstream access was and is blocked by private homes. So, a middle choice.

In Puyallup follow East Main to the bridge over the Puyallup River. Park before crossing.

Walk the dike road ¹/₂ mile downstream, past what was a garbage dump until 1975 and by now (true, the surveyor didn't check it out this time) may be a public green space, to the Momentous Event—the confluence of the Puyallup and the White-Stuck, the two uniting downstream of a long peninsula whereon Sumner is located. Pause to ponder. And listen for loud noises upstream—a distant explosion followed in an hour or so by a sort of giant squishing sound, or however that much mud sounds when doing 50 mph.

That's pretty much the trip, though farther along may be found an enormous sandbar that invites waterside barefoot walking.

Round trip 1 mile, allow 1 hour

Puyallup River and Mt. Rainier at sunset

Morning glories on banks of the Puyallup River

The Turn

Though a walker with only as much gall as the surveyors can do every step from Sumner to Orting, touring trailer parks isn't the happiest sport. This section therefore is best sampled by short strolls from several convenient access points.

The transition is completed to a farming valley, the fields of crops and cows picturesquely framing old homes and barns. At crossroads are little old country store/ post offices. It's hard to believe Tacoma is so close. The near views are over the flat floodplain to forested walls of the Big Valley, 2 miles wide at first, narrowing to 1 mile. The far views are to Ptarmigan Ridge, the Park Boundary Peaks, and Tahoma.

From Highway 410 drive Highway 162 to the bridge over the Puyallup and park on the south side in a fishermen's lot.

A footpath drops to the riverbank slope and follows the river bend (first of three in less than 1 mile) north to a sand point jutting splendidly into the angle. The path is forced from the water by brush and enters a magical place, huge old maples arching over the greensward, a fit picnic spot for Robin Hood and his merry men. Next to the maple grove, and part of the large farm to which all this belongs, operated by Washington State University as the Puyallup Research and Extension Center, is an experimental plantation of cottonwoods in neat rows. Just short of a barb-wire fence a path turns left to the river, the stock fence easily crossed. Soon comes The Turn—an abrupt 90 degrees—and another dandy jutting sandbar. Bar-walking can be continued a bit farther, the river flowing through wildwoods on both banks, before a farmhouse halts toleration.

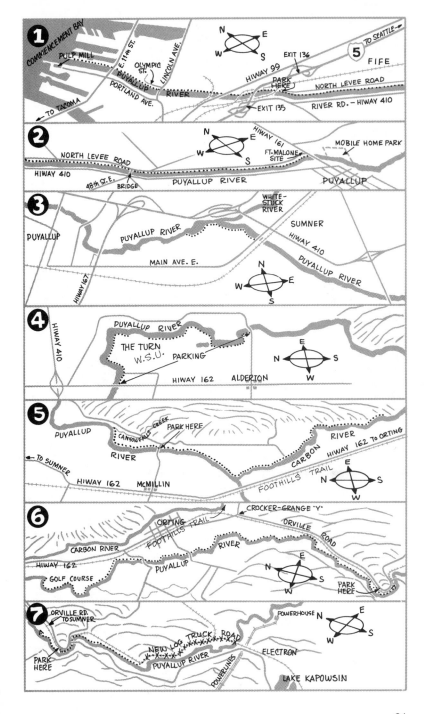

PUYALLUP RIVER

Another Momentous Event has occurred. From Sumner to Commencement Bay the Puyallup flows in a west-east valley. But here it issues from the north-south Big Valley of Pleistocene time, glacier-melt time, the valley that is continuous from Elliott Bay (and Lake Washington) to the Nisqually River, and in this part and that utilized nowadays by a flock of rivers.

Round trip 2¹/₂ miles, allow 1¹/₂ hours

Alderton
Strictly river and wildwoods, only glimpses of farms.
Drive Highway 612 to Alderton and at a "Public Fishing" sign by the post office-grocery turn east on 96 Street 0.5 mile. Just before the bridge is a large Department of Wildlife parking area.
The dike north has a public walking easement donated by Sumner Sportsmen Association. The way is green, passing a large marsh-lake abounding in birds. Subdivision and trailer park halt progress just a shout short of the previous segment.

Round trip 1¹/₂ miles, allow 1 hour

Marsh near Alderton

Fisherman in the Puyallup River

McMillin

Trailer parks and such are left behind, the river becomes purely wild-pastoral. But between the previous segment and this is a long gap—surveyed but not recommended because of brush, awkward farm fields, and dike-side houses.

Drive Highway 162 to McMillin and turn east 0.5 mile to the bridge. Cross and park on a shoulder. Note the pipeline crossing the river—in it flows the Green River to slake Tacoma's thirst. Walk upstream and downstream, but not simultaneously.

Downstream. A gated road bars razzers but permits quiet walkers to amble the lonesome dike. To the right is a slough-marshy forest that has excluded agriculture, established solitude. A wide gravel bar is being mined here; when the truck road ends a sandy trail continues to sheer poetry. Out from under arching alders Canyonfalls Creek stealthily sneaks. Birds chirp and flit in secret shadows. The sand peninsula at the mount is a grand spot to sit and eat peanut butter-and-pickle sandwiches and watch the river and the ducks.

Upstream. The dike road, boulder-blocked to halt wheels, begins with a pasture left, a great bar right. Both sides of the river are now wildwoods. At a scant 1 mile is another Momentous Event, the confluence of the Puyallup and Carbon Rivers. The

63

The Puyallup River and the dike road

walk can continue up the Carbon 1 mile to dike's end at the rearing up of the gravel-and-forest cliff (see Carbon River Parkway Trail).

(Note: The railroad grade from McMillin upstream will be the route of the Foothills Trail, which see.)

Round trip downstream 1¹/₂ miles, allow 1 hour
Round trip upstream 4 miles, allow 3 hours

Carbon River to Canyon Bridge

If cow-watching is your game, here's the Puyallup walk for you. But there are also gulls, ducks, hawks, herons, fish, golfers, and The Mountain.

Due to private roads and fences, this segment has no practical access at the downstream end, or indeed any decent put-in anywhere except at the upstream end. But that's good—difficulties forbid razzers. Drive Highway 612 southeast of Orting 1 mile and at the Crocker Grange Y turn south on Orville Road. In 3.3 miles, as road and river are partway through a horseshoe bend left into the short canyon where Orville Road bridges the river, park on a large shoulder to the left, elevation 350 feet.

Drop to the gravel lane below the road. Follow it down to a lane entering from the highway. Turn downstream on the abandoned rail grade. You're on your way. The dike just goes on and on, crossed by frequent stock fences easily circumvented, the lack of signs demonstrating a high level of toleration of pedestrian trespassers. Except for the occasional farm vehicle, wheels rarely roll the road.

At the start the Puyallup valley is canyon-narrow, soon widening to a modest floodplain, then abruptly to a mile from green wall to green wall, the veritable Big Valley. Cows moo, dogs bark, guns of Fort Lewis boom. From cottonwood forest the river emerges to farms and sorties out in the middle of the broad valley. Off east can be seen the Carbon valley and the tip of Ptarmigan Ridge, Microwave Hill and Spar Pole Hill, and—gasp—Tahoma.

Gravel bars and beaches of black volcanic sand offer alternatives to the dike. Marshes and sloughs are passed, barns and more cows, and at a scant 4 miles, the bridge of the Orting-Kapowsin Road, which due to fences is not an access.

Now, the best part. The river turns westward to the foot of the high, steep, wild-forested valley wall and at a scant 2 miles from the bridge reaches Hi Cedars Golf Club, where golfers quaintly wheel around the kempt greensward in cute buggies. For 1 long mile neat greens and fairways are on one side of the dike, the river and green-tangled wall on the other. Where Orting High students of the Class of 1941 put their numbers on a boulder (as have other classes on other boulders the entire route) is the proper turnaround. Nibble carrots and celery by the river, gazing over the green plain to The Mountain.

The Puyallup River below Electron

PUYALLUP RIVER

It is 1 more mile to the confluence with the Carbon, all but the last bit walkable, but not pleasantly due to mean-it fences and hellberries. The main attraction is the boulder of the Class of 1937.

Round trip 14 miles, allow 9 hours

Canyon Bridge to Electron
Scattered stumpranches display the last cows and barking dogs, the crops become those of the Kapowsin Tree Farm, a lonesome wildwood. Razzers continue to be foiled by lack of access, the walking is free of wheels.

The segment can only be reasonably done from the downstream end. So, park at the same spot as for the previous segment.

Walk the railroad grade upstream through the rock-walled canyon, a notable little spectacularity. Just past the bridge drop off the tracks to river sand, leap or wade Fiske Creek, and scramble onto the start of the dike. For a scant 2 miles the elevated causeway proceeds by marshy woods and stumpranch pastures, the last habitations. (On the far bank construction is madly in progress.) Sands and gravels offer alternative walking. Across the river the torrent of Kapowsin Creek gushes in.

When dike ends, clamber boulders to the rail grade, which here returns to the river after an absence and provides the rest of the route. The way joins a log-haul road and enters clearcuts. However, a fringe of fine trees has been left on the riverbank. In a long 1 mile is the crossing of Fox Creek, which cuts the base of a rock wall; beavers have dammed the small stream. The road leaves the river, whose forest invites exploration of a riverside route. In a final long $1/2$ mile the road returns to the river and crosses it—precisely where it exits from the mountain front, here consisting of the Kapowsin Scarp.

Startling the lonesome walker, at the bridge are houses. Indeed, this is Electron. But you can't get there from here—the bridge is gated and guarded. Go back where you came from.

Round trip 7 miles, allow 5 hours

Electron to the Glaciers
From the bridge it's 1 mile upstream on river gravels to Puget Power's Electron Powerhouse at the foot of Kapowsin Scarp, up which a cog railway once carried tourists to an excellent vista point beside the reservoir. This was a pretty impressive hydroelectric operation in 1904, but interest waned after Grand Coulee and the rest.

The fascinating Electron Flume enters the reservoir, often carrying most of the Puyallup River from the Headworks weir 10 miles upstream. An expedition up the flume was aborted by the umbrella weather that made the narrow plank walkway treacherous; Puget Power probably wouldn't have been too crazy about the scheme anyway.

Yet here, along the 10 miles of the Puyallup valley wall, paralleling if not actually somehow using the flume, the Tacoma-to-Tahoma Trail must ultimately run. This is the wild side of the river, steep and jungled and frequently cliffy.

For the interim, the Kapowsin Tree Farm is the way to go. From the King Creek Gate the Access Road follows the valley upstream to the confluence with the Mowich River. Sideroads lead to or near the river at a number of points.

At the confluence of the Puyallup and the Mowich begins the home stretch to Mt. Rainier National Park, in the Rushingwater Foot-Only Zone of Kapowsin Tree Farm.

Kapowsin Tree Farm

Logging began hereabouts early in the century; the spar pole atop Spar Pole Hill at the mountain front dates from around 1910. Year by year the railroads of St. Paul and Tacoma Lumber Company pushed up the Puyallup River valley, the ridge between it and the Carbon River, and the ridge between it and the Mashel and Nisqually Rivers. At a certain point St. Regis assumed the corporate responsibility and trucks took over from lokies and climbed higher and higher—incredibly, to the very boundary of Mt. Rainier National Park, into valleys and onto peaks that belonged in the park—and still do, though scalped. (Trees will grow. In a few hundred years folks never will know the loggers were here.)

The tree farm served hikers as did no other. The company adopted a policy of no public vehicles beyond the firmly closed gates. Hikers, though, were welcome. To be sure, it was a tree farm, not a wilderness, and there were no trails. But except for the very occasional company vehicle the roads were *footroads*. No pickup trucks to jangle, no motorcycles to enrage. However, due to the closed gates the hiker could not legally get very deep into the tree farm.

Then, in 1981, the last old-growth was clearcut and, in 1984, Champion International Corporation bought the 135,000-acre farm; after a lengthy study, on September 1, 1987, the company announced a bold departure in tree-farm management, giving recreation a recognized (not merely tolerated) status—the first attempt of free enterprise to manage forest lands for multiple use.

The roads were opened to public vehicles the year around, through two controlled gates. No motorcycles, no ATVs! Not even horses. But pickup truck, passenger car, bicycle, and feet, wearing boots or skis.

Not all roads were opened. Seven large chunks of land, totalling 30,000 acres, were set aside as "road-management areas"—which translates to *Foot-Only Zones*! The State Wildlife Department worked with Champion to set aside these as refuges from the roadside hunter. Fortuitously, they also serve as refuges for quiet recreationists—hikers, skiers, snowshoers. Pedestrians formerly were limited to destinations relatively near the gates; now they can drive far up the Puyallup, to the edges of the Foot-Only Zones, and walk to destinations not merely quiet but scenically magnificent.

Remember, this *is* a tree farm. But unlike some others that come to mind, it is not managed on the principle of clearcutting from horizon to horizon and then going off to Alabama for 50 years. The traveler will see forest patches of every age from a few days up to 50 years old, that being the length of the Champion rotation.

The trees are possibly becoming less valuable commodities than their symbionts, the friendly fungi. For many years "Voight Creek Gate" has been a phrase to set the blood of mushroomers a-rushing; parking space near the gate has been hard to come by when the chanterelles are in. A person willing and able to walk a few miles didn't have to compete or search, could stroll the footroads, plucking riches that came readily to hand, and staggering back to the car under a bulging rucksack. Except in the Foot-Only Zones, roadside mushrooms no longer will be found—unless you arrive early in the morning the day they bust out of the moss. But the throngs will be able to spread out over the entirety of the gigantic fungi farm. Will Champion eventually start weighing the plunder at the gate, assessing a fee of so much per pound? (If not, the commercial mushroomers will ship the booty to supermarkets and foreign lands.)

There are marshes, swamps, bogs, creeks, and rivers. The views of Rainier from valley bottoms and high ridges are stunning. Nowhere is it so tall a Mountain as from the Puyallup.

Now, the hook. Champion has taken the other step necessary to give recreation formal status. No large company in Washington state has had the nerve to try the Great Experiment—asking recreationists to pay.

Hunters have been enthusiastic. The test of hiker and family-camping acceptance will come in years ahead. Can modest-fee private lands compete with negligible-fee national parks and no-fee national forests? There are, as well, philosophical issues here that forest-land managers have been debating for years.

As of 1988-89 the daily access fee, the year around, is $10 per person/day and $7.50 for seniors. The fee for 3 consecutive days is $20 per person, $15 for seniors.

The fee for an entire 2-week to 6-week period in hunting season, September 1 to December 31, and for an entire 2-month period January 1 to August 31, is $50 per person/period.

In the fall period, children under 15 are free. In the January-August period there is a family rate (both parents and all children under 17) of $25 per family/day, $75 per family/period.

Permits cannot be obtained at the gates, only from Orting Hardware and Brooks-Kapowsin Grocery or by mail—call (206) 879-5313 or 879-5311 to request a permit order form. For current information, call Champion's toll-free recreation line: 1-800-782-1493.

Try it. See if you like it. Champion is eager to hear what you have to say. Please direct comments and suggestions to Kerry Persing, Champion, 31716 Camp 1 Road, Orting, WA 98360.

About this Survey: In the olden days of locked gates, the older surveyor walked hundreds of miles on Kapowsin footroads from Voight Creek Gate to Montezuma Gate, from King Creek Gate to Spar Pole Hill, from Ohop (Camp 1) to St. Paul Lookout and Ohop Lookout, and from Camp 2 (Mowich) Gate down to the confluence of the Puyallup and Mowich Rivers. Additionally, he sortied in from the Weyerhaeuser and national forest boundaries to The Divide and Busy Wild Mountain.

The September 1, 1987 announcement came during the fire season of the Drought that kept the gates locked tight until far into fall. When the gates were opened at last, the snow was falling. One joyously somber day the older surveyor drove-drove-drove through cloudbursts and blizzards to elevations as high as 3000 feet and turned back in the nick; the next day the ski tows were running at Snoqualmie Pass.

That day set his agenda for the next edition. His old fond favorites mainly have been dumped—nice then, but not worth $10 now. But the explorations he yearned for before now can be done quite reasonably, and some of them distinctly are worth $10.

The surveyors and Champion hope hikers will check it out and speak up. Actually, $10 isn't so much—a person can eat up that much freeze-dried shrimp before finishing the second Sierra Club cup of limeade. The map of the Kapowsin Tree Farm road system supplied on payment of the fee is essential but not to be fully trusted. As of late 1987, roads were on the land that were not on the map and road numbers on the map did not always agree with those on the signs. Carry, in addition, the appropriate USGS maps: Kapowsin, Golden Lakes, Mt. Wow, Orting, Wilkeson.

Driving From the King Creek Gate (map—page 70)

A hiker may very well wish to spend a preliminary day driving the major roads, both to find the trailheads and to soak up the many boggling views of Rainier. If and when the camping areas are improved, as promised, a family might well spend a vacation week in summer, driving each day to vistas, strolls, river-fiddlings.

From Crocker Grange Y south of Orting drive Orville Road south 3.4 miles. Just before the bridge over the Puyallup River, turn sharp left on Brooks Road 2.2 miles to King Creek Gate. Show your permit and pass through the gate onto road No. 6.

At 0.3 mile is a Y. The left is to the three lowland-edge foot-only zones; see Microwave Hill.

Go right from the Y on road No. 6 for 2.4 miles and turn right on road No. 62.

(In 0.6 mile, road No. 62 crosses King Creek, whose box canyon has long been a hikers' favorite. Humiliating to confess, the surveyor never found it; go walking with the Tacoma branch of The Mountaineers—they know where it is.)

Mt. Rainier from St. Paul Lookout

(In 10.6 miles from this junction, park at a turnout and walk the short bit to the Puyallup River. See a house on the far hillside. See a weir. See the great big Puyallup River enter an intake above the weir. See the little tiny Puyallup River exit below the weir. Where is the rest of it? In the flume, on the 10-mile-way to the Electron Powerhouse.)

A bit past the intake is a sideroad right, over the river, to Moose Junction. At 11.1 miles from road No. 6, or 13.5 miles from King Creek Gate, is a Y.

The left is road No. 5, open to wheels, giving sit-down access to some of the most smashing of all Rainier views. Look up the broad, flat-floored valley of the Mowich to the magnificent ice sweep of the Mowich Face. On the left, Tolmie and Hessong lead to Tillicum Point, Echo and Observation, the upper ramparts of Ptarmigan Ridge. On the right, Sunset Ridge (logged to within less than a mile of Golden Lakes!) is part of the panorama continuing over the Tahoma and Puyallup Glaciers to Success Cleaver. And across the Puyallup valley are logging roads and stumps of impressively naked The Divide.

As the viewer drives higher (sidetripping on spurs to more such Big Bang views), he may note waters babbling off west in the bushes. These are Voight Creek, a geological curiosity that "hangs" on the side of the ridge above the Puyallup, paralleling the latter in an "oversize" valley all the way to lowlands. The road climbs to within a very short bit of the Mowich Lake road, firmly gated at the site of Camp 2, a sprawling, famous village in the railroad-logging of the 1930s. Long before that the vicinity was the location of Grindstone Camp, where the Grindstone Trail branched off from the Bailey Willis (Fairfax) Trail and led to Mowich Lake and Spray Park.

Where road No. 5 climbs left, the straight-ahead ends in a few feet at the closed-gate bridge over the Mowich River a few feet above its confluence with the Puyallup. This is the chief trailhead of the Rushingwater Foot-Only Zone, discussed below.

The older surveyor drove here on his December 1987 tour. He recalls his sense of awe and humility and liberation, the time he walked down from Camp 2 Gate, stood at

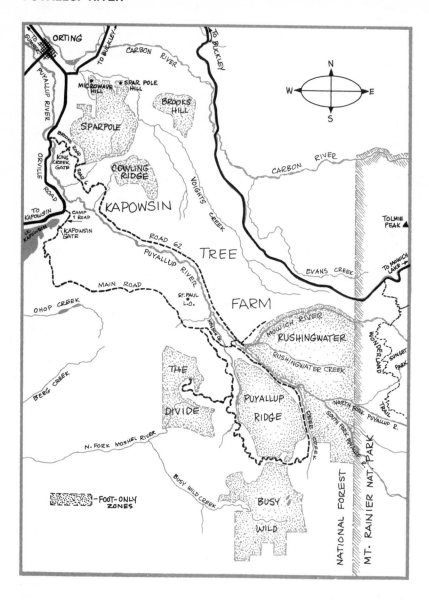

the confluence of the Mowich and Puyallup and looked up from an elevation of 1650 feet the nearly 13,000 feet of The Mountain. On that sunny day he sat with one hot foot cooling in the Puyallup, the other in the Mowich, and reflected that the national park ought to extend to here, at the least. He mused, too, how embarrassing it would be for a foot-soaker if this chanced to be the day for another Electron Mudflow.

Driving from the Kapowsin Gate

(Note: this gate may be closed from January through August, in which case access must be obtained from King Creek Gate—see the maps.)

From Crocker Grange Y south of Orting drive Orville Road south 7 miles and turn left on Camp 1 Road. In 1.6 miles is a Y. The left is to Camp 1 (Ohop); go right 0.6 mile to the Champion headquarters complex and the Kapowsin Gate.

Pass through onto the Main Road. In 3.4 miles go by Camp 1, behind a fence and a never-open gate.

At 7.1 miles road No. 0-522 goes off left to one of the neatest walks in the whole farm, St. Paul Lookout.

The best places to *feel* The Mountain are near but not too near, high but not too high, close enough so it doesn't seem a Hollywood backdrop, far enough so the immensity doesn't overpower a sense of scale. St. Paul Lookout is just right. In fact, St. Paul Lookout is one of the champion viewpoints of 13,000 feet of icefalls and lava ramparts.

The surveyor didn't rewalk the route in 1987; no need; no way to miss the way. Drive road No. 0-522 a bit, turn right on 0-520, and at a convenient spot stop driving and walk.

Windows open as the road contours a subpeak to a 2600-foot saddle and a grand view south. But tarry not, the big show is close. The road starts steeply up the final peak, passes intriguing towers of shattered lava, switchbacks twice, passes a moldering log cabin, a decrepit privy, and at 2970 feet, $3^1/_2$ miles from Main Road, gloryosky!

No matter the lookout tower is gone. The ridge prow is naked, nothing to block the view. A steep 1500 feet below is the great broad flat valley where Mowich and Puyallup Rivers and Neisson Creek join, the valley an awesome 2 miles from wall to wall. Some geological foolery has occurred; one speculates that once the Mowich flowed to lowlands alone in what is now the Puyallup valley, and the Puyallup occupied what what is now used by little Ohop Creek. Did the Electron Mudflow down these valleys have a hand in it?

The view north is to Ptarmigan Ridge, Carbon Ridge, and South Prairie Ridge, and the view south is to scalped heights of The Divide and out to Ohop Lookout and lowlands. But that's not what you came for. Sit on the prow and munch your cookies and stare, and stare, at the Mowich Face enclosed by Ptarmigan and Sunset Ridges, and at Puyallup and Tahoma Glaciers and Success Cleaver. On Klapatche Ridge between the forks of the Puyallup, see the West Side Road on the park boundary. See the logging roads that go to the very boundary, literally into alpine meadows.

The round trip is 5-6 miles; allow 3-4 hours. The high point is 2970 feet and the elevation gain is about 1200 feet. Walk it anytime from April through November.

Now, St. Paul done (or not), back on Main Road at 10.3 miles from Kapowsin Gate is a major Y. The left fork goes 2.3 miles to Moose Junction, a four-way intersection. From it one road goes 0.6 mile to the Puyallup River bridge and the access from King Creek Gate; on the way it passes the Camp 5 road up the Puyallup River and then Deer Creek, between the Rushingwater and Puyallup Ridge Foot-Only Zones, and over a saddle to join the road from Camp 7. From the junction road No. 21 proceeds to a gated entry to the Puyallup Ridge Foot-Only Zone.

From the major Y at 10.3 miles, the right fork, road No. 3, ascends to Camp 7, 2500 feet, 14.8 miles from Kapowsin Gate, and a major junction. Two of the choices presented are back down to Moose Junction and up the side of The Divide. Road No. 32 proceeds up Neisson Creek, crosses the ridge to the Deer Creek road noted above, on the way passing between the Busy Wild Foot-Only Zone and the Puyallup Ridge Foot-Only zone.

Road No. 31 ascends to the right from Camp 7. At 15.6 miles from Kapowsin Gate road No. 311 goes off left. The right continues to a locked gate at 3000 feet, 18.7 miles, and the main access to The Divide Foot-Only Zone.

Sparpole Hill, Cowling Ridge, and Brooks Hill Foot-Only Zones (map—page 70)

These are the portion of the tree farm so long cherished by hikers. At the mountain front, open all year. The locked gates give an unreal, fairy-tale quality. No, not "fairy"—*time travel*, back to the pre-suburb era when there were quiet and lonesome country roads that saw lots more feet than wheels. It simply isn't the same, walking to Spar Pole Hill from Voight Creek Gate along Fox Creek Road, family cars trundling by from King Creek Gate. The older surveyor loved that valley when it was vehicle-free. He also circled the Brooks Hill roads until thoroughly looped and loped to the site of the old Electron Lookout for old times' sake and soaked up views from the newly clearcut (second time) brink of Cowling Ridge.

But you can't go home again. For memory's sake we here subhead a walk that some folks could think worth $10. The surveyors might go as high as $5 in a snowy winter.

Microwave Hill

From the little hill that is the absolute far-out ultimate lower end of Ptarmigan Ridge, look up and up the miles and miles to the upper end on Rainier's white walls. And look down to the green valley where two of Rainier's rivers, the Puyallup and Carbon, hug opposite sides of the Big Valley, enclosing between them the seeming-toy village of Orting.

Drive from King Creek Gate 0.3 mile to a Y. Turn left 0.6 mile on Fox Creek Road (no longer signed as such) and park at the gate that keeps wheels off road No. 104, the Microwave Road. Elevation, 817 feet.

Walk the footroad through the varied stages of tree-farming terrain, passing lesser spurs. At 1 1/2 miles is a four-way intersection; go straight ahead. The microwave tower is now seen ahead, atop the hill around which the road curls. In 1 mile from the intersection are attained the 1448-foot summit and the Bell relay station.

The best view is short of the summit, at the top of a 1977 clearcut (until it grows in—there then will be other clearcuts—the views never quit in a tree farm). Below are green pastures of the Puyallup-Carbon valley, houses of Orting. North are lowlands extending to Issaquah Alps and Seattle, Olympics as backdrop. West are the vast barrens of the airstrips of McChord Field.

Since the surveyors have not been over the ground in several years, and aren't about to pay $15 to do so, they will only remind wealthy readers that there are all sorts of loopings to be done from Microwave Hill. It is no problem to get to Sparpole Hill to pay respects to the spar pole. The older surveyor recalls, on the way to the pole:

Rainier, the full length of Ptarmigan Ridge from glaciers, Mowich Face, Park Boundary Peaks, to Fox Creek. Beyond Cowling Ridge are the Puyallup valley, Adams, The Divide, and the odd Kapowsin Scarp, plus bits of Kapowsin Lake and Ohop Lake, and Nisqually valley and Bald Hills. Then, in a few steps, Rainier is lost but horizons open westward, over Microwave Hill to McChord Field and Tacoma, Black Hills and Olympics. More steps and the north widens, over Puyallup and Carbon valleys to Orting, Sumner, Seattle, Puget Sound, Prairie Ridge and Lake Tapps, Issaquah Alps, Buckley and Enumclaw beyond the White River on the Osceola Mudflow, and Boise, Grass, Pete, Three Sisters. And if you think all this is great, you ought to see the billion-twinkling light show at night.

Conceivably a hiker could get $15 worth of value here.

Round trip from Fox Creek road to Microwave Hill 5 miles, allow 3 hours
High point 1448 feet, elevation gain 700 feet
All year

North Fork Puyallup River

Rushingwater Foot-Only Zone

Here is the preserve that so titillates the hiker's imagination he can't wait to lay down his money. By far the largest of the Quiet Zones, it has three great rivers brawling from the glaciers—the Mowich and the North and South Forks of the Puyallup, offering miles of bottomland and riverbank walking. Then, there is the broad, high ridge between the Mowich and the Puyallup—two ridges, in fact, Rushingwater Creek in the middle, flowing from headwaters in Golden Lakes. To be sure, the ridges are logged— but only to the border of Mt. Rainier National Park. The park—*that* is where the Rushingwater footroads lead.

An intriguing serendipity: way back before the logging began, way back before there was a park, Bailey Willis built his Carbon River-to-Nisqually River trail through here, from Grindstone Camp (modern Camp 2) through the Mowich-Rushingwater-Puyallup valleys and ridges. His Forest Castle (a really nifty camp) probably was on the North Fork Puyallup, or possibly the Mowich. The wildland archaeologist never before has had easy access to the area; the watchful hiker may find artifacts, may pin down the exact Bailey Willis route, long lost to memory.

In the 1970s the old surveyor used to gaze upon what is now the Foot-Only Zone, then a Logger-Only Zone, and dream up trips that would start in Tacoma and conclude on the Wonderland Trail. Now it can be done, legally.

Which footroad to take? The reader's hunch is as good as the surveyor's. The next edition will report our various expeditions.

All the ridge routes start at the 1650-foot Mowich-Puyallup confluence, on road No. 7. Roads Nos. 74, 742, 75, 716, 717, 718, and 71 all terminate a stone's throw (if that) from the park boundary, at elevations of 3000 to 4900 feet. The hiker equipped with the Kapowsin Tree Farm map and the USGS maps (here, Golden Lakes and Mount Wow) can make his choice. Distances from the confluence to the park boundary are about 6-8 miles. A "jeep trail" from road No. 742 enters the park at 4800 feet and is shown on the map continuing 1/4 mile to intersect the Wonderland Trail 1 1/2 miles north of Golden Lakes, in Sunset Park. Road No. 716 ends on Rushingwater Creek at the park boundary, 4200 feet, in the lowest of the Golden Lakes basins.

Valley routes:

From the Y just short of the confluence, drive road No. 5 for 1.5 miles up the Mowich River, park at the gate on road No. 52, and walk this footroad 3 1/2 miles on valley bottom to an end by the braided channels of the river, about 1/4 mile from the park boundary, a long 1 mile from the union of the South and North Forks of the Mowich— which is where the Wonderland Trail crosses them on its way from Mowich Lake to Golden Lakes. (A loop here?)

From the confluence walk road No. 7, then No. 73, 6 miles on bottom to an end by the Mowich, again some 1/4 mile from the park. All this has been logged. But what are the virgin forests like inside the park? The river elevation here is 2400 feet. The trees must be giants. What a magical mile it must be, from boundary to Mowich forks!

From the confluence walk road No. 7, then No. 71, then No. 710 some 6 miles to near the union of the North and South Forks Puyallup. On the way pass (perhaps) the site of the Forest Castle.

From Moose Junction drive Camp 5 road some 4 miles and turn left on road No. 25, which crosses Deer Creek to a gate. Walk a long 1 mile to the vicinity of the forks of the Puyallup. Proceed 1 mile up the south Fork to a split. The left climbs from 2400 feet to 4200 feet in about 2 miles, intersecting the park's West Side Road at Klapatche Point. The right continues up the river 1 1/4 miles to where St. Andrews Creek enters the Puyallup and then switchbacks up near the crest of Glacier View Ridge, to the boundary of Glacier View Wilderness.

Continue on Camp 5 road (here No. 24) up Deer Creek 2 miles, go off left on road No. 243, and switchback up the balds to the big views from Puyallup Point, 5404 feet. Proceed on trail to Lake Helen, Lake West, and Glacier View, in the Wilderness of that name.

The Divide Foot-Only Zone

The spectacularity of this relatively small preserve is The Divide, sufficiently praised in the Nisqually River chapter. Road No. 31 ascends from Camp 7 to within a couple-three miles of the summit, intersecting the route from Beetle Peak (which see). Road No. 8, branching off from Main Road, gets there by a longer route with more elevation gain.

Road No. 3, taking off south of Camp 7, ascends to Mashel Mountain.

Puyallup Ridge Foot-Only Zone

The biggest brag of this enclave, between Neisson Creek and Deer Creek, is The Thing, which apparently is the Bell relay to Jupiter, located atop 4930-foot Thing Peak, former site of the Puyallup Ridge Lookout. The Neisson Creek-Deer Creek loop road crosses the ridge at about 4200 feet, perhaps 1 mile by footroad from the summit.

Busy Wild Foot-Only Zone

From the Neisson-Deer divide, road No. 32 leads to Busy Wild Mountain and Lorraine and Zoffel Lakes, discussed in the Nisqually River chapter.

NISQUALLY RIVER

Southernmost of Rainier's great ice-melts to enter Puget Sound, the Nisqually for generations has been the world's way to The Mountain. For most folks of Puget Sound City, however, the trailheads are too far a drive (too *long* a drive, that is, through the millions upon millions of teeming, screaming cars) to do regularly. Still, there is too much superb walking not to suffer the highway torture occasionally.

Of the several subprovinces, the enormous glaciated tableland of the South Puget Plain is mainly represented here by the Non-Parkway. Private ownership complicates most of the area, as does the public ownership of Fort Lewis. The eastern portion, however, is largely in the Vail Tree Farm, with miles of lonesome roads, quiet roaming through sky-open young plantations and green-tunnel second-growth (and more and more third-growth), by lakes and bogs and marshy-slow creeks. If the shrift given by this book is too short for you, get the Weyerhaeuser map (see below) and go independent.

The northernmost subprovince is that of Ohop Creek, evidencing the derangements of the ancient landscape by glaciers from Rainier and Canada, as well as Electron and other Mudflows. Just an itty-bitty thing, the creek holds title to two oversized valleys, in its upper length occupying an apparent former valley of the Puyallup River (and Glacier), and in its lower the mountain-edge valley of the Really Big River. Ohop stars the best animal show in the Northwest, Northwest Trek.

The main subprovince is that of the Mashel River, a stream known to hardly anybody but loggers; with its major tributaries, the Little Mashel and Busy Wild Creek (poetry does lurk in the hearts of loggers), it drains a broad stretch between the Puyallup-Ohop valley and the Nisqually proper but is cut off by transverse ridges from Rainier and thus rendered obscure. Few areas of the Northwest are so totally privately owned and so absolutely skinned. But oh the views in the big-sky, moor-like land of 50 billion stumps! Among them are supreme vantages for planning the ultimate westward expansion of Mt. Rainier National Park—out on Ptarmigan Ridge to take in the Park Boundary Peaks, out along Sunset Ridge and Rushingwater Creek to the confluence of Mowich and Puyallup Rivers, out across the South Fork Puyallup to take in Puyallup Ridge and Beljica—though it wouldn't be inappropriate to go one more ridge west, over Deer and Neisson Creeks, to take in Busy Wild and Thing and The Divide. Mashel country is split between Weyerhaeuser and Champion International. The latter's roads are open to the public except for those in Foot-Only Zones and are mainly excellent; see Kapowsin Tree Farm. The former's roads are just about always open to the public and are largely rough to impassable.

South of the Nisqually the older surveyor found, in 1978, an astonishing—a bewildering—intermingling of First Wave and Second Wave clearcutting. How, he wondered, did such goggling old trees survive so long at such low elevations, so near the mills? That historical puzzle remains to be solved. The trees do not remain. In the first edition the surveyor ascended Stahl Peak by two different routes and found it altogether bully good. His chief native guide, Ed Alverson, reported in 1982 that the Little Nisqually River trail—the veritable original trail—still existed, in virgin forest dating from an 1830 fire. Neither trip is in this edition. Too much pain.

Other deletions have been made. Glacier View, because it now is in Glacier View Wilderness (and *100 Hikes in the South Cascades*). The Ohop Valley walks because the cows seem less friendly behind "No Trespassing" signs.

The publication deadline clamped down before Ed's favorite, Eatonville Rim, could be investigated: "Two miles from downtown Eatonville where the Really Big River eroded some impressive cliffs and channels in bedrock. Lots of outcrops and moss and twisty madrona trees, and the access is good and easy (incredible clifftop views by going up the back side)."

While in press we learned about a new 4.5-mile Historic Walking Tour in the town of Eatonville; stop at the Visitors Information Center for a free map-brochure.

—And far downstream, both surveyors—1978 and 1987—fell in love with McAllister Springs, near the Nisqually delta, but couldn't find enough walking to justify inclusion in a walking book. But you must go there—contact the Tahoma Audubon Society for guided tours.

USGS maps: Nisqually, Weir Prairie, McKenna, Harts Lake, Bald Hill, Tanwax Creek, Eatonville, Ohop Valley, Mineral, Morton, Kapowsin, Mt. Wow
For a free map of the road system on Vail Tree Farm, write Weyerhaeuser Company, P.O. Box 540, Chehalis WA 98532

The South Puget Plain

Pedestrian accesses to the broad sprawl flats and hills between the Cascade front and the Whulge shore are few, obstructed as the land is by farms and battlegrounds. However, a river runs through it, and a fine river it is. Also offering excellent exercises are certain of the tributaries.

Nisqually River Non-Parkway (map—page 78)

When the governor of Washington proposed a parkway extending up the Nisqually River from the national wildlife refuge to the national park, you'd have thought he'd advocated slamming Mom in the face with her apple pie. Yet a dispassionate survey found little ground for rational objection. The river's rampaging over the ages has resulted in gravel soils unfit for agriculture, uninhabitable jungles and sloughs between unstable scarps of glacial drift, a corridor of wildness from glaciers to saltwater, the only major interruption being the Tacoma dams and reservoirs. What's to be done down there in the Big Ditch but farm trees and re-create people? Not much. Still, the populist passion was backed by big bucks. The governor withdrew.

But lo! The Idea was born again. In 1985 a Nisqually River Task Force was formed under legislative authority, directed by the Department of Ecology, and regiments of bureaucrats and citizens commenced an energetic huffing and puffing. In 1987 they delivered to the Legislature a compromise. Some of the huffers-puffers hail it as a "significant step forward." Others, including the older surveyor, who did his share of committee-sitting huffing-puffing, see it as another in the long list of victories for the Big Bucks. Pretty much the status quo ante, glorified as the Nisqually River Management Plan. However, in 1988 a 21-member Nisqually River Council and a 21-member Advisory Committee are carrying on, to what end remains to be seen.

Candidly, this here surveyor has sort of soured on the Nisqually, not for lack of love, but in the way of the evangelist who strives mightily to save a fallen woman and eventually decides she has fallen one time too many to be worth another round of praying. The recommended walks are fewer than in the previous edition. The present goal is not to save the dang river, but to point to the truly enjoyable walks—those to be done as a pleasure, not a duty.

Harts Valley to Centralia Dam

Ah, serenity. A happy bowl, opening on an emerald plain, a vale of green peace tucked away between river and forest, one of the grandest farm walks in all the *Footsore* world.

From Highway 7 south of Spanaway turn off on Highway 507, signed "Roy, Centralia." In about 1 mile turn left on Harts Lake Road and proceed due south for miles and miles, through Fort Lewis, over the vast South Puget Plain. The road bends west around the rim of the amazingly cirque-like (but that's ridiculous) basin of Harts Lake. At a Y where Harts Lake Loop Road (an alternative approach, from McKenna) proceeds west, turn south, downhill, on Harts Valley Road, signed "Wilcox Farms."

Old barn in Harts Valley

Behold! And wonder—what's the explanation of this horseshoe bowl cupped in 150-foot drift bluffs, this inlet-lacking lake, this wide, river-lacking plain extending from the lake to merge with the Nisqually floodplain? The plunge basin and outwash plain of a great falls of a great river issuing from the ice front? Well, whatever . . . The result has been a large expanse of un-Nisqually-like rich black soil. In 1909, to quote the milk carton, "Grandfather Judson Wilcox established the Wilcox Farm on the fertile land around Harts Lake." The third generation now operates a family factory-farm of 1000 acres with 750,000 chickens in dozens of enormous metal coops plus cows and crops all over the emerald plain. It's a scene from another world. Someplace in Europe, maybe. Farm policy bans public vehicles on lanes but hospitably permits public feet. So, peace be with you in your walking. And blessings on the Wilcox family.

From the Y drive 1.5 miles down by the Wilcox Farm Store (eggs, milk) and farm headquarters (see Rainier!) to the plain. Just after passing the foot of the last hillock and crossing the ditch of Harts Lake Creek, where a lane goes off right, park out of the way, by the ditch, elevation 354 feet.

Walk the lane right, through fields by the creek, 1/4 mile to a Y. Take the left a long 1/4 mile to field's edge, woods, and the upstream end of one of the Nisqually's very few dikes. If little children are in the party the trip likely will end right here, on the enormous wonderful lava-boulder, black-sand bar, with an infinity of material for building castles and tossing in water.

Adults though, will want sooner or later to walk the dike 1/2 mile to the downstream end, wild forest on the across-river wall, and then take a farm lane 1 scant mile, beside a slough, to the Centralia Dam, the weir that diverts water into the Centralia Canal. A gravel bar below gives a view of the structure and a nice picnic.

Round trip 4 miles, allow 3 hours

Cedar Grove and Yelm Ditch

Gravel bars, a grove of great cedars, and a curious artifact of ancient engineers. Drive Highway 7 to Ohop Grange Hall and turn west on Tanwax Extension Road

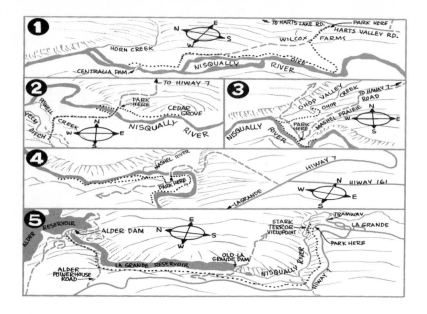

(not so signed at the turnoff). In 1.7 miles, at the intersection with Kreger Road, jog right onto a rough log-haul road. Proceed westerly on the main road, dodging lesser spurs, 1.7 miles to a Y where both forks are equally major. Go left and again dodge spurs another 2.2 miles to a log bridge over the river. Park here, elevation 390 feet.

Walk back from the bridge to a mucky lane that leads right into a grove of cedars up to 4 feet in diameter, 5-foot spruces, and assorted big maples and whatnot. Trail ends by the river in 1/2 mile.

The second star attraction is across the river. Walk the main road over the bridge 3/4 mile to an intersection. Here study a weird waterway, obviously dug by man, now much-dammed by beaver and overgrown with aquatic plants, though the water pushes briskly through. This is the Yelm Ditch, shown on the map as starting upvalley a couple miles, proceeding all the way to Yelm. Was it for irrigation, or electricity? When? No trace of the ditch was found near Yelm itself. Investigating the course might be interesting.

Gravel bars can be walked up and down the river on both sides of the bridge. Upstream on the south side is a scraggly farm, doubtless producing more solitude than sustenance.

Round trips up to 3 miles, allow up to 2 hours

Ohop Creek Confluence

Leaving behind picturesque pastures, Ohop Creek finishes its run to the Nisqually in a swampy-forest valley nearly 1/2 mile wide. This is the southern end of the Big Valley that terminates on the north in Elliott Bay and Lake Washington. A truly Momentous Spot.

Drive Highway 7 south and east over Ohop Valley toward Eatonville. At 0.7 mile from the turnoff to Ohop Valley Road turn right on Mashel Prairie Road. Drive this log-haul road past lesser sideroads 1 long mile to an intersection; turn right 1.5 miles, dropping to the Ohop Creek valley and the river, elevation 450 feet.

Path and gravel bar lead ¹/₄ mile upstream to a rock nose jutting into the water. Wildwoods line the wild river. A 40-foot hard-rock wall continues upward into a 250-foot drift scarp.

Walk fishermen's paths and flood channels downstream beside the river ¹/₂ mile to the far side of the Ohop valley, where slow, dark Ohop Creek is swallowed up by the fierce rock-milk torrent. A woods road leads up the marshy, bird-busy creek.

Round trip 2 miles, allow 1 hour

Mashel River Confluence

A wild river—no, *two* wild rivers. Cool shadows of big trees. Quiet. Solitude.

Drive Highway 7 to a few yards south of the Highway 161 turnoff to Eatonville. Turn right and proceed 1.2 miles, winding down into the canyon of the Nisqually River, which in this stretch isn't messing around on any floodplain. Cross the river and park on the shoulder, elevation 520 feet. Walk upstream and down.

Upstream. Walk through firs and other conifers so big one wonders why they've been spared. Above the river leaps a 200-foot cliff of iron-stained gravel pocked with bird caves—swallows' apartment houses. The forest floor is carpeted in season with blossoms of starflower and candyflower, lily of the valley and trillium, Solomon's-seal and Oregon shamrock. Myriad paths branch off, and gravel bars can be walked, as well as a cutoff river channel. In ³/₄ mile the last path peters out on a "beach" of rock shelving into the water. Above are green shadows of La Grande Canyon and only

Cedar grove near Yelm Ditch

½ mile away is the powerhouse, but you can't get there from here. Not unless you're a fisherman, and insane.

Downstream. Walk the road away from the river around a bend until a way can be found into and out of the moat backhoed to keep wheels out of the woods. Follow an old road by old camps ½ mile to the end. Trail burrows another ¼ mile, ending on mossy slabs shelving off in rapids. Lovely! Lonesome! The route can be continued via scrambles in steep brush to a gravel bar, but the surveyor quit and thus doesn't know how far a doughty adventurer could proceed into wildness beneath the 200-foot canyon-wall jungles that guard the solitude.

On the other side of the bridge paths lead the short bit to the other wild river, the Mashel, and the confluence. See Pack Forest.

Round trip 3 miles, allow 2 hours

La Grande Canyon

The most spectacular section of the Nisqually between glacier and delta. But Tacoma City Light got there before us and drowned it. And since then has done little to ameliorate the crime by exploiting what remains of the scenery. Nevertheless, there is a walk that provides an impressive display of concrete plus a moment of sheer terror.

Drive Highway 7 to the headquarters of Tacoma City Light at La Grande. At the big sign, "La Grande Hydroelectric Plant," turn off right on the gravel road 0.2 mile to a

La Grande Canyon

small parking area just short of a gate. (Alternatively, park by the highway at the picnic area. While walking to the gate take a sidetrip to the top of the tramway and watch the little passenger platform rise or fall from or to the powerhouse 350 precipitous feet below, in the canyon depths, inaccessible to visitors and also invisible, since no vista point has been provided.) Elevation, 940 feet.

Walk by the gate; feet are permitted but not public wheels, so the way is quiet, a very nice footroad for winter exercise in umbrella time. A bit past the gate is a trail signed "Do Not Proceed." A person so foolish as to ignore this advice may descend an old road to concrete supports of an aqueduct, now removed, that once carried water over the canyon. A path leads to the base of the supports—and shrieks, and vertigo, and peril. The canyon here is deeper than wide, and the rock-slab lip overhangs, as one discovers in horror upon peering over to see down the mossy-ferny precipice 300 feet to the riverbed (usually dry, the water diverted through the powerhouse). For a small expenditure Tacoma could erect safety fences and a view platform that would become famous for fainting tourists.

So don't do that, folks. Instead walk the lonesome road up the canyon. Logging trucks can be heard on the highway above but all is peace down here. The best view of the riverbed is in 1½ miles; below rock walls is a green pool at the base of old La Grande Dam, built in 1912, rebuilt in 1944, half-hidden in trees, almost seeming to belong there. A sideroad drops to the dam for a close look at finger-narrow La Grande Reservoir, green with glacier-milled rock flour. In another 1 mile, past a second gate, is a junction with Alder Powerhouse Road, closed to public wheels at the highway. Walk the final ¾ mile to the powerhouse in deep, clammy, perpetual shadows of 840,000 tons of concrete, 330 feet high, 1500 feet long, built in 1944. A stupendous lump. Amuse yourself imagining an Osceola-like mudflow spilling over the dam.

Round trip 6½ miles, allow 4 hours

Fort Lewis

Established in 1917 to train doughboys to fight Kaiser Bill and his Huns, this 140-square-mile military preserve now prepares troops for NATO forces on the North German Plain, whose terrain resembles that of the South Puget Plain. The artillery sounds sometimes for days without cease, 105mm and 155mm howitzers and 8-inch guns firing maybe 50,000 rounds a year, cracking chimneys and nerves in Yelm and often, on dismal winter days, leading lonesome walkers in Cascade foothills to run for the car, supposing a thunderstorm is coming.

Driving the public highways traversing the landscape that reminded Tolmie, in the 1830s, of the parks of 18th-century Whig grandees, one is tantalized by how much walking there is to do in this mostly wild magnificence that extends from Tacoma to the Nisqually River, Puget Sound to the Cascade front. But those guns . . . And those moments when a trespasser suddenly finds himself surrounded by soldiers armed to the teeth and tries to remember how to say "I surrender!" in Russian . . .

As it happens, there is a legal, safe, if complicated way to explore the prairies and woods, notably spectacular in the spring flowering. Obtain the USGS maps covering the fort. Study out a nice-looking trip. Better, several trips. Write an application for an "organized group." Send it, a month or more in advance, to Headquarters, 9th Infantry Division and Fort Lewis, Fort Lewis, WA 98433, Attention: Public Affairs Officer. Not all requests can be honored but if you apply early enough, with enough alternatives, chances are good of a wonderful and legal walk.

Observe while walking: the Fort uses the Nisqually River for training purposes— boat operations, motorized forces fording, engineer bridging, and all like that. In 1984 it gave notice of intent to bring onto the Fort a new force—"a fully motorized division possessing weapons of greater lethality." In 1985 Fort Lewis won the Department of the Army's Environmental Quality Award.

Northwest Trek Wildlife Park (map—page 82)

No zoo, this, but rather a unique 645-acre wildlife park of Tacoma Metropolitan Park District, maintained in cooperation with Tacoma Zoological Society. Northwest Trek began with the loving care by Dr. David and Constance Hellyer, who acquired the property in 1937 and in 1972 gave it to the public. Now hundreds of thousands of visitors a year take the 5½ mile, 1-hour Trek Tour, riding quiet trams through areas where animals roam free, only people are fenced in. The park is open daily February through October, Wednesday-weekends the rest of the year.

Drive Highway 161 south from Puyallup toward Eatonville. (Or, drive Highway 7 south from Tacoma and at a Trek sign opposite Highway 702 jog to 161.) Just south of Clear Lake turn in on the park entrance and drive 0.7 mile to parking areas from which paths lead to Trek Center, elevation 760 feet.

By all means take the Trek Tour and see deer, elk, moose, woodland caribou, bison, wolverine, bighorn sheep, mountain goat, Pennsylvania wild turkey, and more, roaming gone-to-nature farm fields and second-growth wildland woods half a century old.

But do some walking, too, on the 5 miles of nature trails; these are in a different area than that of the Tour, which cannot be visited on foot.

For openers, near the main entrance is Cat Country, with pairs of bobcat, cougar, and lynx. Left from the Center is a loop of blacktop paths totalling ½ mile, passing animals in natural habitats (beaver, porcupine, otter, fisher, mink, skunk, weasel, marten, raccoon), a children's Baby Animal Exhibit, and—supreme thrill—an overlook from which one looks down on nonchalant bear—and wolves loping through woodlands.

For the long walk, go right from the Center toward the Tour Station above Horseshoe Lake, beyond which rise summit snows of Rainier. On the way, opposite uncaged, unchained bald eagles and golden eagles perching there watching the parade, is the trailhead. From it are a number of loops of various lengths, sampling the various forest systems—marsh, young fir, alder-maple.

For an introductory tour, do the perimeter loop, taking all right turns, and thus in about 1 mile reaching the brink of the plateau, the Ohop Valley scarp, and screened glimpses of Ohop Lake. In about ⅓ mile more, at Station 6, starts a sidetrip, the best part. Turn right and proceed along the bluff in cool green lush forest, past the end of

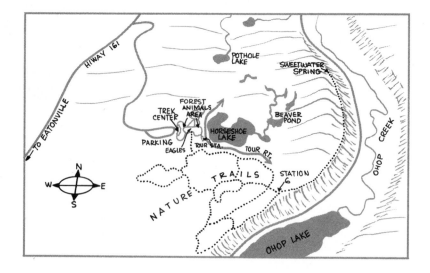

Porcupine at Northwest Trek Wildlife Park

Ohop Lake, out along the slope of Goat Ridge, to Sweetwater Spring, 1 mile from the loop. Sit a while, imagine dipping a delicious sip or so from the boxed-in pool, and return to Station 6. Again on the perimeter, return to the eagles in a final ²/₃ mile.

   Dress and behave appropriately and you may be taken for one of the exhibits, as was the older surveyor, who was eagerly asked by a party of foreigners, "Sir, are you a logger?" The honor modestly accepted, there is now some corner of England where his photo is displayed as representative of the species.

Introductory tour 4¹/₂ miles, allow 3 hours
High point 760 feet, elevation gain 200 feet
All year

Mashel River

Few walkers know the Mashel River, mainly because the loggers have known it so well. There are, however, a splendid rail grade, many miles of excellent footroads, and even a few bits of genuine trail.

The Divide (map—page 84)

Build a highway and put a visitor center on top and The Divide, the high ridge between the Puyallup and the Mashel, way out in the middle of a lonesomeness unknown to the civilized world, visited only by loggers, would depopulate Paradise and Sunrise—*this* would be the visage of The Mountain on every calendar. Well, maybe that's exaggerating a little. But not much.

(Note: This trip was scheduled for resurvey the fall of 1987. But the drought kept the roads closed until there wasn't any more fall, only winter, dangerous mud, and deep snow. The directions given here therefore are from the 1979 original survey. So be careful, out there.)

From the stoplight intersection in Eatonville, turn east from Highway 161 on the Alder-Eatonville Cutoff. In 0.5 mile, at the city limits by the bawfield, turn north on a road maybe signed "Weyerhaeuser High Yield Forest." At a Y in a scant 0.5 mile go left over the railroad tracks and climb into an area first of gravel-mining, then tree-farming. In 2 miles from the Alder Cutoff is a Y of roads Nos. 6000 and 1000. Go right on No. 6000, which leads by many junctions nearly to the summit of Mashel Mountain, pocked on the way by 50 million chuckholes. Drive (slowly) to a Y in 2 miles; stay left and twist up from the plateau onto the west ridge of Mashel. At 5 miles from the 1000-6000 Y is a junction at the foot of the final peak. Elevation, 2050 feet. It may be necessary to park here and walk the rest of the way. In either case, continue right, uphill, on No. 6000. At a spurtop Y at 2300 feet, go left on No. 6000. At a ridgecrest Y at 2500 feet, go right on No. 6000. Aside from that, just ignore obviously lesser sideroads. At 2650 feet, 1.2 miles from the junction at the foot of the final peak, is a promontory of volcanic rubble that has been quarried to a fare-thee-well. It may be necessary to park here because the views become so stupendous they leave no time for a steering wheel. (East over the headwaters maze of the Mashel River to scalped ridges decorated with gaudy gashes of logging roads in ocher volcanic soils. Atop a 4930-foot nakedness is a monster boxy Thing one speculates is the Bell System's Outer Space Connection, designed to pick up TV programs on the UFO Network. Beyond is Puyallup Ridge, partly stumps—Kapowsin Tree Farm—and partly green— Clearwater Wilderness. And then just ice, just Rainier, and beware that bulging eyes don't pop out of your skull.) But the trip is only just beginning. Road No. 6000 proceeds a scant 1.5 miles from the quarried promontory into the saddle between the north and south peaks of Mashel Mountain. From here, at 3200 feet, proceed 0.7 mile, passing

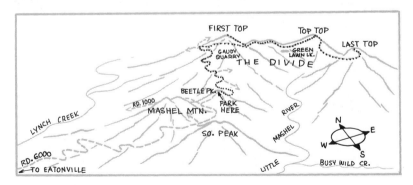

Mt. Rainier from The Divide

a pair of sideroads right, bending left around the east side of Mashel to a 3240-foot saddle. Turn right on the sideroad here, climbing to the top of 3370-foot Beetle Peak, named in honor of the survey vehicle which despite great suffering in three days of struggling over miserable Mashel roads bravely conquered this summit at the creaky age of 105,926 miles. Park the car here. In fact, maybe junk it.

To the right of the summit knob (views the equal of those from Mashel) find an old cat road adopted by the elk and follow it down the north ridge of Beetle. In a short way, where the rude trail splits, go left. Down more, after a very steep stretch, when the trail splits, go right. And so, after losing some 300 feet in maybe ⅓ mile, congratulations! There in the 3070-foot saddle, step onto a logging road—you have broken through the No Man's Land from the Weyerhaeuser road system to the Champion International road system. (To spare your vehicle much pain, drive near here on Champion roads, as described in Kapowsin Tree Farm. However, the roads at this point, and the entirety of The Divide, are in The Divide Foot-Only Zone. You'll never see public vehicles, 4-wheel or 2-wheel, here. Thank you, Champion.)

Follow the road left, rounding into a tiny-creek draw and a Y; the right is to a 1978 logging show, one of the last there'll be around here until the 22nd century; go left. Ascend around another corner to nice little Lynch Creek and a monster gaudy quarry in the yellowish volcanic rubble. Another sideroad goes right to the 1978 logging; continue straight, bending around another corner, by a smaller quarry. At 1¼ miles from hitting the Champion road the way tops the west ridge of The Divide at 3300 feet. At the junctions here, take the first right, along the ridgecrest.

Now the eyes turn from the South Puget Plain to the view over Mashel headwaters to Thing Peak and The Mountain. Now begins a classic walk in the sky, following the ridge, high in the air, views everywhere, Rainier framing itself in a series of stunning photographs with foregrounds of googols of stumps and shrubs. At a scant 1 mile, at 3650 feet, the road tops the ridge just past First Top, to whose 3760-foot summit a sideroad leads.

Always on or near the crest, the road proceeds 1 scant mile to a saddle at 3600 feet. In a basin below right is lovely "Green Lawn Lake." Above is a handsome slope of black stumps and white sticks, a masterpiece of geometric desolation. From the saddle are roads left and right—to deadends. Instead take the system of cat tracks between them, staying on or near the crest. In ⅓ steep mile is the 4100-foot plateau of Top Top—and, on the survey day in early June, a glory of blooming beargrass. Continue over the plateau to the east end and a logging road. Pick a spot on the brink to spend a couple hours goggling.

(For variant views even closer to Rainier, continue on logging roads curling around 1 mile to the 4000-foot summit of Last Top.)

Below east is the deep valley of Neisson Creek, which makes The Divide an "island" by connecting the Puyallup and Mashel valleys, evidencing some mystery of a prior drainage. Beyond is the ridge that rises to the climactic box of The Thing, then Deer Creek and scalped Puyallup Point.

Below north is the enormous gulf of the Puyallup, divided from the oddly wide Ohop valley by the ship prow of St. Paul Lookout. Beyond are Ptarmigan Ridge, from the summit icecap to Spar Pole Hill, and the Mowich Lake Road.

Ah, but the centerpiece. Success Cleaver. Tokaloo Rock. Klapatche Ridge and the in-park West Side Road. Tahoma Glacier cascading from the bowl ringed by Point Success, Columbia Crest, Liberty Cap. Sunset Amphitheater. Puyallup Glacier. Sunset Ridge. Mowich Face. Mowich and Puyallup Rivers far below, rattling their gravels.

Round trip to Top Top 8 miles, allow 6 hours
High point 4100 feet, elevation gain 1600 feet
May-November

Big Mashel Gorge and Little Mashel Falls
(map—page 87)

Walk lonesome, wheelfree woods past views of a Christmas-card village to a pair of astounding phenomena, one sponsored by the Mashel River, the other by the Little Mashel.

From Highway 161 in Eatonville turn southeast at the stoplight onto the Alder Cutoff. In 0.5 mile, at the city limits and (unsigned) Paul Kreger Memorial Field, turn north on a road with a "High Yield Forest" sign. Drive 0.5 mile to the railroad tracks and park, elevation 890 feet.

Hit the tracks south ½ mile to the high-in-the-sky bridge over Mashel River. (The bridge won't be every stroller's bowl of cherries; for a bridge-dodging approach, use the alternative starting point, below.) Across the bridge, skid down right to river level

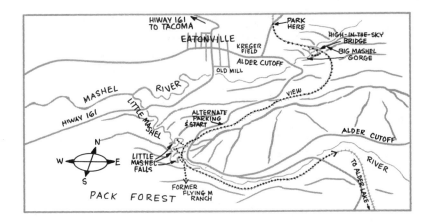

and follow a woods road to the gorge. Lordy. If one has walked over the bridge, now, looking up to it in consternation, one may wish one hadn't. But the river and its walls are the superstar. Downstream it widens to pools, becomes just a nice wild river. Upstream, though, it issues from a slot gorge through which mountain tea flows in black deeps as narrow as 4 feet wide under vertical cliffs 200 feet high. Sit on water-carved slabs and admire.

Return to the tracks, pass a path down left (to the head of the gorge), and emerge from woods into a late 1970s clearcut now sprouting houses right up to the tracks. At 1 scant mile from the bridge, where the tracks round a nose of lichen-black rock, a garden of alumroot, ocean spray, and goatsbeard, is a fine prospect. Ever seen a town nestle? That's what Eatonville does, in the Mashel valley, amid its hills. Look across to the fabulous Ohop Wall, the other way to Hugo Peak, and down to the moldering Eatonville sawmill that closed some 30 years ago but may still pose picturesquely, wasteburner and all, beside the ducky old millpond. And look out over lowlands to Bald Hills and Black Hills. Humming "O little town of Eatonville" proceed ³/₄ mile to where the tracks pass under a bridge of the Alder Cutoff at 2¹/₄ miles from Eatonville; just before the bridge is a wide parking space and alternative start, elevation 1100 feet.

In ¹/₃ mile is the second feature. A short, no-sweat bridge over Little Mashel River is the overture. From both sides find paths down the mossy, flowers-in-spring, rock slot the river has sliced to the uppermost of three falls. Carefully pick a slick way down by potholes to the plunge basin.

Now for the real action. Return on the tracks 150 feet from the bridge and spot a dirt track up the cutbank. Follow the trail along the gorge rim. Rude paths go off left to poor looks down to the middle falls, but they're nothing much. The main tread leads to the top of the lower falls. They're something, okay. Arched over by maples, the stream flows on lichen-dark, water-rounded, exquisitely sculptured rock, down a small cataract into a black pool of foam-flecked mountain tea. There it gathers itself and hurls over the brink—to a preliminary drop, then out of sight in the forbidding chasm. Gracious. At one time or another Eatonville got water from here and toyed with a ridiculous hydroelectric scheme, but now the falls area is preserved in Pack Forest (which see).

The bottom of the lower falls—actually a double falls totalling about 150 feet—can be reached by a perilous skidway. Exploration of the ¹/₂-mile gorge in which the Little Mashel drops 270 more feet was not carried out by the surveyor, stricken with terror.

From the upper falls a closed-off backdoor road-trail leads to Pack Forest. The railroad is worth walking another 1 forest mile up the pretty little river. Then farms start, changing the mood from wildwood to pastoral. But that's nice too. For one so minded,

it's another 6 miles or so to Alder Reservoir. There's a citizen plot to put the trains back on the tracks, from Tacoma to Rainier. As of 1989 there is a Mount Rainier Scenic Railroad, a steam locomotive hauling passengers 14 miles along the Nisqually River. For schedule, call (206) 569-2588.

Round trip 8 miles, allow 6 hours
High point 1200 feet, elevation gain 600 feet
All year

Busy Wild Mountain (map—page 91)

What! Not yet another brain-spinning vista of Rainier? Yes, but more too. As a foreground for The Mountain That Was God, there is some of the most staggering clearcut scenery in the Cascades. The drama is explored on a five-destination melange of overlapping hikes.

Drive Highway 7 to Elbe and continue on Highway 706. At 3 miles past Ashford go left on road No. 59, signed "Lake Christine and Glacier View." Climb climb climb on this narrow but solid road, at all junctions sticking with No. 59.

The first destination, on a snowline-prober of winter or spring, depends on where you start and how long you walk. Wherever, it's great. The road leaves the highway at 1850 feet in virgin forest, climbs by lovely Copper Creek and others, proceeds through big old second-growth to more virgin, passes a broad vista of the Nisqually valley, crosses pretty Christine Creek, and swings into the logged-to-the-last-stick upper valley of Copper Creek, with wide views.

(On the way, at 4 miles, road No. 5920 goes right to Lake Christine and Glacier View Wilderness—see *100 Hikes in the South Cascades*.)

For the second destination, drive 5.7 miles from the highway, to where the road makes its first switchback to climb from Copper Creek onto Beljica Ridge. Park here, 4200 feet.

Ascend a linked succession of cat roads up the clearcut. Razzers are halted by Champion International barricades as the way leaves Mt. Baker-Snoqualmie National Forest. In 1/2 mile is a hillside landing at the end of a road coming from Copper Ridge. Go left on this road to a saddle, then up to the 4520-foot southernmost high point of the ridge. The specialty of the walk is the look straight down to silver-shining braided channels of the Nisqually River, and hamlets and highway. But there is a goodly share of the sights described for subsequent destinations.

Round trip to Copper Ridge 3 miles, allow 2 hours
High point 4520 feet, elevation 350 feet
May-November

For the third destination, shun the road from Copper Ridge and continue straight up from the landing on a cat track 1/4 mile to the ridge crest. To the north 1/4 mile is the totally clearcut 4850-foot summit of Copper Knob. Walkers who wish to spend hours simply ogling need go no farther. Rainier is the big news, but there are also Adams and St. Helens, the cliff of High Rock, Storm King, The Rockies, Stahl, and Bald Hills. The tree-free Copper Creek valley. The Mashel valley out past Mashel and Dobbs to Ohop.

Round trip to Copper Knob 2 miles, allow 1 1/2 hours
High point 4850 feet, elevation gain 650 feet

To rest is not to conquer. A cat track drops 200 feet in a scant 1/4 mile to join a major road—just about the end of the long tortuous line from Kapowsin Lake. Turn right and gently descend the sidehill of stratified lavas, crossing a divide to headwaters of Busy Wild Creek.

Glaciers were once here, briefly. After a long 1/2 mile on the road, having dropped 4300 feet, look down left to a meadow-marsh in a cirque. And look right to shallow, reed-grown Lower Busy Wild (Zoffel) Lake. Strike off in open woods, perhaps on vestiges of ancient trail, and in 1/4 mile find Upper Busy Wild (Lorraine) Lake, 4320 feet, a tiny, cool-shadowed nook of virgin-forest serenity, ringed by hellebore and beargrass and huckleberry.

But, back to the sun-blasted outer bleakness, exclaiming at the satanic beauty of yellow-white road gashes curving around yellow-brown basins green-dotted with fir shrubs. The last scraps of virgin forest were liquidated by 1981 or so. Then the call of

Pre-1980 photo of Mt. St. Helens from Busy Wild Mountain

the Yellow-Shafted Talkie Tooter died out, a great silence began which will enwrap the land for centuries—because that's how long it'll be before another crop is ready up here. One hopes the backcountry poet who named Busy Wild Creek was not doomed to see his world destroyed.

At a Y where the logs used to flow left, downhill, turn right, uphill, to the ridge crest. Round a subsummit to a spur shoulder and where the road contours left, leave it for a cat track and walk the naked crest between Deer Creek and Busy Wild Creek. At 1¹/₂ miles from Busy Wild Lakes, attain the 4850-foot summit of Busy Wild Mountain.

Whoopee! Settle down for a minimum 1 hour of swinging the horizon. Trace every feature of Rainier from Ptarmigan Ridge to Success Cleaver. In front of it, look down to Deer Creek and across to virgin green of the Clearwater Wilderness and to Beljica and Wow. North are Echo and Observation, Tolmie, Park Boundary Peaks, Carbon Ridge. Westerly are Mashel, Dobbs, Ohop. And Whulge. South are Goat Rocks and Adams and St. Helens and Bald Hills. In season, blooming amid summit stumps, are glacier lilies and lupine.

Round trip to Busy Wild Mountain 6 miles, allow 4 hours
High point 4850 feet, elevation gain 2000 feet
June-October

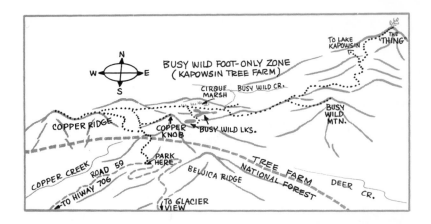

The route to the final destination is obvious to any eyeball. Where the route to the top of Busy Wild turns onto the cat track, stick with the road as it gently descends, joins another major road, and contours around to the saddle between Busy Wild and Big Creeks. When the road to Kapowsin Lake swings left, turn off right and climb to the summit of Thing Peak, 4930 feet, once the site of Puyallup Ridge Lookout. Visiting The Thing, and perhaps having your blood curdled by radiation, are extra added attractions.

Round trip to Thing Peak 11 miles, allow 8 hours
High point 4930 feet, elevation gain 3000 feet

Pack Forest

At the interface of lowlands and foothills, on a "mountain island" enclosed by Mashel and Nisqually Rivers, is Pack Forest, a 4110-acre laboratory of the University of Washington's College of Forest Resources. Miles and miles of lonesome footroads wind around hills and valleys in woodland and meadow and views from Rainier to Puget Sound, a walker's paradise. Snowline-probing and animal tracks in winter, flowers in spring and summer, colors and mushrooms in fall. And—peace be with you—on weekends the gates are closed to public wheels, but not feet. Ah, quiet!

Aside from pedestrian pleasures, Pack offers a unique opportunity to observe a wide range of forest-management techniques and experiments. Tree-farming was pioneered here, including some of the earliest plantations in the Northwest. Thinning began in 1930, and in the 1940s the first forest-fertilization studies anywhere in the world. Through the years there have been programs in forest nutrition and in harvesting methods, clearcut and shelterwood. Presently in progress is a project using forests to dispose of Metro sewage sludge and wastewater and studying the effect of these on forest growth and groundwater purity. It was for such purposes that Charles Lathrop Pack made the initial gift of land in 1926, establishing a teaching and research laboratory for teachers and students, a demonstration area for the forest industry, and, for the general public, a living textbook.

The andesite ridges of Pack, glaciated and drift-covered down low, rock-outcropping up high, were thoroughly burned about 1800, only a few relict trees escaping. Some of this 1800 forest survived the big Eatonville Fire of 1926 and other blazes of the period. A management plan has been adopted to make for greater age

Ancient red cedar in Pack Forest

diversification of Pack's forest groups and thus enhance the educational value: 10 percent of the land, including the 33-acre relict-tree Ecological Area, will be reserved in a natural state; 14 percent, including the 94-acre Hugo Peak Transect of 1800 forest, will be specially managed with only limited salvage logging of fire-damaged trees; and 76 percent, including the almost two-thirds of Pack burned since 1920, will be intensively managed on a conifer rotation of 80 years, approximately 30 acres to be harvested annually. On a single walk a person thus can see trees from seedling age to centuries old, and a variety of planting and tending and harvesting methods.

Drive Highway 161 through Eatonville to Highway 7 (or drive 7 direct from Tacoma). At 0.2 mile south on 7 from the junction is the Pack Forest entry. Just past the entry and just before the gate (open weekdays to 4:30 P.M. closed weekends) is the public parking area, elevation 800 feet.

Change is a constant on Pack Forest, as on any other tree farm. Roads are improved or built; each year some 30 acres of clearcut open new views—as the growth in plantations is closing old ones. Pack, however, is much more than a tree farm. Though 95 percent self-supporting from harvesting, the income is incidental to the teaching, the research, and the "demonstration" which is so integral to the purposes that visitors are not merely tolerated but warmly welcomed. The hiker is as much a part of the picture as the forester.

A person could wander Pack for days (but not nights—no camping allowed) on modern management roads and old farm lanes and CCC roads dwindled to trails; everywhere are routes for shortcuts or trip extensions or independent explorations. A favorite quick introduction is the Hugo Peak Trail, built and maintained by the Tacoma Branch of The Mountaineers and forestry students. The comprehensive introduction is the 1000 Loop (Lathrop Drive). To this the energetic can tack on the 2000 Loop, and the added sidetrip of the Canyon Loop. The long-legged explorer may be particularly pleased by the far reach of Bethel Ridge. But these are only the start. The ingenious routefinder can devise inside loops and outside loops and loop-the-loops until the birds get dizzy watching. Be sure to pick up the free trail map, which shows much more than is discussed here.

The gate is open to public vehicles 7:30 to 4:30 weekdays, permitting advanced starts for shorter walks or even straight-out car-touring, but closed to wheels weekends, when Pack Forest becomes a de facto wilderness area. Hikes are best taken from the gate and are so described.

Hugo Peak (map—page 94)

Find the trailhead ¼ mile up the entry road to the administration building near the greenhouse-nursery where are grown the 55,000 seedlings planted each year. Turn right on South Lathrop Drive (road No. 1000) and in ½ mile spot the trail sign on the left.

The path ascends steeply, with switchbacks, through mixed forest, then alder-maple, then Douglas fir-madrona, and finally a fir plantation. These are research plots and it is very important to stay on the trail in order not to disturb the sites. From the plantation the way crosses road No. 1400 and enters a beauty of a forest—large cedar and smaller maples and fire-scarred old-growth firs. Above a spring-fed meadow the way switchbacks on old roads, levels out in a corridor of fir and hemlock, and goes up and down through spindly trees. Peek-a-boo views begin in a stand of young alder. The trail swings along the side of the peak and up to a borrow pit in the summit plateau. Here is a sign, "Hugo Peak Trail—Tacoma Mountaineers." Road No. 1080 finishes the scant ½ mile to the highest point of Hugo Peak, 1740 feet.

Located at the exact abrupt front of the Cascades, since being partially clearcut in 1974 to salvage trees dying from fire damage Hugo has been the classic grandstand of Pack Forest. From the 1740-foot peak, and the 1720-foot peak, and the 1693-foot peak are views. Below is the Mashel valley, the Ohop valley joining from the north.

From Hugo Peak over the South Puget Plain

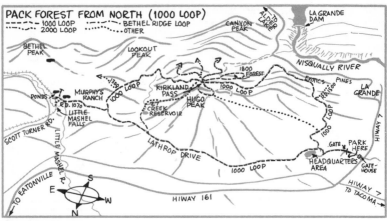

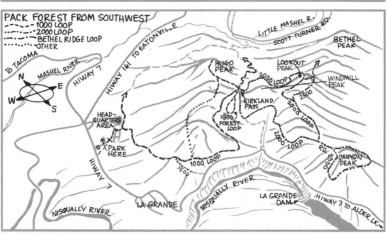

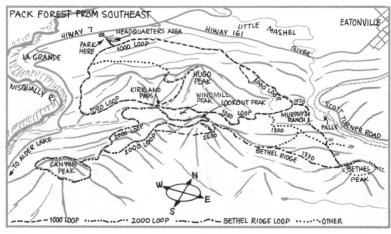

Beyond are the Nisqually, Bald Hills, and woods and farms and lakes of the South Puget Plain, over which Nisqually and Deschutes Rivers run to Nisqually Reach and Budd Inlet, respectively. Beyond saltwaterways rise Black Hills and Olympics. The Simpson Kraft steam plume marks Tacoma. The Issaquah Alps point to Seattle.

From the gravel dig road No. 1080 drops ¼ mile to Kirkland Pass and road No. 1000.

Round trip 3 miles, allow 2 hours
High point 1740 feet, elevation gain 1000 feet
All year

1000 Loop (map—page 94)

From the administration building walk left on road No. 1000, signed "Lathrop Drive North, Murphy's Ranch." Pass above the millpond of the former sawmill and proceed along the road through forest experimentally treated with municipal sewage sludge in 1977, pioneer project in the system now being employed on forest lands throughout the region, and then a plantation of 1978. Cross 27 Creek and at 1½ miles from the administration building come to a sign on the right, "Reservoir."

Reservoir Trail

Turn right on Reservoir Road ¼ mile to the 27 Creek Reservoir, intended by the CCC to provide water for fighting fires, but now an abandoned, moody, black pool. Here is the trailhead. The route, another project of the Tacoma Mountaineers, ascends ¾ mile to Kirkland Pass and thus is another way to Hugo Peak. Loop as you please.

From the trailhead cross the reservoir dam, turn left up the old road, and at a "Trail" sign go off right into a plantation featuring snags and masses of deer ferns. Views out left to Lookout Peak, down to Mashel and Ohop valleys. In ¼ mile the trail turns steeply up through fir 200 years old, most of the way beside a dry creek. Near the pass the forest crown opens and the ground is lushly green in spring-nourished grass and sedge.

Cross the dry creek to a cat track. This leads to road No. 1080; walk left down the road to Kirkland Pass. The trail also goes there, taking off across the cat road and paralleling it a ways.

Round trip 1½ miles, allow 1 hour
High point 1620 feet, elevation gain 460 feet
All year

Murphy's Ranch

Back on 1000 Loop, in a scant ½ mile from 27 Creek is a Y at the forest edge, 1160 feet, and the takeoff of two sidetrips, Murphy's Ranch and Little Mashel. Or maybe you'll want to bag the loop and spend the whole day here.

As soon as you've recovered from the impact of Rainier's huge whiteness, which here ambushes the eye, go left on road No. 1070 into the broad pastures of 650-acre Murphy's Ranch, which under the name of Flying M Ranch was famed in the 1960s for rock concerts, and in 1975 was acquired by Pack Forest.

In ½ mile, where the farmhouse used to be, is the former ranch entry road from the Alder Cutoff. Continue through fields to the two fish ponds, now devoted to floating ducks and providing foregrounds for photos of The Mountain.

Round trip 1½ miles, allow 1 hour

Little Mashel Falls Trail

Walk 1/4 mile on road No. 1070 to the far end of an experimental plantation of cottonwoods. At the end of a fence look left for a muddy track through the grass, start of the Falls Trail, unsigned. The old road bends left, shortly reaching an uprooted sign, "Little Mashel Falls Trail, BSA Eagle Project, 1984." Stay left past a small grove of firs on the right and above a pond on the left. The trail winds around and down the hill on a cat track. At the foot of the hill ignore a path continuing straight ahead and down (a good exploration) and turn right into mixed forest. A flat stretch comes to a Y, an old road-trail straight right, the trail to the left. Now, on the descent, the roar of the falls grows loud and the way soon arrives at the top of Bridal Veil Falls (the middle and largest) and enchanting deep pools below the upper, or Tom Tom Falls—which plunges into other superb pools. From Tom Tom a path can be found upstream to lovely little falls.

Return up the trail and watch on the right for an obscure track that drops down, down, down—slippery, slippery, slippery. Bridal Veil comes in view—wowee! Slipslide on and down to a promontory ridge between the middle and lower falls. Turn right to the rock-slab pools at the base of Bridal Veil Falls.

No safe route can be seen down to the lowest falls. Be satisfied.

Thus spake the surveyor of 1987. For the comments by the surveyor of 1978, see the railroad route to the other side of Little Mashel Falls.

Round trip 1 mile, allow hours

Ecological Area

Back on 1000 Loop, from the 1160-foot Y proceed upward on road No. 1000, passing road No. 1300 left to Bethel Ridge. Forest grown up since the 1926 and other fires abruptly yields, at the edge of the burn, to wonderful big trees of 1800 forest, plus a few older relicts. Note fire damage to the big trees, many of which are dying—thus the salvage logging. In 1 1/4 miles, gaining 460 feet, is the Pack hub, Kirkland Pass, 1593 feet. Five roads come to the pass, so watch it. A mandatory sidetrip from here is to the Ecological Area, for a 1-mile round trip through 1800s forest, tall trees and deep shadows. In the heart of the area are relicts from a more ancient past. Walk the Trail of the Giants down the valley of usually waterless Newton Creek. The trail branches, forming a loop. Don't go fast, take your time—time to feel the dimensions of big hemlocks and cedars, and especially of the Douglas firs up to 9 feet in diameter, 250 feet tall, maybe 450 years old.

The way back, on 1000 Loop, is short and downhill. Descend on the middle road, No. 1000, signed "Highway." In 3/4 mile leave the 1800 cathedral and enter "Nisqually Canyon Salvage, 1981." Views are smashing down to the drowned Nisqually Canyon and the La Grande Dam that done it. Shortly after is a plantation of exotics established in 1927, including Japanese red pine, redwood, Oriental cedar, Port Orford cedar, Korean pine, Arizona cypress, and big-cone spruce. Off left a bit on road No. 1500 are Ponderosa pines grown from seeds gathered in a dozen areas of the West. The Hugo Peak trail is passed, and the administration area, and at 2 miles from Kirkland Pass the loop is closed.

Loop trip with all sidetrips 12 miles, allow 8 hours
High point 1740 feet, elevation gain 1200 feet
All year

2000 Loop (map—page 94)

Here is a loop off the 1000 Loop, and then a loop off *that*. Kirkland Pass is the start-end. Set out on unsigned road No. 2000—which is *both* the roads to the left of No. 1000—take the one on the far left.

Hikers in Pack Forest

The way alternates between 1800 and 1926 fires, a textbook illustration of how fingers of fire follow natural flues up the slope. In ¹/₃ mile views open out to Eatonville and Rainier. In a scant 1 mile is Lookout Peak, 2034 feet, highest (?) point of Pack Forest's "island." The tower was built in 1929, pulled down in 1983; it should have been preserved as an historical artifact and to give parents of daring children hysterics.

Road No. 2000 bends around and descends to a junction with road No. 2040; off on the latter a short way is the summit of Windmill Peak, another claimant for the title of highest point of Pack Forest and site of a windmill and acid-rain gauge. The summit is cleared and views are superb.

At 1³/₄ miles is a junction with road No. 2500, signed "Bethel Ridge." At a long 2 miles, in fine stands of hemlock and fir, is a junction, 1700 feet, with road No. 2300.

For the Canyon Loop (off the 2000 Loop), walk No. 2300 out along a spur ridge, up and down, and circle 1855-foot "Canyon Peak," with clearcut views to Alder Dam and Reservoir, Stahl Mountain, and the Little Nisqually. Loop back to road No. 2000 for a total sideloop of 1¹/₂ miles.

Back on 2000 Loop, road No. 2000 ascends 1³/₄ miles to close the loop at Kirkland Pass.

Loop trip from Kirkland Pass 5¹/₄ miles, allow 3 hours
High point 2034 feet, elevation gain 500 feet
All year

Bethel Ridge (map—page 94)

Things have changed here since the survey in late 1978 and we didn't resurvey in 1987. Lazy? No, no! We decided to leave something to your imagination. For historical purposes we will tell what the trip was like in 1978:

"Walk 2¹/₃ miles from the entry gate on road No. 1000 to Flying M Ranch and go left on road No. 1070 over pastures to the fish ponds. Continue on an old farm lane that climbs the pasture to forest edge and becomes an old woods road. At 1500 feet, 1 mile from road No. 1000, is another dammed reservoir, a lovely secluded pool now so greenery-invaded as to be mostly a marsh. From this pretty bowl the road-trail climbs to a 1650-foot saddle in Bethel Ridge and splits. The left fork climbs ¹/₄ mile to the 1824-foot highest point of Bethel Peak, which when sawed open will give famous views to Mashel and Nisqually valleys.

"For the loop go right on a wildwood trail that will become road No. 1330. Dodge branches that descend left and right (or why dodge? why not explore?), stick with the ridge, and at 1¹/₄ miles from the pretty bowl-pond hit road No. 2500, precisely at a 1790-foot saddle where a new cut has opened a delightful picture of Eatonville.

"Follow road No. 2500, passing a clearcut with a sublime vista of Rainier over a middleground of Mashel, Thing, and Busy Wild, rounding slopes of Lookout Peak, in ³/₄ mile reaching road No. 2000. (An easy shortcut can be made on an obscure old road, as noted on the map.) Turn right on 2000 and follow it 1³/₄ miles up to Lookout Peak and down to Kirkland Pass. Return the 2¹/₃ miles on road No. 1000 to the administration building and the Pack gate."

Loop trip 10 miles, allow 7 hours
High point 2050 feet, elevation gain 1500 feet
All year

Mashel River Trail (map—page 94)

As for what may well become the most popular hike on Pack Forest, we can only say: eat your heart out; it hasn't been built. And the terrain is so formidable and the vegetation so hyperhealthy a route cannot even be faked very politely. The old-growth jungle at the confluence of the Mashel and the Nisqually, only recently acquired by Pack Forest, is considered by those who have battled through its thorns to be one of Nature's masterpieces. The canyon of the Mashel has broad river terraces guarded by precipitous walls. The 5-mile loop from the Pack entrance down to the canyon floor, through the incised meanders, to the Nisqually, and return, is a gigantic coming attraction.

The historical significance is at least as great as the ecological. The original residents, the Nisquallies, remember how one fine day in March of 1856 a doughty company of real estate speculators, calling themselves the Washington Mounted Rifles, mostly composed of colonels, rode into a village on the Mashel, discovered the men were away, and vented their frustrated patriotism by murdering 17 women and children. If the site can be identified, a sidetrail would be appropriate, and an interpretive center for the Mashel Massacre.

THE SOUTHERN FRONTIER: BALD HILLS, THE PRAIRIES, BLACK HILLS

At the south end the *Footsore* world rises to heights that may seem home hills only to the Olympia neighborhood. However, though halfway from Seattle to Oregon, they are still familiarly "Puget Sound." Yet with differences, a touch of the foreign. Ah, viva the differences—even folks for whom the frontier is well beyond the Two-Hour Circle, who fear falling off the edge of the world, must come for excitements not to be found otherwise. There's more to walking than exercise.

Ends. The Whulge ends, and its feeder streams; here is a momentous hydrographic divide. From the Bald Hills flows the Deschutes, southernmost river of the Cascades to enter Puget Sound. Also from the Bald Hills flows the Skookumchuck, which turns south to the Rainier-born Cowlitz and thus the Columbia. But also from the Bald Hills flows the Chehalis, joined from the prairies by the Black, the two together nearly enwrapping the Black Hills and then proceeding west to Grays Harbor, augmented on the way by streams from the curious system of little parallel valleys in the gap between Black Hills and Olympics.

Ends. Here ended the Puget Lobe of the continental glacier. A hiker from the north senses a peculiarity in the hills—they remind of the Western Cascades of Oregon, the Ozarks or the southern Appalachians. The reason is that the ice rode up the north flanks (on the east side of the Black Hills, to about 1460 feet) but not over the highest tops; the terrain is not ice-shaped and youthful—as say, the Issaquah Alps—but mainly stream-sculptured, maturely dissected.

The Puget-Willamette Trough extends south, but here where it narrows between Bald Hills-Black Hills "portals" are the enigmatic prairies. What is Eastern Washington doing west of the crest? What are Oregon-like oak groves and western gray squirrels doing so far north? Tolmie in the 1840s remarked on the contrast with lush forests of uplands all around; declaring the prairies unsurpassed in elegance, he compared them to the open parks amid artfully landscaped estates of English nobility. The art, of course, is Nature's (though prior to 1850 aided by regular burning done by Indians to encourage the camas and the deer). The flats are the outwash plains of rivers from the front of the ice in its farthest advance toward Oregon. The soil is composed of river gravels with poor water-retention; no matter that the skies are Puget Sound-drippy—so far as plants are concerned the sites are semi-arid.

Ends. Here the Really Big River carried ice-dammed waters of the Cascades through today's Chehalis valley to the ocean, joined west of the Black Hills by the Really Big River from the Olympics.

Ends. On prairies and their upland counterparts, the "balds," and in adjoining woodlands, are the northern limits of some plant species. And the southern limits of others.

Merely high-graded here, due to the driving time from northern population centers, the Bald Hills are a westward thrust of the Cascades seeming as unrelated to that range as their northern counterpart, the Issaquah Alps. Logging only recently has reached the center of the subrange, the headwaters of Deschutes and Skookumchuck Rivers, but the outer north ridges sampled here, mostly in Weyerhaeuser's Vail Tree Farm, were railroad-logged decades ago; the Second Wave clearcuts are opening views. What views they are! The outrigger position gives unique grandstand perspectives over the South Puget Plain to Tacoma and Seattle. Elevations are high enough for long vistas, low enough for all-year walking.

Called "Klahle" ("black") by the Indians, the Black Hills are an isolated uplift some 15 by 12 miles in size seeming to belong to neither nearby mountain range. Like the Olympics, though, they are largely pillow lavas and breccias from submarine eruptions of basalts, deeply weathered to a reddish-brown clay soil that when wet and horse-churned and wheel-rutted becomes a boot-sucking red goo. Elevations from 120 to 2668 feet offer walking the year around, though the heights can be deeply white for spells in winter. Most of this chapter is devoted to the Black Hills because there, unlike on the tree farms of private enterprise, recreation is not merely tolerated but recognized. Capitol Forest has its serious faults (motorcycles are not merely tolerated but positively cheered by the DNR) but very great virtues, too.

Sadly, we note two grievous losses in this edition. This is what we said before about Deschutes Falls:

"Everybody knows the Deschutes River ends in a lovely splashing tumble to saltwater. Few but locals know that near its headwaters is another falls and the supreme beauty spot of the Bald Hills—a big-fir virgin forest where the little river plunges into spooky, spray-billowing depths of a dark deep narrow gorge.

"But be warned. The owners, descended from pioneers of the area (none other than the Longmires) and just two removes from the original homesteaders, admit the public to the 290-acre private park only in order not to hog a notable wonder of nature. . . .

"The falls are at hand but for full drama should be approached from upstream. Therefore walk the forest road through the picnic ground to the end in 1/4 mile. Continue on trail 1/2 mile to a general petering-out. Admire the old-growth Douglas firs and understory tangle of this isle of virgin wildness, yearly more precious. Sidepaths lead to the river, rock slabs to sit on and wade from under arching maples.

"Returned to the picnic ground, continue downstream on green-mossy buttresses of andesite conglomerate stream-carved in slots and bowls and potholes—and little lazy-green swimming pools safe for little kids, to the alarm of the dippers.

"And then—sacre bleu!—the falls! A cable restrains the foolish from too-close looks; even so, folks prone to giddiness often will retreat to get a grip on a tree. The plunge basin is a Darkness far below, a clammy green chasm. From it extends downstream a slot with 100-foot vertical walls—which at one point virtually touch. The brink path proceeds from one gasp to another, then slip-skids to the gorge bottom. Himmel. A fearsome spot. The sky is a thin strip of brightness half-screened by leaning firs and maples. Drips from overhangs flash in the sun. The dank precipices are a saxifrage garden, hung with flowers in crannied walls, draped with ferns, shrubs festooned with old man's beard dancing in the breezes. Slow-flowing river, floating leaves and flecks of foam, issues from the gorge, surges by enormous green boulders, around a sharp corner, out of sight."

Attempts have been made to interest the county parks department, State Parks, any government agency that might obtain funds to purchase the spot. As of 1988, no success. And the cost of liability insurance in this age where *caveat emptor* has yielded to *purveyor look out* has forced the owners to fence out the public.

The previous edition spoke thus of Grand Mound Prairie:

"There is no trail system and none needed. One loop samples both the creek and the prairie. Walk west past the headquarters building, the gracious old farmhouse of the Brewer Homestead dating from about 1858. Past the barn trend right, down the Scatter Creek, wide and slow and deep, much of the course through a great dismal swamp. Wonderful. Push through snowberry thickets in fir forests to secret spots where lichen-somber maples and oak lean over the creek. Wild things live here. Birds. Beaver. Golly knows.

"Emerge into big sky of Scotch Broom Prairie, views of Rainier and Black Hills and Bald Hills. Stroll through brown straw (winter) or yellow-blue-white-red flowers (spring and summer). At the west boundary fence loop back east. Where burrowing critters (pocket gophers?) have dug it up, note the gravelly soil that makes the prairies. Note a few subdued Mima mounds, the rest obliterated by a century of ploughs. Note the large grove of oak trees whose acorns support the big squirrels—western grays at just about the northern limit of their range. Watch out for acorn-loving bears. A bit off right is the site of Fort Henness, where during the alarms of 1855-56 the 224 pioneers of the Five Prairies holed up for 16 months—and never saw an Indian."

Though this portion of the Scatter Creek Wildlife Recreation Area may be spared,

Deschutes River in the slot gorge below Deschutes Falls (As of 1990 the area is not open to the public but is being proposed for park acquisition)

as of 1988 much of the prairie is being split into five-acre housing tracts, saving only a fisherman's easement along the creek. We could further point out that though the Mima Mounds Natural Area is a joy, less that 2 percent of the mounded prairies are legally and intentionally protected. *The Mima Mounds Coalition needs YOU!*

USGS maps: Bald Hill, Lake Lawrence, Vail, McKenna, Yelm, Maytown, Tumwater, Tenino, Rochester, Shelton, Malone

For a free map of the road system on Vail Tree Farm, write Weyerhaeuser Company, P.O. Box 540, Chehalis, WA 98532

For a free map of Capitol Forest, write Department of Natural Resources, Olympia, WA 98504

DESCHUTES RIVER—SKOOKUMCHUCK RIVER

As a general rule, the attractions of rivers flowing through tree farms must not be overpraised, certainly not in comparison to those flowing through old-growth forests. Here, however, are several walks offering not only unusual views but unique ecosystems.

Bald Hill Lake and Bald Hill East (map—page 102)

At the absolute mountain front, on the tip of the ridge jutting into the angle between Nisqually and Deschutes Rivers, lies an ecological community—or better say, community of communities—that may best be introduced in the words of the surveyors' (and just about everybody else's) expert guide, Ed Alverson: ". . .lake, cliffs, canyon, prairie 'balds,' old-growth forest, oak-madrona woodland, and marsh-swampland, in a compact area . . . a wider array of rare and interesting wildflowers and plants that anywhere else in the Puget Trough. . . spring is the ideal time."

Man has done such things here as make a person ashamed of his species—groves of outstanding old-growth forest reduced to stumpage, bald meadows ravaged by motorcycles. Yet latterly man has done something to redeem himself. The Nature Conservancy and the state Department of Natural Resources have combined to establish a Bald Hill Lake Natural Area Preserve. Be warned: boots, too, are the enemy of such fragile terrain; most of the preserve is closed to public entry, protected for botanical research.

However, adjoining the closed area, both on the lake and on the hills above, the walker can encounter all or most of the plants in the preserve. And on the hills there are views, too.

Drive Highway 507 south from McKenna to Four Corners (known as such but not so signed), intersection of highways from Yelm, Vail, KcKenna, and Lake Lawrence. Go southeast on Bald Hill Road, marked by a large "Lake Lawrence" sign, 9.5 miles, to 1 mile past Single Tree Estates on Clear Lake. Turn left on Weyerhaeuser's road No. 1000, a great wide mainline haul road. In 0.2 mile turn right on an unsigned, double-entry road.

Bald Hill Lake

Drive 0.2 mile to a Y and turn left. In 0.4 and then 0.1 mile are two road-trails going left; they join and are the route of the round-the-lake-walk. Continue from the second of these 0.4 mile to the road-end and parking space, elevation 640 feet.

Walk the way you came to the first road-trail, turn right, and simply follow your nose. Stay with the near-shore road around to its end. There two trails offer short sidetrips.

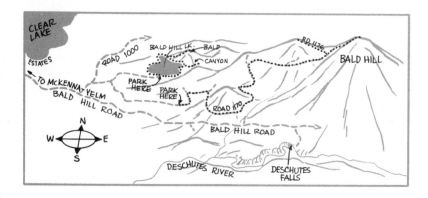

Oak grove and prairie "bald" in the Bald Hill Lake Natural Area Preserve

One ascends steeply and roughly to oak groves and prairies. The other goes a short way into the mouth of the canyon, featuring enormous boulders (small mountains, more like it) and old-growth Douglas fir. Returned from sidetrips, complete the lake loop on road-trail.

The history of the area over the centuries was one of repeated fires, creating and perpetuating the "balds." Yet in clefts of the mountain scarp old-growth forest survived the blazes. But not the loggers, who in 1976 clearcut the shores of Bald Lake, one of the crimes for which the forest industry someday will be made to answer. However, Nature Conservancy acquired some 336 acres, including the canyon and the balds, which here have been only lightly grazed and thus are quite "natural." The area now is managed by the state DNR as a Natural Area Preserve. Some 35 grasses have been

THE SOUTHERN FRONTIER

found, half of them native. The display of ferns includes a number of the unusual and rare. More than 300 plants have been identified. many are at their northern limits and remind of Oregon; many "don't belong" on this side of the Cascades and remind of Eastern Washington. The flower show changes completely every few weeks. The April beginning is the little *Synthyris reniformis*; the July ending is farewell-to-spring.

So says Ed Alverson, so it must be true.

Round trip with sidetrips 1½ miles, allow 3 hours
High point 800 feet, elevation gain 160 feet
Spring

Bald Hill East

Bald Hill East

From the Y at 0.2 mile from road No. 1000, keep right a scant 1 mile to a Y, elevation 830 feet.

It is possible to drive onward and upward, but since one of the two reasons for the trip is plants, the foot is the only fitting machine. Walk the left fork, road No. 1170, dodging lesser spurs and climbing steadily, then dipping into a creek valley. At several spots, due to the combination of repeated fires (set by the original residents to make "camas farms"?) and the dry sites resulting from near-surface, glacier-smoothed, conglomerate bedrock, are prairie-like balds. Groves of Oregon white oak grow amid fields of common camas, poison camas, sea blush, monkeyflower, buttercup, paintbrush, shooting star, strawberry, large bittercress, serviceberry.

At 1¾ miles the main road rounds a ridge tip at 1420 feet and the views begin and continue without a break in clearcuts of the middle and late 1970s and early 1980s. Below is the odd cliff of Fossil Rock. In 1 mile more is a saddle at 1700 feet. To the right is the 2026-foot summit of Bald Hill, one of the viewpoints. For others, turn left on road No. 1176 a final scant ½ mile, over the tops of two 1740-foot bumps. From pieces here and there assemble a 360-degree panorama.

East beyond the Nisqually River are Ohop Lookout, Hugo, Dobbs, Wow, and Rainier. To the north spot nearby lakes—Kreger, Silver, Cranberry, and Rapjohn— and Ohop Valley, Kapowsin Scarp, Spar Pole Hill, Carbon Ridge. South over headwaters of Deschutes River are Bald Hills—and more of them west, Clear and Elbow Lakes at their foot. Farms and villages and woods dot the enormous sprawl of the South Puget Plain; out there boom Fort Lewis cannon. On a clear day see Olympia, Whulge, Olympics.

Round trip 8 miles, allow 6 hours
High point 2026 feet, elevation gain 1500 feet
All year

Porcupine Ridge (map—page 105)

Here is the 50-yard line of the Bald Hills game, the royal box of the scenery opera. From a 1970s clearcut the scarp plummets, nothing to block unique views over the amazing vast expanse of the South Puget Plain, from here appearing table-flat, a sprawling dark green of forests patched with light green of prairie farms. Off right is the monster white bulk of Rainier, off left the dark rise of the Black Hills. Beyond are Whulge, Olympia, Tacoma, and Seattle. Fantastic.

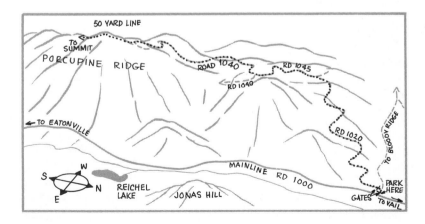

Mt. Rainier from Porcupine Ridge

From Highway 7 south of Tacoma drive Highway 507 to McKenna. Just out of town, across the Nisqually River, turn left on Vail Loop Road, here signed "Lake Lawrence." In a scant 1 mile cross Bald Hills Road at Four Corners. (If driving from Olympia, reach here on Bald Hills Road from Yelm.) Continue 9.5 miles to the outskirts of Vail and turn left on the unsigned Weyerhaeuser Mainline (road No. 1000). In 1.7 miles, where No. 1000 goes straight and No. 2000 goes right, park, elevation 450 feet.

The gate policy of the Vail Tree Farm is to open them to the public weekends from fishing season through hunting season, except in fire season. However, recreationists are too few hereabouts to deserve much consideration. The gates are undependable. Best never to leave one in your recreational rear.

In the angle between big roads Nos. 1000 and 2000 is little old gated woods road No. 1020, the start of the route, which will, however, finish on road No. 1040. Begin with 1 1/2 steep miles switchbacking up a spur, then a valley, in big second-growth, passing a road right, attaining the Porcupine crest at 1221 feet. At the Y here go left a long 1/2 mile on the crest to a Y. Go left, upward on the crest, 1 mile, passing a road left, to 1500 feet. Drop 1/3 mile on the north side of Point 1610 to a Y at 1340 feet. Go right, up, passing a road left, a final 3/4 mile to the wide plateau. Any handy stump on the lip of the north scarp provides the box seat and picnic table, at 1860 feet, about 4 1/4 miles. You can't miss it.

(Sentimentalists may wish to continue upsy-downsy on the crest 2 miles to the summit of Porcupine Ridge and the site of the old lookout, 2252 feet; the grassy field ringed by 50-foot firs is moody but viewless.)

Just below is Reichel Lake. The oddities of Shell Rock Ridge and Jonas Hill interest, and waters of Lake Lawrence, and cows on green prairies. The Deschutes River can be traced over the South Puget Plain to Olympia on Budd Inlet, as can the Nisqually from Rainier to Nisqually Reach. Tacoma is in view and also, pointed to by the long westward thrust of the Issaquah Alps, Seattle. Green and Gold Mountains mark the location of Bremerton. And the horizons include Black Hills, Olympics, Cascades.

Round trip 8¹/₂ miles, allow 6 hours
High point 1860 feet, elevation gain 1800 feet
All year

Bloody Ridge (map—page 107)

From plantations on the westernmost heights of the Bald Hills, the southernmost vista of the *Footsore* world, look down to where the Puget Glacier halted in its Oregonward rush and died. See the hydrographic divide: the extension of the Puget Trough in which the Cowlitz flows south to the Columbia, and the Chehalis also flows south before turning west to Grays Harbor; and the Deschutes and Nisqually flowing over the South Puget Plain to Puget Sound.

Drive to the 1000-2000 junction (see Porcupine Ridge) and park, elevation 450 feet. Gates are often open but always treacherous—don't trust them.

Walk right on big broad road No. 2000 for 1 mile and reverse-turn right, uphill, on lesser but good road No. 2020 (unsigned). At a junction in ¹/₄ mile, follow the good road in its switchback left. Continue 2 miles, climbing, swinging around a ridge to the Skookumchuck valley, turning up Baumgard Creek to a Y, 1120 feet. For the full tour, do a loop; for a shorter walk (round trip 10¹/₂ miles from the car) take the concluding leg.

Go left for the loop, in and out of beaver-marshy, clearcut Baumgard valley. The old logging-railroad grade enters cool lush second-growth, rounds Miller Hill, and emerges in the skinned valley of "Short Run." Moor-like fields open broad looks over the Skookumchuck valley (and reservoir) to Blue Ridge. At 3 miles from the 1120-foot Y are the 1400-foot crest of a spur ridge and an experimental plot fenced to keep out deer and elk. In ³/₄ mile pass a sideroad to Miller Hill, former lookout site. In 1 more

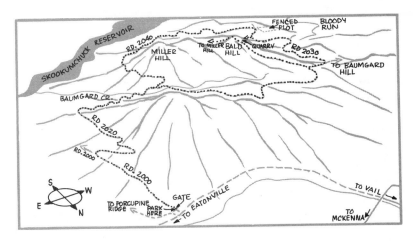

Fenced-in experimental plot on Bloody Ridge

mile, at all junctions going upward, the way attains the plateau crest of Bloody Ridge at 1573 feet.

The road of the route thus far proceeds ahead to Baumgard Hill, the best destination if it has been re-logged. If not, turn right on a good sideroad which quickly leads to a T, 5 miles from the 1120-foot Y. The loop return is left, but the immediate job is a sidetrip right, along the crest, in climax views north and west and south. Views don't get better than this but for neatness continue a final 1 mile to a quarry in rotten volcanic rock and through a field to the summit of Bald Hill West, 1750 feet.

There's Rainier, big, white, close, beyond Porcupine, Bald Hill East, Mashel, and Wow. Close below north are Weyerhaeuser headquarters at Vail and the Deschutes River flowing to Olympia. And through towns and farms of the plain flows the Nisqually River. See cities, and Issaquah Alps. However, this is distinctively the place to view Bald Hills south, Black Hills west, and Doty and Willapa Hills southwest. And almost Oregon. Just below west, above Tenino, is the bitter end of the Bald Hills and the edge of the prairie province.

For the short concluding leg of the loop, from the ridge-crest T go downhill north, swinging around the head of Baumgard Creek, regaining the Y in 2¼ miles.

Complete trip 15 miles, allow 10 hours
High point 1750 feet, elevation gain 1300 feet
All year

Skookumchuck Falls (map—page 109)

Even guidebook writers—*especially* guidebook writers—need native guides. Ed Alverson not only has a keen eye for precious flowers and rare ferns but a sharp nose for snooping out interesting nooks. Though the older surveyor had established the first ridge south of the Deschutes River as the boundary of the *Footsore* world, Ed went over the line and discovered a treasure that requires a boundary adjustment.

Drive Weyerhaeuser road No. 1000 to the gates at the junction with road No. 2000 (see Porcupine Ridge). Park here, elevation 450 feet.

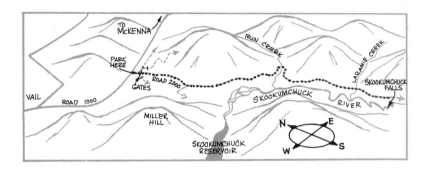

I cannot improve on my guide's description:

"We walked road No. 2000 (gated, and thus quiet and peaceful on weekends) up through an odd sort of 'pass' (probably a peri-glacial drainage channel), at 620 feet, 1 mile, and into the Skookumchuck valley, continuing upstream at about the same elevation. The road sits up above the river on a level bench, but if you wander a few feet off the road, you come to the brink of a sheer 150-foot cliff that drops straight down to the river. The river, then, flows through a mini-canyon, and the side-streams waterfall down to the river. At the upper end of the canyon, some 4 1/2 miles from the gate, the Skookumchuck tumbles over a series of cascades, with perhaps a 30-foot drop. Elevation, 700 feet. 'Tis a splendid patch of wild river, a mere 25 miles from downtown Olympia. A trail on the non-roaded side of the river would be ideal. Columbines grow along the river, on the mossy bedrock. Thin wisps of waterfalls thread cliffs on the far side."

Round trip 9 miles, allow 6 hours
High point 700 feet, elevation gain 300 feet
All year

Capitol State Forest

Another name for Black Hills is Capitol State Forest. From 1901 to 1941 several cut-and-get-out companies operated here—the Bordeaux brothers' Mason County Logging, Vance Lumbering, and Mud Bay Logging. They progressed from bullteam to "lokie" logging and built more than 100 miles of railroads, the basis of today's road and trail systems. In the mid-1930s a far-sighted State Forester, Ted Goodyear, and his assistant, Mike Webster, purchased 33,000 acres of logged, burned lands for 50¢ an acre, supplemented these with gifts, and assembled them with trust lands managed by the state for the common schools and counties. Some of the earliest tree-farming was here, seedlings set out by the CCC, then by Cedar Creek Youth Camp.

Since the 1960s the successor of the State Forestry Board, the Department of Natural Resources (DNR), has been authorized by RCW Chapter 79.68 to practice multiple-use sustained-yield forestry on the National Forest pattern. In a sense, and to an extent, DNR has done so, using state and federal funds distributed by the state Inter-Agency Committee (IAC) to exploit the recreation resource.

The DNR has seven large multiple-use areas: Capitol Forest, 80,000 acres; Tahuya (see Kitsap Peninsula), 33,000; Sultan-Pilchuck (see *Footsore 2* and *3*), 81,600; Yacolt, 73,000; Hoh-Clearwater, 105,000; Ahtanum, 63,000; and Okanogan, 176,700. (The newer Tiger Mountain State Forest also is a multiple-use tree farm, but somewhat different due to its near-urban location. See *Footsore 1*.)

Capitol Forest has some 75 miles of management roads, mostly gravel, suitable for ordinary automobiles; there are excellent campgrounds, picnic areas, and vista points, all reached by several approaches. The excellent, free DNR map is indispensable.

THE SOUTHERN FRONTIER

Since the 1960s conquest of the world by razzers, the Forest has gained an evil reputation among hikers. Some 90 miles of ATV routes have been developed by DNR and user groups, attracting a veritable ATV industry to the Black Hills, including sales and service outlets, rental agencies, and "staging areas" of private clubs. The DNR has striven to eliminate conflict by splitting the Forest into an ATV Zone and a Hiker-Horse Zone, the deadline being the Black Hills Crest. A good idea. Unfortunately, ATVs are permitted on all roads and from them readily trespass on trails officially banned to wheels.

Capitol Forest often is cited as a model of how tree-farming, automobile recreation, and backcountry trail hiking can coexist amiably. We wish we could be more enthusiastic about the walks in deep valleys by small streams in second-growth wildwoods. Walks on moor-like broad-view heights with breathtaking vistas from Olympus to St. Helens to Rainier to Baker, from Puget Sound and Hood Canal to the Pacific Ocean. But the DNR says it all in a brochure, "Trailbiking is the single most prevalent use of Capitol Forest."

Still, it's too good to be abandoned. As DNR currently counts the vote, wheels are winning. But that's because the feet are staying home from the polls. Difficult, sometimes, to believe, but there *are* more feet in the world than wheels—even more feet than wheels in the backcountry. It's just that they cast a silent ballot.

Though this book is a hiking guide, the view-driving cannot be ignored. Capitol Peak, described herein as a walk, can be done as a drive. So can scores of miles of ridge-climbing roads. We particularly call attention to the Chehalis Valley Vista. Ascend the short path to a cleared knoll, 1150 feet, on the brink of the plunge to the floodplain 1000 feet below. You are standing on the absolute southern boundary of the *Footsore* world, beyond the limits of ancient ice, looking to Oregon, to the ocean, and a goshamighty more. See Rainier, Adams, and St. Helens, and the hamlet of Rochester out in Baker Prairie, and Willapa Hills beyond the Doty Hills, and the enormous plume rising from the Chehalis Steam Plant, where stripmined coal is burned to generate electricity. Directly below, the Black River meanders at the foot of the Black Hills scarp. Across emerald pastures 2½ miles, the Chehalis River meanders at the foot of the opposite scarp. But they didn't dig this valley—that was done millennia ago by the Really Big River, several times the size of today's Columbia, the sum of all the rivers of the Cascades dammed from more direct routes to the sea by the wall of Canadian ice.

The hikes described in these pages are the surveyors' favorites. We have omitted the maze of paths on the Mima edge of Capitol Forest, where the Black Hills rise abruptly from the prairie, miles of walking through mysterious wildwood valleys. Ease of access gives special value in winter, when higher roads may be mucky or snowy. However, due to the muckiness-snowiness, in winter the DNR permits ATVs here, out of their zone; even when they aren't on the scene, their scat is, their reek.

How is it possible to omit Rock Candy Mountain? Northernmost of the three highest peaks of the Black Hills and giving the choicest views straight down to petering-out saltwaterways of Puget Sound, its panoramas extend from Whulge and Tahoma, from Rainier to Adams, Stahl, Bloody Ridge, Tenino in the prairies between Bald and Black Hills, and St. Helens. Directly below is the Waddell Creek valley, site of Hollywood, above which rise Big Larch and Capitol. Out there in the Puget-Willamette Trough are the plume of the Chehalis Steam Plant, and the Cowlitz draining to the Columbia. The name was given by the brush apes who lived in Hollywood Camp, from the 1920s to 1947 site of Mason County Logging Company's Camp 4; after a day in the cold rain, rassling big sticks, the dry and warm railroad-car bunkhouses may actually have seemed as sybaritically magnificent as the entertainment capital of the world. The mountain honored the hobo's dreams of bulldogs with rubber teeth and cops with wooden legs, cigarette trees and hens that lay soft-boiled eggs, and a lake of booze where you can paddle around in big canoes. All very well. But Rock Candy Mountain lies in the ATV Zone. (A native pedestrian has revealed that a foot-only trail exists to the summit, never molested by wheels. A bit brushy. Hard to find. (Danged if this book

Beaver lodge on the McLane Creek Nature Trail

will give away the secret.)

The 75 miles of recreational roads in Capitol Forest are so interconnected that any of the five entries to the Forest gives easy access to the trails. Porter Creek Entrance and Cedar Creek Entrance are not described here because they are on the west side, the most distant for most hikers. Rock Candy Mountain Entrance, on the north side, is actually the quickest from Olympia, but the north part of the Forest is the ATV area, and there are enough fun wheels in the *non*-ATV area. Driving directions for the other three, closely grouped on the east side:

Delphi Entrance: Go off I-5 on Exit 104 in Olympia and drive US 101 west 2 miles. Turn south at the exit signed "West Olympia, Black Lake," on Black Lake Boulevard 4 miles to a T with Delphi Road. Turn left 2 miles and then keep right on Waddell Creek Road. The Delphi Entrance is passed and at 3 miles from Delphi Road is a Y. The left is C-6000, to McKenny Camp and the Waddell Creek Entrance. The right is signed "Hollywood 2.2, Capitol Peak 10.9."

Waddell Creek Entrance: Go off I-5 on Exit 95 and drive Highway 121 west to Littlerock. Proceed straight through that hamlet on the road signed "Capitol Forest." In 1 mile is a T. Go right on Waddell Creek Road, pass Mima Mounds Natural Area, the Waddell Creek Entrance, and a sideroad to McKenny Camp; at 4.8 miles from the T is the Y junction with the Delphi Entrance road.

Bordeaux Entrance: Drive 1.3 miles south from the T west of Littlerock and turn right on Bordeaux Road 2.5 miles to the entrance, where the road changes name to D-Line.

McLane Creek Nature Trail (map—page 113)

Beaver ponds, beaver dams, beaver lodges, and—if you're quiet and lucky—beaver splashing about their business oblivious to the audience. And an encyclopedia of woodland plants and marsh plants and swamp plants, on a mere 41 acres of DNR land that seem ten times that.

Drive Black Hills Boulevard to Delphi Road (see Delphi Entrance) and turn right 1 scant mile to the DNR sign and access road leading to the trailhead parking area, elevation 150 feet.

A self-guiding pamphlet and interpretive signs aid understanding of sights along the way, the most spectacular of which are three beaver ponds, the centerpiece broad and strewn with lily pads and wiggling with salamanders; view platforms are comfortable spots to lie in wait for the beaver. The path proceeds on plank walks through marshes and swamps, on bridges over McLane Creek. Partway along the 1.1-mile outer loop is a shortcut connector along an old railroad grade, passing close by one of the two beaver lodges. There are skunk cabbage and devils club, alder and fir—including at least one monster "wolf" disdained by the loggers. Ancient cedar stumps nurse young cedars. A two-legged maple arches over a trail "tunnel." Picturesque snags house bird families.

Complete trip 2 miles, allow many hours
High point 175 feet, elevation gain 25 feet
All year

Mima Mounds Natural Area (map—page 116)

To quote from an old Nature Conservancy postcard, "Mima Prairie is the type locality of the mysterious Mima-microrelief or pimpled plains of western North America. Scientists agree that the spacing of the mounds is a 'squeeze pattern.' Biologists claim that the mounds were built by gophers and (along with beaver dams) are the largest structures created by any mammal. Geologists claim that the mounds are the result of freezing and thawing. In 1966, The Nature Conservancy leased part of the prairie as an emergency measure to save it from damage by grazing, mining, and other commercial uses."

To update the story, geologists have found the same mounds in process of formation, by a complicated process of ice melting and dumping in morainal material, at the toes of stagnant glaciers, and since this is precisely the farthest advance of the Puget Lobe, that might have ended the debate—except that hereabouts there was no permafrost as there is farther north. So, gophers? A new hypothesis is that a layer of

1.5 miles W of Littlerock on Waddel Creek Road

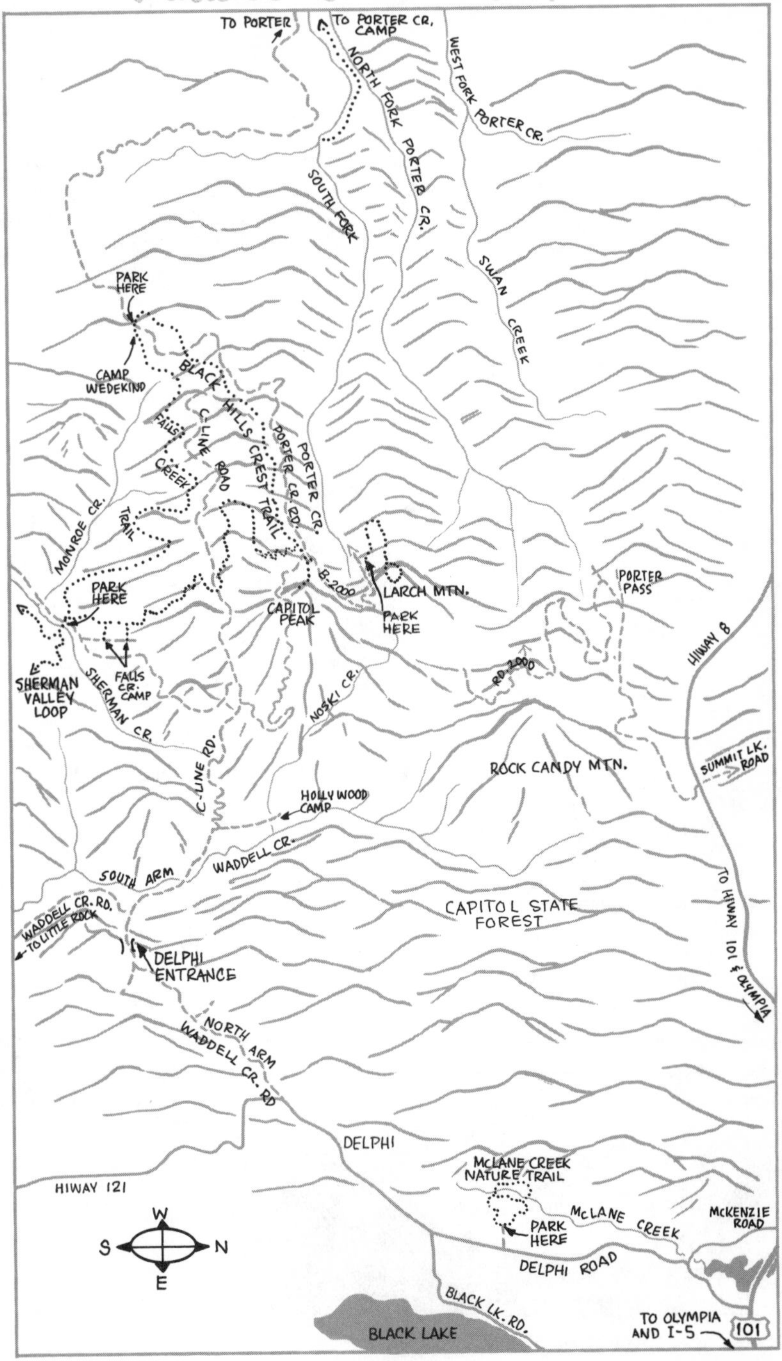
TO PORTER
TO PORTER CR. CAMP
NORTH FORK PORTER CR.
WEST FORK PORTER CR.
SOUTH FORK
SWAN CREEK
PARK HERE
CAMP WEDEKIND
BLACK HILLS CREST TRAIL
FALLS CREEK TRAIL
C-LINE ROAD
PORTER CR. RD.
PORTER CR.
MONROE CR.
PARK HERE
B-2000
LARCH MTN.
PARK HERE
CAPITOL PEAK
PORTER PASS
HIWAY 8
SHERMAN VALLEY LOOP
FALLS CR. CAMP
SHERMAN CR.
NOSKI CR.
RD. 2000
ROCK CANDY MTN.
SUMMIT LK. ROAD
C-LINE RD.
HOLLYWOOD CAMP
WADDELL CR.
SOUTH ARM
CAPITOL STATE FOREST
TO HIWAY 101 & OLYMPIA
WADDELL CR. RD. TO LITTLE ROCK
DELPHI ENTRANCE
NORTH ARM WADDELL CR. RD
DELPHI
McLANE CREEK NATURE TRAIL
HIWAY 121
W
S
N
E
PARK HERE
McLANE CREEK
McKENZIE ROAD
DELPHI ROAD
BLACK LK. RD.
BLACK LAKE
TO OLYMPIA AND I-5
101

Aerial view of Mima Mounds

loess or silt deposited atop a plain of glacial deposits was sculpted into mounds by flooded mountain valleys bursting their ice dams. As for protection, that grew steadily more urgent with burgeoning motorcycle hoodlumism; of the nearly 1,000,000 mounds originally scattered over some 30,000 acres of prairies, most not already leveled by plows and cows and bulldozers were being ravaged by razzers. In 1967 the site of Mima Prairie was declared by the National Park Service as a Registered National Landmark. Evergreen State College took over the lease for study and protection purposes. Now the land manager, the state DNR, has built a trail system that will preserve the site while permitting public enjoyment of the phenomenon.

Drive Waddell Creek Road (see Waddell Creek Entrance) about 0.7 mile and at the DNR sign turn left on the entry road a scant 0.2 mile to the parking area and trailhead, elevation 240 feet.

Begin at the dome of the interpretive center. Study the displays, then walk the paved 1/2-mile self-guiding nature trail, consulting the pamphlet that explains the evolution of the plant community.

Next, wander the less formal trails any old way, any old how. The Natural Area Preserve, 445 acres, is thoroughly sampled—fields, forest, and clumps of shrub-like firs pioneering the fields. (The cessation of regular burning by the Indians, done to perpetuate their "camas root farms," has resulted in expansion of forests.) The spring flower show is famous—the grassland turns blue with camas blooms. In summer come the bluebells, wooly sunflowers, oxeye daisies. Then the prairie turns to gold as the grasses dry. Even late October usually has a profusion of bluebells-of-Scotland amid the golden grass and the airy balls of yellow-green lichen. Birds: little flitterers in the grass seeking seeds and bugs, raptors patrolling above on the lookout for little critters in the grass.

And mounds. Some in the woods, covered with moss and ferns. Some in the prairies, covered with grass and herbs. Contrast those seen from highways, low bumps nearly or completely flattened, to those here, with full original relief.

Don't rush. Take your time. Feel the vibrations. Watch out for Ancient Astronauts.

Round trip about 5 miles, allow 5 hours
High point 240 feet, minor elevation gain
All year

Cedar Creek (map—page 116)

The biggest stream in the Black Hills, intimately experienced on a foot-only path particularly swell for leading tiny children by the hand, introducing them to splashing-type puddles, throwing-type rocks, and frogs.

From the Bordeaux Entrance drive the D-Line 3.2 miles to Sherman Valley Y. Go straight ahead on the D-Line (Cedar Creek Road) to the west end of Sherman Valley Camp. At the parking area with the sign, "Foot Trails Only," park, elevation 388 feet.

Walk down into the delightful streambank campground to a dandy foot-only bridge over Cedar Creek, which has just received the waters of Sherman Creek. The water seems a dark tea—until one realizes the color is from algae-covered bottom pebbles. Black water for the Black Hills. The path often is precisely beside the water, on a bottom carpeted with thousand mothers, sometimes on an elevated alluvial terrace, sometimes high on the sidehill. Lichen-silvered alders lean over the stream, lacing branches high above the bird avenue. Stare into spooky depths of black pools. Show the kiddies a beaver-gnawed giant cottonwood. Pause to let them play on gravel bars—or, at one point, an outcrop of black basalt where white suds fleck black water.

The trail fords the creek and at 2 miles hits Cedar Creek Road. Don't bother; go back the way you came.

Round trip 4 miles, allow 3 hours
High point 600 feet, elevation gain 400 feet
All year

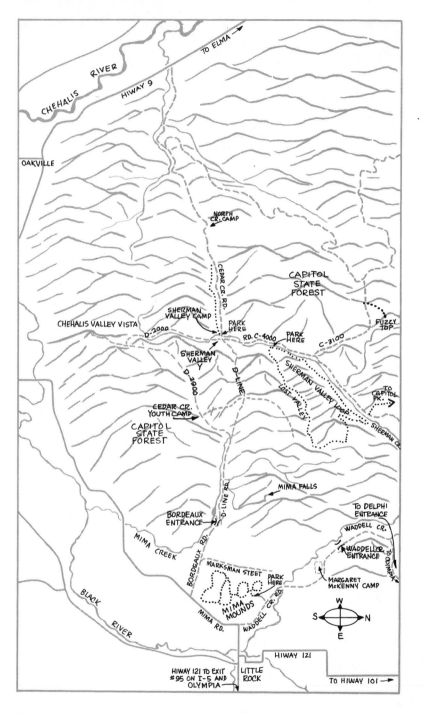

Cedar Creek

Fuzzy Top (map—page 116)

Golly knows the railroad loggers tried to take 'em all, leave nothing taller than a huckleberry bush. Here and there they were defeated by a "long corner"—an area just beyond the reach of the yarding rigs and not quite worth pushing a rail spur to another setting. Now and then, too, the terrain was too steep and mean. Thus it was that a knob topped by 200-year-old Douglas firs and hemlocks escaped the misery whips and the chokers and amid the scalped ridges stood out as a "fuzzy top" knob. Assuming stewardship of the land, the state foresters gave it brownie points for broadcasting seed to reforest the bushland. Perhaps they grew fond of it for its own sake. Possibly, now, they wouldn't dare molest it.

From the Sherman Valley Y (see Cedar Creek) turn north on road No. C-4000 a long 2 miles and turn left on road No. C-3100 and climb 2 miles to the trail sign, elevation 1500.

THE SOUTHERN FRONTIER

The path is closed to motorcycles and horses. So, walk in peace, through vistas of the Black Hills Crest, into the old-growth. In a scant ½ mile is the summit, 1720 feet. Not the highest knob around. But the only noticeable part of Capitol Forest harboring trees older than—in human equivalence—7 years. The giants in their early middle age look out in all directions to children, infants.

Round trip 1 mile, allow 1 hour
High point 1720 feet, elevation gain 220 feet
February-December

Sherman Valley Loop (map—page 116)

The longest and richest valley walk in the Black Hills, following an old rail grade up one stream through skunk cabbage and beaver ponds in splendid mixed forest, then crossing a ridge and switchbacking down firs and ferns and descending another creek in the supreme alder bottom of the area.

Mushrooms on a fallen tree in Sherman Valey

From Sherman Valley Y (see Cedar Creek) turn right on Sherman Valley Road (C-4000) 1.2 miles upstream to a trail sign on the right, "Sherman Valley Trail." Park here, elevation 450 feet. (There's a second trailhead 2 miles up the road but in the surveyor's opinion this is the most esthetic start.)

Cross Sherman Creek, wide and black-bottomed and alder-overhung, to a T. The loop, equally esthetic either way, here is described counterclockwise. Turn right, signed "Mima Trailhead," round a corner into tributary Lost Valley, and hit one of the Bordeaux boys railroads. The little creek is pretty, the huge cedar stumps are crowned by salal gardens, the firs are big, the alders moss-green or lichen-silvery, Rusted ironware and rotten trestlework are passed, and a stump with a cable groove and spikes. Beaver dams. The creek is crossed and recrossed repeatedly. Inside-out flower and foamflower and youth-on-age and trillium and ginger and all.

At 2½ miles, 1000 feet, near the ridge crest at the valley head, is a Y. The right leads 7 miles to McKenney Camp via Mima Falls; go left, climb above the creek head in the now-silent valley, ¾ mile to another Y at 1100 feet. The right leads in 4¾ miles to McKenny Camp and 5¾ to Mima Trailhead; go left, signed "Fall Creek Camp 2.1." (Note: As of 1988 the trail between the Ys is closed and it is temporarily necessary to detour on the adjoining road No. C-5000 for 1 mile. Go off the trail at the first Y, to the road, and leave the road to reach the second Y.) Now not on rail grade but new trail, sidehill through a saddle, 1150 feet, and leave Lost Valley for another tributary of Sherman Creek. The trail makes long, lazy switchbacks down the steep hill in fine fir and massed ferns, crossing and recrossing trickle creeks. Capitol Peak is glimpsed.

Dry-hillside ecosystem is left for that of lush valley. At 2 miles from the 1100-foot Y is Sherman Creek, 580 feet. A bridge crosses to the road and upper trailhead. Go left, downstream, swinging in and out of tributary valleys, sometimes close by marvelous wide Sherman Creek, sometimes up on the slope with grand overlooks of Sherman Valley and down to the creek in interwoven billows of alders. The way crosses waterfalling creeks and carpets of Oregon shamrock, tunnels thickets of vine maple, with screened views of the Black Hills Crest and Fuzzy Top. At about 2½ miles from the upper trailhead the loop is closed.

Loop trip 8 miles, allow 6 hours
High point 1150 feet, elevation gain 900 feet
All year

Capitol Peak (map—page 113)

One of the two tippy-tops of the Black Hills, Capitol commands a grand sweep of horizons from Cascades to Olympics, Bald Hills to Willapa Hills, saltwater fingers of Puget Sound to infinity of the Pacific Ocean. The ascent excellently samples the second-growth wildland from green depths of Sherman Valley to wide-sky heights.

Drive to the upper trailhead of Sherman Valley Trail (which see). Across the road is the Capitol trailhead, signed "Greenline #6" as well as for Camp Wedekind and Porter, elevation 580 feet. The claim is made that Capitol Peak is 3.2 miles. A sign in the woods a few steps away says 4½ miles. Preposterous. The surveyor's feet added up 5½.

In second-growth fir and Second Wave clearcuts the trail sidehills out of Sherman Valley, passing several alternative entries from Fall Creek Camp. At ½ mile, in cool alder bottom, is the crossing of West Fork Fall Creek. The first of many old logging railroad grades is joined for a lovely passage through alternating alder and fir forest. The grade is left, the trail climbs, hits another grade and contours, leaves and climbs, and so on, the pattern repeated. At 1250 feet, 1½ miles from the creek crossing, C-Line Road is crossed. (An alternative start for a shorter ascent—but missing the nicest woods.)

View east from Capitol Peak

Contouring above the road, the trail passes screened views over Sherman Valley to Fuzzy Top, its dark-green 200-year-old firs prominent in the lighter green of 50-year-old firs. At 1350 feet, ¹/₂ mile from the C-Line, is a bridge over West Fork Fall Creek, clear, cool, waterfalling, tasty. In a scant ¹/₂ mile, at 1525 feet, is a T with a rail grade that goes left to the C-Line and right, in maybe 3 miles, to the Capitol Peak Road. Go right a few feet and then left, leaving the grade for resuming foot trail, signed "Capitol Peak." Then another rail grade, another contour. But at 1650 feet, something different.

Switchbacks, by the dozen. And spindly young firs with lots of holes between—views south to the Chehalis valley. For a scant 2 miles the trail alternately climbs and maddeningly contours (for the comfort of horses). A trickle is appreciated on a scorching day. A "meadow" opens up a view over the head of West Fork Fall Creek to—ta! da!—Capitol Peak, which has begun to seem a myth. At 2350 feet the trail attains the saddle between the peak and the long Black Hills Crest (which see) west. And (sob) the Porter Creek Road.

The final long ¹/₂ mile is all road. Turn right from the trail a few steps to Capitol Forest Vista and a triple fork. The right is the Capitol Peak Road, B-2100. The left leads to Big Larch Mountain (which see). Take the middle fork and climb the crest in fir shrubs and flowers to the summit, 2667 feet, 5¹/₂ miles. If one comes on a spring Sunday, one realizes the ideal time for this ascent is winter, when at least the family sedans are missing from the vehicle parade, maybe the motorcycles if the snow is deep enough, leaving only four-wheel sports and the regiment of service trucks always here tending the forest of radio towers, testimony to the American revision of Descartes: "I communicate, therefore I exist."

Move from one side to another of the summit plateau, then to the other summit, for the best views in various directions. South: the big valley of Sherman Creek, Prairies (Mima, Baker, Grand Mound, and other), Chehalis valley, Doty and Willapa Hills. Easterly to northerly: the big valley of Waddell Creek, South Puget Plain, Bald Hills, St. Helens, Adams, Rainier, Glacier, Baker. Northerly: the big valley of Porter Creek, Big Larch and Rock Candy. Totten, Eld, Budd, and Henderson Inlets and Nisqually Reach, Black Lake and Olympia, Issaquah Alps, Green and Gold Mountains, Olympics—starring the home of the gods, Olympus. West: what that Spanish chap saw from a peak in Darien.

Round trip 11 miles, allow 8 hours
High point 2667 feet, elevation gain 2300 feet
February-December

Falls Creek Trail (map—page 113)

Tour the history of railroad logging in its highest and latest days hereabouts. Squish through skunk cabbage, hop over creeks, look out through young forest to the hinterland. If not so big-sky dramatic as the Black Hills Crest which it parallels, the Falls Creek Trail gets more intimate with the juices of the Black Hills.

Drive to Camp Wedekind (see Black Hills Crest), elevation 1896 feet.

The trail takes off east of the shelter, signed "Greenline #8, Fall Creek Trail." The beginning is in alder forest on old rail grade. Springs are crossed on puncheon bridge. A glimpse of Fuzzy Top. More springs, more puncheon, maidenhair fern, oxalis ("Oregon shamrock," the Irish call it). A bridge over a creek leads to an eye-catching structure of crisscrossed, 6-foot-diameter logs at the edge of the steep scarp of Monroe Creek. A loading dock? The grade proceeds in more springs and creeks, all draining to Monroe Creek, by remnants of trestles.

At about 1 mile the way opens out to views the first time. A railroad causeway (locomotives hate wet feet) is carpeted with ginger. Beyond a swamp and an eerily dark tulgeywood is another view opening. Back in forest, the railroad at last is left behind as the trail commences a gradual descent, coming to another bridge and then the largest stream yet, still another branch of Monroe Creek, and a long long bridge over springs and marsh.

The trail nicely winds out around a perky little 1300-foot peaklet but then, at 5 miles, enters a recent clearcut. The route continues 2 miles down to Falls Creek Camp on road No. C-4000, but here, at 1000 feet, is the proper turnaround. Return to Camp Wedekind. Squish squish.

Round trip 10 miles, allow 7 hours
High point 1896 feet, elevation gain 1000 feet (on the return)
February-December

Black Hills Crest (map—page 113)

The five-star scenic supershow of the Black Hills. It ends atop Capitol Peak and has all those views. But in addition are kaleidoscopes from the trail along the crest of the range's longest, highest ridge, between the valleys of Sherman and Porter Creeks. Stroll for miles in bilberry and bracken and alpine-seeming shrubby firs, the sky-surrounded crest eerily moor-like. Enough to make a Scot homesick. Or an Ozark Mountain boy.

From the Y west of Delphi Entrance take the right fork, straight ahead, 1.4 mile to a split. Go left on the C-Line, signed "Capitol Peak, 9 miles." Stay with the C-Line 7 miles to a junction on the ridgecrest, 2150 feet. Turn left on road No. B-2000 for 1.5 miles to Camp Wedekind, site of the 1947-1965 planting camp from which better than 10,000,000 seedlings were set out amid the stumps. Park at the pleasant little camp, with picnic shelter but no water, in a field atop broad-view Wedekind Pass, elevation 1896 feet.

Walk Porter Creek Road a couple hundred feet and turn right on road-trail signed "Trail No. 30, Trail No. 6, Capitol Peak 4 miles." In another hundred feet diverge right toward a quarry on a still lesser track signed "Fall Creek Camp 9.4 miles, Porter Creek Camp 6.5 miles, Capitol Peak 4.1 miles via Trail No. 30 or Greenline #6." Ascend to the quarry top and a sign, "Capitol Peak 3.8, Porter Creek Camp 5.1." Ascend gently a long ½ mile to the crest of 2150 feet and a Y. The left, unsurveyed, descends to Iron Creek Road and Porter Creek Camp; go right, signed "Capitol Peak 3.5."

Now, stroll. On wings, almost, liberated from heavy Earth. A little up, a little down, from one "moor" to another. Grass and salal, huckleberry and salmonberry, old stumps and young firs—including plantations of alpine-appearing nobles. Lumps of weathered basalt columns poke through thin soil. In season the way is colorful with alpine-seeming flowers. Moors fall off right to Sherman Valley and Chehalis Valley draining to the ocean, left to Porter Valley and lacework of blue inlets and green peninsulas of South Sound and the Great Bend of Hood Canal. Ahead are the stump ridge of Big Larch and the surreal summit decorations of Capitol—and huge clean Rainier looming whitely beyond.

Twice the road is crossed and twice more can be briefly spotted, but mostly the walker is totally unaware of wheels, so skillfully is the trail placed. The second crossing can confuse. This is at the 2150-foot saddle where the C-Line tops the ridge (see above). Take a few steps right from the junction along the C-Line and go left on a lesser road obscurely signed "Trail." In a couple hundred feet the trail indeed takes off up left to the crest. After a final grassy, rocky, meadow-like knoll at 2450 feet, the trail drops the short bit to a final 2150-foot saddle, that of Capitol Forest Vista, there meeting the top of the Capitol Peak (which see) trail from Sherman Valley. The final ¾ mile is on the road to Capitol Peak, 2667 feet. But if the razzers are thronging you may not want to go. No matter. You've already had a trip.

Round trip 8 miles, allow 6 hours
High point 2667 feet, elevation gain 1500 feet
February-December

Big Larch Mountain (map—page 113)

The highest peak in the Black Hills (by 1 foot, according to the USGS), Big Larch is also the best of the lot. Though in the heart of the ATV Zone, it's the only high summit that's wheelfree. And it has neither trees (larches or any other) to block views nor radio towers to clutter—and to spawn parades of service vehicles and razzers. At the end there's no trail, just game traces through a garden of silver stumps and logs, little shrubs and pretty flowers. And the views! Actually, the other peaks have the approximate equal. But the older surveyor is prejudiced because he came to Big Larch on a crystalline day of late October and for the first time in all his *Footsore* travels saw, grandly ice-chiseled in the depth of the Olympics, none other than Olympus. And by golly, out west was none other than the really-truly ocean. Not salt haze but the water, the waves, shining in the low sun. Boy.

Drive the C-Line to the junction on the Black Hills Crest at 2150 feet (see Black Hills Crest). Turn east on road No. B-2000 for 2.5 miles to the junction of Capitol Forest Vista (see Capitol Peak). Continue on No. B-2000, descending in 1 mile to the pass

Hiker near the summit of Big Larch Mountain

between Porter Creek and Noski Creek, 2200 feet. At the junction in the pass turn left, sidehilling 1 mile to a Y, about 2200 feet. Park here.

Walk the lesser fork, uphill, 1/4 mile to an intersection with a rut signed with a picture of a motorcycle. (Remember, you are on the ATV side of the Forest.) Go right, up the bike trail, a short way to a small open area. Ascend the clearing, watching for obscure tracks made by trucks in the early 1970s during the setting out of seedlings. Follow these along the ridgecrest through shrubs and salal, until they end. Then forge ahead atop or near the hogback, ascending gently to the summit plateau.

Ah, the stump garden, the sculptured silver wood. So sun-scorched and wind-blasted is the crest, so hot and so cold, that even though noble fir has been planted, trees won't grow big here for a long time. As grace notes to stumps and alpine-seeming shrubs are myriad alpine-seeming flowers (in season, not October). Peace! No wheels! Stumps and chunks of weathered basalt contrast with the mess on Capitol. To enjoy the views, walk to edges of the plateau, 2659 feet, for separate panoramas.

What's the view? See the catalog for Capitol Peak. Big Larch has all that, in a different perspective, and more. Bring a big lunch. Maybe dinner, too, for the evening light show.

Round trip 3 miles, allow 2 hours
High point 2659 feet, elevation gain 500 feet
February-December

WHULGE TRAIL:
TACOMA TO OLYMPIA TO ALLYN

Walkable the whole year, close to homes of nearly everybody, the Whulge Trail is the region's single most important walking route. Even if their various governments don't, Whulgers know it. Folks flock to exchange the gloom and clutter of dank winter forests for the freedom and simplicity of the sands, hobnob with ducks and admire pretty boats, open eyes and souls in panoramas of waves and islands and mountains and sky.

The way begins in Tacoma, where the steam plume is the showiest, the smelter stack the tallest, and Point Defiance the greatest city park for at least a few thousand miles. Two parallel strips of steel lead through The Narrows, under the most esthetic bridge in the region, past some of the most enormous gravel mines. Then commences the longest stretch of the most utter wildness on the entire Trail, the triple sequence of Fort Lewis Military Reservation, the old and empty Dupont explosives-making preserve, and Nisqually National Wildlife Refuge on the delta of the Nisqually River, emptying into the South Sound.

The "South Sound." How does it differ from the "North Sound"? The boundary is less a line than a zone of transition, but the Nisqually may be said to complete the change that starts at Tacoma.

North is Main Street carrying traffic of the world. South is lonesomer, with few ships, some tugs-barges, mainly pleasure craft. North is where the glaciers came from and stayed the longest. In the South the Vashon Glaciation, the most recent, was relatively brief and its drift is more mixed with the older Salmon Springs deposits, the gravels partly iron-cemented to conglomerate, the sands nearly sandstone, the blue clays often iron-stained and compacted to rubbly shale, forming quite vertical walls—but not so tall as North, usually less than 100 feet and often mere banks that let houses crowd the water.

South is the hotbed of history: the historical museum in Tacoma; the reconstruction of Fort Nisqually at Point Defiance; old homes of Steilacoom; the site of Fort Nisqually, first European settlement on Puget Sound; Treaty Tree where were signed the Medicine Creek Treaties that started the Indian Wars; and Tumwater, first American settlement on the Sound.

North is characterized by broad sweeps of water and wind, long views and violent storm surfs, high bluffs, often of naked drift, and wide beaches beaten from the cliffs; drama.

South is what Vancouver called "the sea in the forest." A complexity of bays and spits, a maze of passages and inlets and reaches and islands. Estuaries lovely to look at, delightful to boat, appalling to boot, the intermingling of muck and brush and water often forming absolute route-stoppers. Birds enjoy the protected waters—everywhere in winter are small flocks, vast fleets—and the population of great blue herons and kingfishers may be the largest in the world. Seals, too, are happy here. So are people who appreciate the intimacy, the coziness, of narrow waterways where waves are feebler and thus beaches narrower. When trees slide down the bluff and topple to the sands they are not, North-like, battered to driftwood in a winter and carried away by longshore currents; they just lay there growing seaweed and barnacles, awful to crawl through. Vegetation grows to the very edge of the beach, swordferns root in the sands, and maples and alders lean far over the gravels, enclosing green-lit alcoves of waterfalls and maidenhair fern; if they lean too low they give a walker the brushfits. The shallow bays drain at low tide to become enormities of mudflats, seeming alternative routes and brush escapes, but often sucking in boots, knees, thighs, maybe entire hikers. It's a whole new beach-walking game, brandnew to the explorer from the North. Worth the learning. South is different. But good.

Abandoned dock at Titlow Beach Park

WHULGE TRAIL

The mile-by-mile description of the Trail ends at Tumwater Falls. Puget Sound, though, goes on and is traced through its fascinating frittering away into long, narrow fingers (let it be noted, with few public put-ins, and little evidence much will be preserved from subdivision) to its westernmost waters at Shelton, its north-westernmost at Allyn. But, you say, the South Sound has another shore. Yes. For that see following chapters.

USGS maps: Tacoma South, Tacoma North, Gig Harbor, Steilacoom, McNeil Island, Fort Lewis, Nisqually, Lacey, Longbranch, Squaxin Island, Tumwater, Shelton, Potlatch, Mason Lake, Vaughn, Belfair
Walkable all year

Mile 0-7½: Union Station-Old City Hall-Bayside Trail-
Historical Museum-Garfield Gulch Park-Puget Park-
ASARCO Smelter-Point Defiance Park (map—133)
The fitting commencement is Union Station, superb example of the 19th-century Railroad School of architecture, preserved in all its beautiful ugliness, reminding that Second City began as a rail promotion when Seattle's principle industry was real-estate speculation. The Trail proceeds along Pacific Avenue ½ mile to 11 Street, then a long ⅓ mile through downtown, which quits before it gets tiresome, to Old City Hall at S 7 Street. Here Pacific splits. The right fork is Schuster Parkway, with a splendid sidewalk at the foot of the drift bluff that separates up-high downtown Tacoma from its down-low commercial waterfront. Take the left fork, atop-the-bluff Stadium Way, a scant ¼ mile to the start of the Bayside Trail.

Most city trails are purely of local interest; this one, some 2¼ miles long, is worth coming a distance for; with sidetrips, it can richly fill a day. The trail has a half-dozen easy accesses served by buses and several convenient parking areas, the first on Stadium Way at the trail start at S 5 Street, via a stairway down from the sidewalk. The path contours upsy-downsy along the wildwood bluff, sometimes in a spooky "ivy forest" where that exotic parasite has exterminated native ground cover, often in great views to the Simpson Kraft steam plume, waterways and industry of the Puyallup flats, ships in Commencement Bay, Cascades and Olympics. Five rustic picnic shelters are nice spots to get out of the rain and eat your kipper snacks. Soon after the third shelter is a sidepath uphill to the Washington State Historical Society Museum, worth days of browsing; parking at N 4 Street and Stadium Way. Also notable here is the natural amphitheater, the stadium, famed in the pre-electronic era for its acoustics, letting Fourth-of-July oratory reverberate. Another wonder is Stadium High School, housed in a majestic old railway hotel of French Provincial style, replete with spires and turrets and garrets. What a crazy place to go to school! Past the fifth shelter, and around a point above old red sheds of Sperry Ocean Dock, the way swings into Garfield Gulch Park. A short path drops to the gulch mouth. A longer path swings up the gulch to Garfield Playground (street parking on Borough Road at N D Street) and a view of rambling Annie Wright Seminary, then descends the gulch to the end of the Bayside Trail on sidewalk of Schuster Parkway. No parking just here.

Cross under the parkway skyway, over the tracks, and walk the seawall to a park strip (with parking) leading to McCarver Street, where Schuster Parkway ends, the arterial becoming Ruston Way. Here the shore is designated as Commencement Park, extending 2 miles to N 49 Street. Have a fresh seafood lunch: stop at Ocean Fish Company, go out on the public Old Town Dock, sit on a bench, and peel shrimp while watching the fishermen, human and feathered, and enjoying views down Commencement Bay to Mt. Tahoma. First seen by Europeans (Vancouver) in 1792, named in 1841 by the Wilkes Exploring Expedition, which here commenced its work, the bay was first settled in 1852. In the 1860s Job Carr homesteaded at Chebaulip (Old Town, Old Tacoma). On behalf of the railroad. McCarver renamed the projected metropolis for The Mountain and moved the center up the bay. Now, however, Old

Union Station

Town is undergoing a renaissance—restoration of historic buildings, establishment of nice little places to buy good things to eat.

Parking is plentiful as Ruston Way proceeds by a picturesque old derelict sawmill on a pier, a fish and chips bar (oh the aroma!), Harbor Lights, and a boat company. A paved bikeway-footpath comes in from Alder Way and goes along beside the seawall.

For a sidetrip at Alder Way, walk the trail 1 mile up the green ravine of Puget Gardens, a fine wild scene.

At 49 Street a monster sign, "ASARCO TACOMA," used to announce entry to the City of Ruston, a chunk of Butte plunked down by the Sound. An interestingly cruddy industrial beach gives a great view back to Commencement Bay and the Cascades and down the Sound to Vashon and Maury Islands and Glacier Peak. The public highway to Point Defiance tunnels through the smelter—too dangerous to walk. Actually, few folks will wish to walk from here on. This spot, 5 1/2 miles from Union Station, makes a nice day's tour—with the option of riding back on the bus.

But, for the purists, a detour continues the Trail. From Ruston Way climb the bluff on N 49th, switchbacking up Waterview to Ferdinand. Turn right on 48th, cross Huson to the hilltop, to Baltimore. Turn right, downhill, passing the very foot of the gigantic masonry heap of the smelter stack, visible from Cascades to Olympics. Stand a while, struck dumb. Until the smelter closed in 1985, after a century in operation, the 572-foot, 10-inch stack—tallest in the world when built in 1916—emitted 310 tons of arsenic a year. (The stack may be dynamited to earth in 1989.) At the bottom of the hill, in the mill area, turn left on Ruston Way and continue along streets and sidewalks to the entrance to Point Defiance Park.

Bus: 13, Oakland, to Historical Museum; 11, Point Defiance, to the park

A Shay locomotive at Point Defiance Park

Point Defiance Park (map—page 133)

The greatest city park in the nation? On the nomination list, anyhow. The greatest in the Northwest? No contest. The average city park is dandy for the folks for whom it's handy, but nothing to justify a long trip. Here's no average park. Acquired from the Army in 1888 (formal title transferred in 1906) this peninsula ¾ mile wide and nearly 2 miles long juts out between The Narrows and Dalco Passage, providing some 3 miles of mostly wild beach from which drift cliffs leap to an upland of big-tree virgin forest interwoven with 50 miles or more of trails. There also are gardens, zoo, and aquarium—and Camp Six and Fort Nisqually, by golly. Second-largest municipal park in America, 698 acres, exceeded only by New York's Central Park, this is not merely a city asset but a regional treasure.

All roads (and a bus line) lead to Point Defiance. The easiest way for foreigners to get there is to leave I-5 on Exit 132, follow Highway 16 toward Narrows Bridge, and turn right on Pearl Street.

Five Mile Drive, looping the perimeter, has numerous parking areas to permit short walks on blufftop or in forest. For the beach walk, up to 6 miles round trip on a low-medium tide, drive to parking at the Vashon ferry dock or Owen Beach; the walking is discussed below, when Trail narration resumes. A good introduction is a perimeter survey. For this, park at the first opportunity, just inside the Pearl Street entrance, elevation 100 feet.

Not to overburden with elaborate and unnecessary instructions, the plan is to head for the water but stop short, atop the bluff, and except for one deviation, stay there all around the peninsula. The trail system is not signed and there are a dozen times more paths than shown on maps—just take the outermost (nearest the bluff) path and, that failing, walk the road or cross into forest to find a path there. Following are sights along the way:

Overlook of Vashon Island ferry dock, the black-slag (from the smelter) peninsula on which is built the Tacoma Yacht Club and Commencement Bay and the Cascades. Japanese Gardens. Job Carr home, moved here from Old Tacoma, built 1864, the settlement's first post office. A sign on Five Mile Drive, "Big Tree Trail—This is the Forest Primeval," leading on a 3/4-mile loop up one side of a ravine, down the other, sampling glorious old Douglas firs and other splendid wildland vegetables. Rhododendron Gardens. A major ravine, one of several slicing the bluff, this one carrying the road down to Owen Beach; for perimeter purposes it is best to follow the road down to the beach and on the far side of the ravine find meager paths up the bluff to more formal trails. Vashon Island viewpoint. Another superb green-riot ravine, with the loop's last decent trail down to the beach. The Mountaineer Tree, a fir 220 feet tall, a circumference of 24 feet, about 400 years old. Another great viewpoint, up Colvos Passage. Point Defiance Viewpoint, atop a sand-gravel cliff above the light, with views across to Gig Harbor. Here, in 1841, Lieutenant Wilkes declared that with a few cannon he could defy the fleets of the world; in 1868 President Johnson signed the order reserving the site for coast artillery, but guns never were emplaced. Walking distance to here, about 4 miles. Onward to:

Madronas leaning over the bluff brink. Eagle-perch fir snags. Narrows Bridge Viewpoint. Never Never Land, a Mother Goose World (optional). A viewpoint noting the camp made May 20, 1792 by Peter Puget, when detailed by Captain Vancouver to explore this "sea in the forest."

Fort Nisqually—allow at least an hour here. The first fort, built in 1833 by Hudson's Bay Company, was destroyed by Indians and little is known about it except the location near the beach just north of the Nisqually River. The second fort was built in 1843 at a more inland site at Dupont, 17 miles south of here. Remnants were moved here in 1933 and the entire fort faithfully reconstructed. Among the fort's firsts: first European settlement on the Sound, first cattle, sheep, and chickens on the Sound, first European marriage, first European child, first religious instruction, first murder. The only original buildings are the granary, the oldest surviving building (1843) in Washington, and the factor's house, now a museum, open afternoons, featuring rooms with pioneer furnishings, other relics, and a small souvenir shop. Replicas, displaying pioneer artifacts: blacksmith shop, two lookout towers, kitchen, washroom, Nisqually House (the warehouse that was located on the beach below the fort). Also original is the boiler of the wood-burning *Beaver*, launched in England in 1835, arrived at Nisqually in 1837, the first steamship on the Northwest Coast, wrecked off Vancouver, British Columbia, in 1888. Onward:

From a group camp just below the fort, bluff-near paths lead to the Salmon Beach community and the Narrows Bridge (see Whulge Trail below).

Camp Six—allow another hour, especially if you've spent a lot of time in second-growth forests among evidences of railroad logging, for here are a logging railroad complete with locomotive, a Shay No. 7, invented 1880, a huge Lidgerwood Skidder, a Dolbeer Donkey, a loaded log car, other donkeys, yarders, and loaders, a 110-foot fully rigged spar tree, and two complete logging camps, one (formerly Camp 7 in the Kapowsin Tree Farm, described in this book) resting on the ground, the other (Quinault Car Camp) on flatcars. Onward, now inland, the bluff having been left at the fort:

Northwest Native Gardens. Via a detour left, the zoo (the owls are particularly outstanding); the aquarium, best on a rainy winter day when the seals and walrus and otter are lonesome and will stage a swimming show for your solitary benefit; and the 1906 carousel. Rose gardens. Pond full of islands, bridges, and ducks. Waterfalls. And so back to the Pearl Street Entrance, some 3 walking miles from Point Defiance.

Perimeter loop 7 miles, allow 7 years
High point 300 feet, elevation gain 800 feet
Bus: 11, Point Defiance

Mile 7¹/₂-14: Point Defiance Park-Vashon Ferry Dock-Dalco Passage-Point Defiance Light-The Narrows-Salmon Beach-Bennett Tunnel-Narrows Bridge (map—page 133)

From the park entrance walk road or path down ¹/₄ mile to the Vashon ferry dock and follow the shore on an old, closed-off road a scant 1 mile to Owens Bathing Beach. From now on the beach is wild, and wilder, beneath the 200-foot jungled bluff of sand and blue clay, views over Dalco Passage, north to the Issaquah Alps. In 1 mile is the last path up the bluff—the last easy beach escape in the park. In a long ¹/₂ mile more the shore curves around to Point Defiance and the light, at the base of a great sand precipice. An exciting place—Dalco currents colliding with Narrows currents, fishermen, boated and winged, clustered at the rip, views over the water to Gig Harbor and up and down the Sound.

It's a good spot for thoughtful, cautious folk to turn around. The next section of Trail—to Bennett Tunnel—is recommended only for the doughty, and maybe a little dumb. The saving grace (and what saved the surveyor's neck) is that a person needn't hike the stretch twice in a day but can loop back to the start by Tacoma bus. Actually, at low tide the 1¹/₂ miles south of the point, to park's end, are safe and partly easy— and the most rewardingly wild section of the park. And though there is no safe way up the bluff, a rude path of sorts blunders along the bluff foot, through the clumps of alder forest riding sand blocks down to block the beach with brush; an explorer doesn't risk drowning, only exquisite suffering, with the possibility of cracking wide open, as happened to the surveyor, who at last said the hell with it and went wading in The Narrows, water to his waist.

At the park's end (unsigned) begins Salmon Beach, supporting a truly Alternative life style. Ever-menaced by the unstable sand precipice above, on a southwest shore open to storms, beside The Narrows which at change of tides runs river-swift, boat and trail access only, are some 50 residences built on pilings of driftwood and scraps stacked and tacked together, ingeniously designed, gaudily painted. Crazy, man. And to attempt to describe the 1 mile by Salmon Beach to Bennett Tunnel also is. On the ground, though, the route is self-evident, and goes something like this:

From the start of the shanties find a path up the bluff to the main access trail and ascend a scant ¹/₄ mile to a turnaround circle, by the bluff edge, find a fairly decent trail climbing a scant ¹/₄ mile to a gravel road, 260 feet. The road goes left to civilization, right down toward the beach; go straight on a woods road along the flat near the bluff edge a scant ¹/₄ mile to a turnaround with garages sized for cars of the 1920s and with (late 1977) 44 mailboxes. (Note trails in the woods north—for chickening-out purposes, these lead to the Fort Nisqually section of the park.) On the south side of the turnaround circle, by the bluff edge, find a fairly decent trail climbing to a gravel road, 260 feet. The road goes left to civilization, right down to the beach; go straight on a woods road along the flat near the bluff edge a scant ¹/₄ mile to a turnaround with parking area. Find a good old trail dropping off the lip into confusion. The next scant ¹/₂ mile is beyond description. Paths go everywhere in the largest, finest madrona forest in the older surveyor's experience. Avoid those that go inland to civilization and those that drop to houses of Salmon Beach. If you get onto poor trail, or dangerous, retreat, because there is at least one easy, safe way. At last find a path that drops directly onto the top of the mouth of Nelson Bennett Tunnel, and thence to the railroad tracks. Fun, wasn't it?

Tacoma Narrows Bridge ("Sturdy Gertie") from War Memorial Park

WHULGE TRAIL

Now the way is plainly marked by the two parallel strips of steel. Above left, the wildland bluff continues—a 6-mile jungle from Point Defiance to Titlow Beach that would make a famous trail, and indeed doubtless has a network of paths familiar to many local residents under the age of 16. Below right is the water—and rarely any beach, due to the railroad invasion. The view is south to Narrows Bridge and across to Point Evans and Point Fosdick. Grebes ride the currents, and gulls on bits of driftwood, apparently for the sheer thrill of the speed.

At ³/₄ mile from the tunnel is a little waterfall-creek and a trail up the bluff—to where? A bit south is a large creek valley and a woods road—from where? Here are square miles of in-city wilderness, guaranteed by the bluff's treachery to remain so. The way passes under powerlines carrying Lake Cushman electricity to Tacoma and at a long 2 miles from Bennett Tunnel crosses under the awesome Narrows Bridge. In the wonderful wild valley just beyond is (what else? you maybe expected a park?) another sewage plant. The service road winds up the bluff ¹/₄ mile to parking at War Memorial Park.

Bus: 11, Point Defiance, to Vashon ferry dock; 12A, University Place, to 6 Avenue and Jackson; walk ³/₄ mile to War Memorial Park

Mile 14-21¹/₂: Narrows Bridge-Titlow Beach Park-Days Island-Sunset Beach-Chambers Bay-Sunnyside Beach Park-Steilacoom ferry dock (map—page 133)

From I-5 take Exit 132 and drive Highway 16 to the first exit before the Narrows Bridge, onto Jackson Avenue. Go through the light, downhill to War Memorial Park. Park here, elevation 120 feet.

Walk out on the bridge for views up and down The Narrows (skinniest segment of the main channel of Puget Sound) from Point Defiance to Steilacoom. It's exciting as trucks cross and the entire monstrous structure *bounces*. The Pictorial Center in the toll plaza tells that The Narrows are 4600 feet wide, 120 feet deep, with 12-foot tides running as fast as 8 knots. A campaign begun in 1923 culminated in the 1940 completion of the first bridge. Called "Galloping Gertie," it never rested, but walked and trotted in breezes, at winds of 35 mph galloped, and on November 7, 1940, at 42 mph, snapped, killing a hysterical dog. On October 14, 1950, was opened the present bridge, "Sturdy Gertie."

From the park walk the switchbacking road (gated against public vehicles but not feet) down to the Western Slopes Treatment Plant and onto the railroad tracks. In ¹/₂ mile begins Titlow Beach Park, ³/₄ mile long and extending inland as much as ¹/₄ mile, mostly wildwoods on both sides of the tracks, a maze of paths everywhere. Leave the tracks for ¹/₃ mile, walking the beach or the top of the low clay-till bank in forest of fir and madrona, a picnic ground. Then follow the top of the seawall on an old, closed road some ¹/₂ mile tto park's end at 6 Avenue, in the community of Titlow. Inland from the tracks is the developed section of the park, with playfields, duck ponds—and if a sidetrip is wanted and a way around the cyclone fence is available, the 1¹/₂-mile or so Fit Trail looping over the greensward, around Titlow Lagoon, up the hill and through the woods. At each of 20 stations the pedestrian is commanded to halt and do pushups or situps or jumpups or leaps over bars or swings across creeks on rings. This gives the ducks fits, and thus the name.

Titlow, with plentiful public parking and a bus line, is reached by driving Highway 16 to where it curves right to the Narrows Bridge and keeping left on 6 Avenue down to the water. Remnants remain of the pre-bridge ferry dock.

Walk the tracks south from Titlow 1 mile through boatworks and marinas in the bay sheltered by Days Island, which is totally covered with houses. In the next 1¹/₄ miles the bluff rears up, keeping houses at a respectful distance atop, the route a strip of wildland. Sunset Beach interrupts, a row of outside-the-tracks cottages on a bulkhead fill. Wild shore resumes for a long ¹/₂ mile.

Now for something completely different. The next 1¹/₂ miles are one of the most gigantic gravel-mining operations on the Whulge—probably in the world. Two gigantic

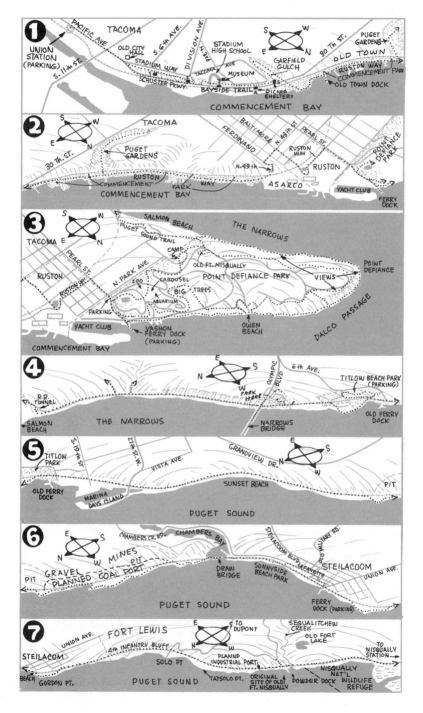

"cirques" gouge the bluff. One looks into the big holes, up the mountains of sand, and expects to see a Foreign Legion patrol ride over the skyline, pursued by a pack of snarling camels. The gravel factories fascinate, with clanking rumbling conveyor belts and washers and sorters, and hoppers for loading rail cars, and docks for loading barges. Let it be noted, though, that the noise and machinery are confined to two spots and most of the 1½ miles is empty and lonesome, and most is excellent sandy beach, a favorite place for private swimming and whatnot. (But the companies are mulling the building of a coal port that would ship 50,000,000 tons a year to Taiwan, Korea, et al. This would raise heck with the skinnydipping. The seals might not like it either.)

Views have been over the water to Fox Island, now left behind, yielding to McNeil Island, whereon appear the penitentiary buildings. At the end of the gravel mines the way crosses a drawbridge over the mouth of Chambers Bay, an estuary in the canyon of Chambers Creek (which see). Marina, lumber yards, and pulpmill steam clouds at the inlet head are picturesque. Just south of the bay, on the shoulder of the Steilacoom-Chambers Creek Road, is public parking.

Now begins the outside-the-tracks bulge of land occupied by Steilacoom's Sunnyside Beach Park, featuring (where else would you put it?) a sewage plant. Parking beside the highway, here named Lafayette Street. Soon comes the ferry dock.

Bus: Tacoma 12A, University Place, to Titlow and to within ¾ mile of Narrows Bridge

Gravel-mine dock near Chambers Bay

Beautifully preserved Victorian building in Steilacoom

Mile 21¹/₂-24¹/₂: Steilacoom ferry dock-Gordon Point-
Cormorant Passage-Solo Point (map—page 133)

From I-5 take Exit 129, singed "Steilacoom," and drive a tortuous and confusing route by a thousand stoplights, all red, past Steilacoom Lake and Western Washington State Hospital, to Steilacoom. Before reaching the ferry dock turn right on the closest-to-the-water street, Commercial, and park somewhere between the dock and Pioneer Orchard Park, on the hill north at Main Street.

Devote an hour or more to touring the town, one of the earliest European settlements on Puget Sound, incorporated 1854, and never growing to such size as to wipe out the old buildings. From here to Bellingham ran the Military Road built in the Indian Wars (or, as Indian historians call them, the White Wars). Numerous houses have plaques identifying them as built in the 1850s. Pioneer Orchard Park is the site of a log cabin used as a school and an Indian Wars refuge. Visit the museum in the Town Hall on Lafayette and Main (1-4 P.M. Tuesday-Thursday, 1-5 Sunday).

Another thing to do at Steilacoom is ride the little ferry to Anderson Island (which see). The shuttlings of the vessel now enliven the water traffic, which south of Tacoma consists mainly of tugs-barges and pleasure craft; this is still Main Street, but down at the lonesome end.

From the ferry dock hit the tracks south. In a short bit is little Salters Point Beach Park. In a long ¹/₂ mile is Steilacoom Bathing Beach Park on Gordon Point, and Steilacoom Marina. Walk out to scan the view north to Narrows Bridge, Fox Island,

and Carr Inlet, westerly over McNeil Island to the Olympics, and to Ketron and Anderson Islands.

Proceed along Cormorant Passage, separating the mainland from little Ketron Island. Bluff rears up to keep houses from the tracks—and soon there are no houses because ³/₄ mile south of Gordon Point begins Fort Lewis, reserved for warfare and wilderness. Little creeks cut ravines through the jungle of 4th Infantry Bluff. What wildwoods are up there? What walks?

At some 2¹/₂ miles from Gordon Point wild solitude is briefly interrupted by the public road at Solo Point.

Mile 24¹/₂-30¹/₂: Solo Point-Tatsolo Point-Dupont Powder Dock-Sequalitchew Creek-Nisqually Delta-Nisqually Station (map—page 133)

Go off I-5 on Exit 119, signed "Dupont, Steilacoom." Turn right at the interchange stoplight to a Y and take the right fork, signed "Steilacoom." At 2.2 miles from the exit spot an obscure fish symbol on the left, denoting a Wildlife Department public access to water, and signs saying "Ft. Lewis Water Pollution Control Plant" and "Solo Point." In 0.7 mile, at an unsigned intersection, go right, in 1.5 more miles passing the sewage plant and winding downhill to a ravine and the large parking area on Solo Point. (Just before the sewage plant is Scout-built Ecology Park, with a self-guiding nature trail, a fine view over the Sound, and a path of sorts down wildwoods to the shore.)

Head south on the tracks, in views to Anderson Island, in some of the most total solitude of any stretch of the Whulge Trail. Something else new: the forest changes from the usual alder-maple mix on clay-sand-gravel-till bluff to Douglas fir on a moderate slope of loose gravels—outwash from the final push south of the Puget Glacier. Inland begin the prairies, and here their notable flower shows extend to the very shore. Tatsolo Point is rounded and views open south past the tip of Anderson Island to the Black Hills—and to the Nisqually Delta. Old pilings are passed, and an old wagon-like road down the bluff, perhaps a settlers' landing predating the fort, maybe even the railroad.

At 2 miles from Solo Point the long pier of the old Dupont powder dock juts out. Fort Lewis has been left for the even more complete wilderness of the 3200 acres where formerly explosives were manufactured, beginning in 1909, an activity that required much empty land around, just in case. Weyerhaeuser Company acquired the property in 1976 and planned to build a major—an enormous—log-and-lumber-products warehousing and shipping port, and perhaps mills as well, and perhaps a major "industrial park" with other companies as tenants. Environmentalists opposed the project for reasons: immediately south is the Nisqually National Wildlife Refuge, crucial to the survival of wildfowl migrating on the Pacific Flyway, as well as resident wildlife; plentiful shipping facilities are available at Tacoma and north and elsewhere in the state, rendering unnecessary a major port on the South Sound, which ought to be left free of the risk of pollution catastrophes; this is the wildest, most peaceful section of the Whulge Trail; Sequalitchew Creek's canyon, down which would come the truck highway to the docks, is the largest and most magnificent wildland gulch on the entire Whulge Trail; the site is among the most historical in the Northwest, with a major village of the Nisquallies, Nisqually House built in 1832 and the first Fort Nisqually in 1833, both at the canyon mouth, an American church mission in 1840, the second Fort Nisqually (see Point Defiance Park) in 1843, up on the bluff where are planned a truck road and rail spur. Weyerhaeuser ignored all this but shelved the plans when the export market weakened. Temporarily. But in 1988 it announced plans to build a new town of 14,000 people, "Northwest Landing," on the property. The Nisqually Delta Association, if it can raise the funds from public contributions, intends to carry on the contest whenever and wherever necessary.

A few steps past the powder dock a pilings jetty juts out at the edge of the vast muds of the Nisqually Flats; here is the boundary of the Wildlife Refuge, where oil and

Nisqually National Wildlife Refuge

organisms should never mix. Fir forests end and "normal" muckycliff deciduous forest resumes. Tracks leave shores of Nisqually Reach and swing into 2-mile-wide Nisqually valley. Above are wildwoods. Below are delta sloughs and marshes and pastures and continous "No Trespassing" signs; in future there may be an entrance here to the Refuge. Mounts Road is crossed on a bridge, then the twin torrents of I-5, and at 3³/₄ miles from the old Dupont powder dock is the site of vanished Nisqually Station.

To get here for walks north to Solo Point and all, go off I-5 on Exit 116, signed "Mounts Road, Old Nisqually." Drive a scant 2 miles from the interchange toward Old Nisqually and shortly after crossing the railroad tracks spot the station site. Ample parking here, elevation 60 feet.

Nisqually National Wildlife Refuge (map—page 133)

The last major unspoiled estuary of its kind on the Pacific Coast of the United States, and an important stopover on the Pacific Flyway for migratory waterfowl, the Nisqually Delta has recorded some 50 species of mammals, 200 of birds, 125 of fish, and 300 of higher plants in its ecosystems of open freshwater and saltwater, mudflats, freshwater marshes, saltmarshes, mixed coniferous forests, deciduous woodlands,

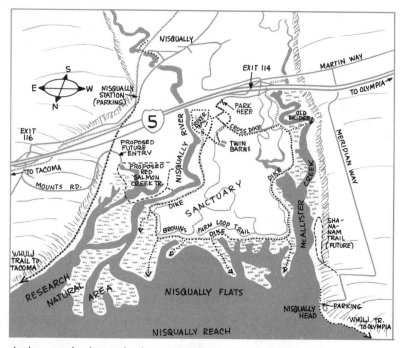

shrubs, grasslands, croplands, and the tidally influenced fresh waters of Nisqually River and McAllister Creek. On one winter trip the older surveyor saw a coyote dive from a dike into a slough, swim across, and run a mile over fields; he also saw (and was closely inspected by) a group of three otters; deer were numerous, and more birds than he knows. Led by the late Margaret McKenny and the Nisqually Delta Association, in 1974 a movement culminated in the establishment of a Nisqually National Wildlife Refuge, managed by the U.S. Fish and Wildlife Service, authorized for an ultimate 3780 acres.

Go off I-5 on Exit 114, signed "Nisqually." Cross under I-5 and turn right 0.2 mile to the refuge entry—no hunting, no pets, foot traffic only, no jogging, daylight use only. Park here, elevation virtually nothing.

For a very great short trip, walk past the open-air interpretive center 1/4 mile to the Twin Barns and the start of the Nisqually River Trail, a 1/2-mile, self-guided, nature trail loop over a slough, through cottonwoods to the river, and back.

The classic long walk is the perimeter loop around the Outer Dike. Now named the Brown Farm Trail, remembering what the delta used to be, it remains the big show. But please keep in mind: until a controlled hunting program can be instituted, the dike will be closed—for the safety of walkers—during the waterfowl hunting season. To avoid disappointments during the development period, visitors are encouraged to call in advance, (206) 753-9467.

From Twin Barns walk to the river and the dike, which follows the Nisqually, gray-green with rock milk from Rainier's glaciers, 1 1/2 miles to the vicinity of the mouth, where diked freshwater marshes yield to saltmarshes open to the tides. Look north to Ketron Island, Steilacoom, Narrows Bridge, ASARCO Smelter. Over Nisqually Reach to the Olympics. Turn around and—holy cow!—that's Rainier!

The dike turns left (west). Saltmarsh reaches out in long, inviting fingers. The wildfowl display depends on the season. Nearly always there are clouds of peep—by the hundreds, the thousands.

In a long 1 mile, at McAllister (Medicine) Creek, the dike turns left (south), following the slough back into the delta, the sluggish water meandering through tidal marshes. In 1½ miles the trail leaves the Outer Dike and turns east on the Cross Dike, which leads in 1¼ miles back to the refuge entrance.

And what besides walking are you doing all that way? Watching herons blunder out of bulrushes into the air, hawks circle above, waterfowl feeding and flying, little birds flittering. And maybe coyotes swimming, otter diving.

Brown Farm Trail loop trip 5¼ miles, allow 4 hours
High point 10 feet, minor elevation gain
All year (presently, except bird-hunting season)

Mile 30½-38: Nisqually Station-Nisqually River-Medicine Creek-Nisqually Head (map—page 138)

The next segment of the Trail is not recommended at present, through it has history and scenery in the first stretch and farther along might become great in a future development of the Nisqually Wildlife Refuge.

At Nisqually Station leave the tracks and walk the Old Pacific Highway, crossing the Nisqually River, going from Fort Lewis to the Nisqually Indian Reservation; downstream a bit is Frank's Landing, scene of opening battles in the Indian (White) Wars of the 1970s.

Just beyond the river turn east on 6 Avenue SE (not so signed, but only "Public Fishing") a long ¼ mile to a Wildlife Department public access on the riverbanks. A woods road-trail leads upstream, and a dike downstream by houses; a person could put together a walk of 1-2 miles, mainly interesting for watching Indian fishermen speed up and down the stream in motorboats, tending nets.

Proceed along Old Pacific Highway to cross Medicine Creek, now called McAllister Creek. At a Y by a grocery store is a monument commemorating December 24-26, 1854, when Governor Stevens hornswoggled the Indians into signing the Medicine Creek Treaties that triggered the Indian Wars of the 1850s. Nearby is the Treaty Tree where the signing took place.

At the monument turn right on 7th, then right again on Steilacoom Road to I-5 and Nisqually Plaza. A trail could be developed from here along the wild-jungled 3-mile wall above McAllister Creek to Nisqually Head. As things stand, if some knucklehead really were determined to walk every step from Tacoma to Olympia he'd have to do it via Martin Way and Meridian Road (which is north-south on the Willamette Meridian) and onward to Nisqually Head.

Mile 38-41: Nisqually Head-Hogum Bay-De Wolf Bight-Beachcrest-Butterball Cove-Big Slough-Tolmie State Park (map—page 138, 141)

Go off I-5 on Exit 114, signed "Nisqually," and drive Martin Way west 1 long mile from Nisqually Plaza. Turn right, north, on Meridian Road 2.5 miles. Turn right on 46th, signed "Public Fishing," and in 0.2 mile turn left and on D'Milluhr Drive and follow the winding road to the Wildlife Department picnic and boat-launch site at Luhr Landing.

South is Audubon Nature Center, open noon to 4 P.M., Wednesday, Saturday, and Sunday, and an unsafe old dock that looks like a ferry slip. Luhr Beach is an entry point to Nisqually National Wildlife Refuge.

The beach west is formidably private and there is no walking except in the high-toleration season (winter weekdays, small, quiet parties) at low-medium tides. A few beach-near bank-top houses are passed and in ¼ mile is an enchanting spot, the first of several tidal lagoons in creek estuaries; sneak up on gangs of floating waterfowl. The bluff lowers, permitting beachside houses, and in another ¼ mile a "point" of oyster shells juts into Hogum Bay. See the conveyor belt bringing shells from the opening room. See the oyster dredge working offshore, bringing in cargoes, picking up shells for returning to the oyster beds, as nowadays is required by law. Oysters may be purchased from the factory's retail outlet.

Tolmie State Park

Unusual for this area, there now is ½ mile of beach mysteriously wild. In the middle is another valley, another estuary lagoon in a cove behind a grassy baymouth bar, wild-tangled forest ringing the waters. Wildness ends in the first of two private beaches of Beachcrest community. Each beach is a little valley; the second has another dandy lagoon. The scant ½ mile of Beachcrest ends in a third valley-estuary-lagoon, this a boat moorage. At low tide one can go inland, leap the mucky creek, and battle brush to retain open beach.

Now comes another long ½ mile of wilderness—this one no mystery. In the middle is a derelict dock led to by a woods road from the the blufftop. Up there, in the middle of the large emptiness usual for such business, Atlas Powder manufactured explosives. Weyerhaeuser has acquired the property and is planning an enormous industrial and port complex, the twin of a complex planned on the other side of the Nisqually National Wildlife Refuge, which thus straddled and menaced would not be much of a refuge. The Nisqually Delta Association stands guard, waiting for Weyco to make a move.

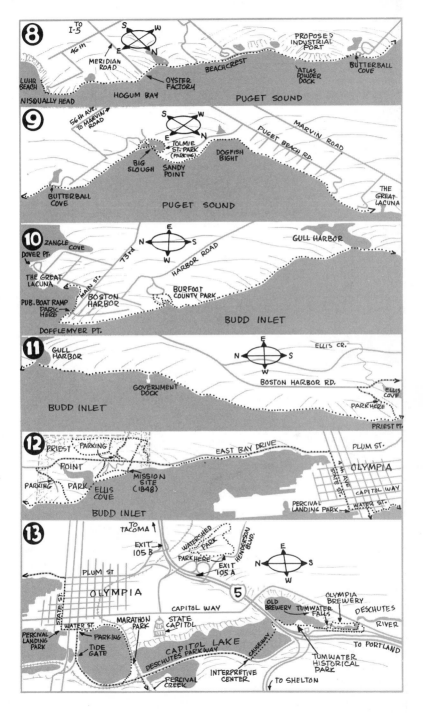

What is presently a great stretch of wildness, potentially a magnificent park, ends in another great valley, baymouth bar, and lagoon at Butterball Cove, with two cute little houses on the bar sharing the beauty with the ducks. At the south end is a 50-foot cliff of wavy-banded, yellow-brown riverbar sands; this handsome cliff, and a companion north of the cove, block walking at all but rather low tides.

The bank is crowded with houses, some by the bulkhead-invaded beach, the final 1/2 mile to the cove of Big Slough and Tolmie State Park.

Mile 41-73: Tolmie State Park-Sandy Point-Dogfish Bight-The Great Lucuna-Henderson Inlet-Dofflemeyer Point (map—page 141)

Go off I-5 on Exit 111, signed "Yelm, Marvin Road," turn right on Marvin Road and drive 5 miles, following signs that lead relentlessly to Tolmie State Park. Park either in the blufftop lot or down in the valley near the beach.

In an area so densely subdivided the public hardly can glimpse the water, this little park is a jewel beyond price, much worth a visit even in the bright, warm season when toleration of trespassing is zero and walkers must stay strictly on public property. A delightful stroll of maybe 2 miles can be put together from these materials: the 1/4 mile of beach to Sandy Point; the woods trail to Sandy Point; the grassy baymouth bar that nearly closes off charming (little) Big Slough; the path down a ravine from the bluff to the beach; a path up the lush-green, wild-tangled valley of Big Slough Creek. A historical display tells about Dr. William Frazer Tolmie (1812-1866), who spent 16 years with Hudson's Bay Company at Nisqually House and Fort Nisqually as physician, surgeon, botanist, and fur trader, and on his botanizing tour of 1833 was the first European to set foot on slopes of Rainier.

But to proceed on the Trail. A scant 1/4 mile from the valley parking lot is Sandy Point, the start of private beach and almost continuous houses. In 1/2 mile more is the splendid slough of Dogfish Bight, the enclosing bar solid with houses. So is the shore north 2 miles to Mill Bight, an estuary that means business, a boot-stopper. And so the Great Lacuna . . .

The hiker's pal, the beach-guarding bluff so nearly omnipresent on the Whulge, dwindles; permitting houses near the beach, even on the beach. And the sheltered, feeble-wave beaches are narrow, often brushy. And the beach repeatedly is interrupted by impassable estuaries. And the Privates have rigidly fenced out the Publics.

The surveyor spent hours probing roads and rarely even saw the water, so expertly is it guarded from alien feet and eyes. The very concept of a Whulge Trail is tenuous here and is maintained only from stubborness as an expression of faith in the future. In this generation, only for residents and guests and roving sailors are the 7 miles from Tolmie State Park by Mill Bight and Baird Cove to Johnson Point, and the 8 miles to the head of Henderson Inlet, first of the frittering-away fingers of the South Sound, and the 10 miles up Henderson Inlet by Woodward and Chapman Bays, where Weyerhaeuser's log railroad used to dump the bay full of wood, to Dana Passage, and the 7 miles by Dickenson Point and Big Fishtrap and Zangle Cove to Boston Harbor and Dofflemyer Point, at the mouth of Budd Inlet.

However. In 1987 the Legislature empowered the state DNR to convert income-producing "trust" lands and other lands that might be acquired to Conservation Areas. The four areas named in the legislation as the start of a statewide system were, Mt. Si, Cypress Island, Dishman Hills—and *446 acres on Woodward Bay* formerly used as a Weyerhaeuser log dump. As of 1988 the surveyors don't know what all this means, but it involves a heronry, bald eagles, and the second-largest seal haulout on South Puget Sound.

Mile 73-78: Dofflemyer Point-Budd Inlet-Burfoot County Park-Gull Harbor-Priest Point Park (map—page 141)

Drive Boston Harbor Road via East Bay Drive from Olympia (see Priest Point Park) to the cozy old village of Boston Harbor. Turn left on Main Street 0.2 mile to an

Inlet north of Burfoot County Park

unsigned public boat-launch and parking area.

Though solidly populated, the shore can be strolled the 1 mile to Dover Point at the mouth of Zangle Cove; the route was not surveyed beyond there but might continue.

Olympiaward the shore of Budd Inlet is just about all private and a fence goes down the left side of the boat ramp to the water; the signs cry "Keep Out—Private Tidelands." Presumably the walker would have to have a minus tide, baring the beaches that are "public." (Ha!) For the hiker from the north this second of the frittering-away fingers, the first to be walked, is a new experience—what from now on is the standard experience. Here is the "sea in the forest," seeming more a lake than an arm of the ocean. Rarely any surf here. The water snuggles.

Dofflemyer Point, with a little old light, is immediately rounded and Budd Inlet entered. In ¾ mostly wild mile is Burfoot (Thurston) County Park. From Boston Harbor Road the park entrance leads to parking areas, elevation 80 feet. A trail system twists and loops around in lovely woods on the bluff slope and descends a cool green ravine to a tiny cove nearly closed off by a little baymouth bar.

The 1½ miles south from the park have a drift bluff 60-100 feet high that keeps all but a couple houses away from the beach. The dome of the Capitol is glimpsed. Once in a great while a ship passes, to or from the Port of Olympia. Beyond the waters rise

Forest trail in Priest Point Park

the Black Hills. A naked till bluff, bright in season with yarrow and vetch and lupine (and poison oak!), announces Gull Harbor. But it's not a used harbor, rather a wonderful little wilderness of forest and estuary lagoon and birds. A baymouth bar nearly closes off the harbor—only at low tide can the channel reasonably be hopped-waded. This makes a good turnaround for a pleasant walk from the park.

Though a few breaks in the bluff permit waterside houses, the next 2¾ miles are mostly in solitude. After 1 mile of just about perfect wilderness are a dock and some sort of small federal-state port and research facility; on the day of the survey, the lightship *Relief* was docked. Beyond is a wooded bluff down which a few staircases come from unseen houses. A picturesque group of floating boathouses, with other houses nearby atop a 30-foot bluff, nourish a fleet of moored sailboats. Pretty. Then a point is rounded and Priest Point Park begins.

Priest Point Park (map—page 141)

Forests of big firs and lush ferns, very deep and greenly wild ravines, a cozy little duck and heron harbor, and a mile of beach with views to ships in the Port of Olympia. And like most everywhere around here, some history, too.

Go off I-5 on Exit 105-B and turn right on Plum Street, which at the shore becomes East Bay Drive; continue on it straight north. Where houses yield to forest, spot a park sign on the median lawn of East Bay, which bisects the park, and turn right on the entry road, which winds uphill a bit to a parking lot, elevation 100 feet.

With proper design the 254-acre park easily could hold a weaving, looping trail system of 5-10 miles. Presently, despite a maze of paths and service roads, there isn't a coherent lengthy walk. But there are a mess of nice little ones. However, the two gorges of Ellis and Mission Creeks have no paths at all. Nevertheless, a person can spend a few hours poking around in the park's hillside-forest and blufftop, beachside-forest segments. No route description is needed. Just go.

For an alternative starting point, at the north end of the park go off East Bay Drive on Flora Vista Road and in several feet turn left on an unmarked gravel road. Where the road becomes a private driveway is a small turnaround-parking area from which a path descends a gully to the beach at Priest Point, just south of where houses mark the boundary. At a low enough tide the beach can be walked south and Ellis Cove, at high tide always floating a flotilla of birds, squished across on mudflats to the main picnic-area portion of the park.

Though no traces remain, at the mouth of Mission Creek the Oblate priest, Father Pascal Ricard, in 1848 built his mission to the Squaxin people.

**Introductory loops 3¹/₂ miles, allow 2¹/₂ hours
High point 140 feet, elevation gain 200 feet**

Mile 78-83¹/₂: Priest Point Park-Olympia-Percival Landing Park-Capitol Lake Park-Tumwater Historical Park-Deschutes River-Tumwater Falls Park (map—page 141)

Not with a whimper but a bang-bang-bang ends the Whulge Trail. The individual bangs can be separately visited from any number of parking areas or linked together on an 11-mile round trip from Priest Point Park that will render you shell-shocked with ecstasy.

From Priest Point Park the way is on the sidewalk of East Bay Drive, pleasantly viewful over the beach houses, and then if desired on low-tide sandflats. Across waters of Budd Inlet are the fill peninsula on which is built the Port of Olympia, and the Black Hills rising beyond. In 1¹/₂ miles is State Street, which leads west ¹/₂ mile through beautiful downtown Olympia to Water Street.

Here is Percival Landing Park. (Go off I-5 on Exit 105-B, turn right on Plum, then left on State. At Water turn right to limited parking or left to very large lots by Capitol Lake. And if these are full there's a ton of parking along Deschutes Parkway.) Walk the promenades of Percival Landing and tour the mile of boardwalk along the shore. Look at the pretty little boats, out past big boats and ships along Budd Inlet to Washington, The Brothers, Constance.

Urban park is continuous from here to the end of the Trail. Walk Water the 2 blocks to Capitol Lake Park. Formerly Budd Inlet did at low tide what comes naturally for these long skinny fingers of the South Sound—it became a mudflat. For years this gave state politics a distinctive reek. In 1949, to bring the Legislature the odor of dignity, a dam was built to let the Deschutes River maintain a lake. Partly ringed by lawns, partly cattails, partly wild tanglewood bluff, it provides a postcard/calendar foreground for the Capitol come rising from green forest into clouds of circling gulls. The ducks love it. And the joggers.

Proceed on sidewalk and waterside path over the dam-tidegate, where in season salmon and steelhead can be seen coming upstream to spawn, and beside Deschutes Parkway. Directly across the lake from the Capitol is the peninsula of Marathon Park with ample parking, pretty views of the skyline of downtown Olympia. (Across the bridge at the park end a cheaters' path rounds the fence to the railroad tracks for a shortcut return.) Past the park Percival Creek enters the lake; railroad tracks lead up the valley, which was not surveyed but appears to offer a 1-mile wildland, worth a sidetrip.

From Marathon Park a walkway leads 1¹/₂ miles to Capitol Lake Interpretive Center. A causeway trail then goes over the lake and under I-5 to Tumwater Historical Park, 60 acres that include paths, picnic shelters, and a boat-launch featuring canoes. (Get here by car via Grant Street from Deschutes Parkway).

The history begins to get thick. Up Grant Street from the lake, which here narrows to become the mouth of the Deschutes River, is a handsome antique dwelling, a

Telephoto of Olympia and the state capitol building from Priest Point Park

registered Historic Place, built in 1854 by Nathaniel Crosby III, Bing's grandfather. Find a path to the riverbank and look across to noble brick bastions of the original Olympia Brewery, built in 1905, converted to other purposes with the coming of Prohibition to the state in 1916. The new brewery, on the hill above, was opened with Repeal in 1933.

Here, too, are the first looks at the lowermost falls of the Deschutes, called Tumwater Falls, partly retaining the Indian name, "Tumtum," for the throb of the heart suggested by the sound. Walk uphill, parallel to the river, to Deschutes Parkway, and past the entry road to Olympia Brewery and past Falls Terrace Restaurant enter Tumwater Falls Park, ¾ mile from Capitol Lake. (To drive to the park, leave I-5 on Exit 103 and follow signs to Deschutes Parkway and the park entrance.)

Soak up the history. The headquarters exhibit has a huge granite erratic from Hartstene Island with a petroglyph of mountains, sun, bow, arrow, a bear, and assorted other animals. A panel of photos shows scenes of the falls in olden times and buildings that were here: Horton Pipe Factory (1872), the first power plant (1890), Ira Ward house (1860), George Gelbach Flour Mill (1883), Tumwater Falls Powerhouse (1904), and so on. A monument tells the story of Colonel Michael T. Simmons arriving here in 1845 with 32 companions and establishing the first American settlement (which they called Newmarket) north of the Columbia River.

Soak up the scenery. Southernmost of Cascades rivers to enter Puget Sound, here the Deschutes got hung up on a stratum of hard rock precisely at tidewater; a series of foaming cataracts strung along a slot of spring-dripping, fern-and-moss-hung rock cliffs, drops a total 115 feet. In the ¼-mile length of the gorge are trails along both sides, artfully placed to experience the clouds of spray billowing from plunge basins, smaller falls of tributary creeks cascading off the walls into landscapings of native shrubs. Sidepaths lead to rock outcrops scoured and potholed by the river, view platforms of the falls and fish ladderways, where in season spawning salmon and steelhead can be watched battling up the torrent. So, walk up and down both sides of the gorge, crossing at lower and upper ends on quaint bridges, in ¾ mile doing the whole park. But better plan on doing it twice or more. And don't hurry.

The imposing structures atop the cliff ought not be ignored. The large sign announces daily visiting hours. So, climb the cliff trail, here in Tumwater, where begins the Inland Passage to Alaska, and thus end the continuously walkable portion of Whulge Trail. It's a long walk from Bellingham. Makes a person thirsty.

146

Watershed Park (map—page 141)

Walking shores of Capitol Lake, one admires wildwoods on the far shore. No simple connection presently makes a sidetrip, but the 150 acres of Olympia's old watershed on Moxlie Creek are worth a separate visit.

From Exit 105-A or 105-B on I-5, drive Henderson Boulevard southeast to a small trailhead parking area. Elevation, 100 feet.

The volunteer-built, foot-only path drops into the fine wild ravine to a Y; do the loop in either direction. The way winds through big cedar and fir and hemlock, fern-draped maples. It crosses and recrosses the creek on neat little bridges, weaves through soggy alder bottoms on plank walks, climbs and descends the sidehill, tunnels through shrubs of the valley floor, and generally extracts all the juices from the in-city wilderness. Still to be seen are miscellaneous machinery and wire-wrapped wooden pipes that until the 1940s diverted Moxlie into city faucets.

Loop trip 1¹/₂ miles, allow 1 hour
High point 100 feet, elevation gain 100 feet

Eld Inlet (map—page 147)

Third in sequence of the ice channels (then), inlets (now), Eld is formidably privatized most of its length and where not, at the head in Mud Bay, is unfit for energetic walking, though fascinating to poke about in saltgrass and mudflats. However, on each shore the survey found a gap in the defenses against public feet, a way to the water.

Evergreen State College

Our youngest state college has the state's largest campus, more than 1000 acres, mostly second-growth wilderness, and 3300 feet of natural waterfront. A splendid trail samples trees and waves.

From Exit 104 on I-5 drive US 101 for 3 miles and exit on Evergreen Parkway. In about 2 miles enter the campus, turn left at the sign, "Campus Plaza, Parking," pay the small fee, and park just beyond the booth in Lot B (left) or C (right). Elevation, 190 feet.

Walk through the campus core, first over the plaza to the library, then between the latter and the Activities Building, by the Recreation Center and Residence Halls, and cross Driftwood Road to Parking Lot F. Bear left and on the far side of the lot, about ³/₄ mile from the start, spot a sign, "Nature Trail." The path expertly savors the varied systems of the wildland: great big old stumps from the long-ago logging, alder bottoms

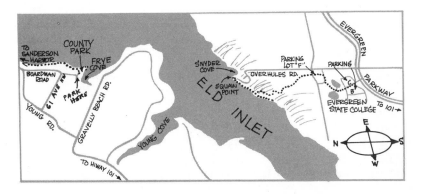

with gurgling creek, a pond, an old pasture, ferny-mossy maples, handsome stands of cedar and fir and hemlock.

At ³/₄ mile from Lot F is a T. The left leads a few yards to the beach and a little baymouth bar enclosing a little lagoon. In the season when the woods are bright with blossoms the beach should only be visited by the liberal-minded, since students come here to gain overall tans; on the survey day the flowers of snow were coldly blooming and the only waterside sport was snowballing the ducks.

The right leads ¹/₄ mile along the slope in fine firs and madronas, salal and twinflower, to Geoduck House, the college's marine ecology studies center, on Squaw Point. Sit on the grassy lawn under a big old fir, look to the college's boats in Snyder Cove, and across the inlet to Young Cove and Flapjack Point, and to Black Hills and Olympics.

Round trip 4 miles, allow 3 hours
High point 190 feet, elevation gain 190 feet

Frye Cove County Park

An excellent Thurston County park, undeveloped, virtually unknown.

Drive US 101 a scant 2.5 miles past the crossing of Eld Inlet (Mud Bay) and turn right on Steamboat Island Road. In 1 mile turn right on Gravelly Beach Road. In 2.2 miles turn left on Young Road. In 0.7 mile turn right on 61 Avenue NW and proceed 0.5 mile to the end at Boardman Road. Turn right on Boardman 0.2 mile to the end. Park here, elevation 100 feet.

A sign says "Path to Beach. Welcome. Observe Park Rules." It doesn't say what park. At the bottom of the trail take either the left or right fork to the beach. For the gem exprience, walk south to the mouth of Frye Cove, uninhabited and lonesome, one of those charming estuaries appalling to boot but intriguing to gaze into, wondering what would be found around the sinuous corners, deep in forest, if one had a boat. Firs lean over the water, framing the scene.

At a low-medium tide, head north along the inlet, under a steep forest that roofs the beach and often blocks it with logs and branches. A glorious maple extends 35 feet over gravels and waters. A Douglas fir 5 feet in diameter grows out of the very beach! Duck into a green-dark alcove of overhanging alders to find springs dripping down a clay cliff hung with maidenhair fern. Climb patiently over seaweedy, barnacled logs— or, at low tide, squish around in boot-swallowing mud. Look out the inlet to its mouth at Cooper Point.

Though several houses are hidden up in the woods in the first 2 miles, scarcely so much as a trail betrays their presence. Beach-near houses then begin and continue the 1 mile to Sanderson Harbor, which halts progress.

Round trip 6 miles, allow 4 hours

Totten and Skookum Inlets (map—page 150)

There simply aren't enough people yet to fill all the many miles of waterfront; as a consequence, though choice spots are inhabited, wildness grows more common on the fourth of the "seas in the forest" and its offshoot, the fifth.

Kamilche Point

But *this* access has fallen to the private dollar since the original survey in the late 1970s. Go there no more, you public.

However, the surveyor noted that the opposite shore of Totten Inlet is (was) wilderness only sporadically molested by humanity. How would one get at it? By driving Steamboat Island Road (see Frye Cove County Park) and its sideroads.

Totten Inlet

Arcadia Point

At the tip of the peninsula separating the fourth and sixth of the finger seas begins an excellent, long-as-you-like exploration of Totten Inlet.

Drive US 101 past Kamilche 1 mile and turn right on Lynch Road, which joins Arcadia Road, which at 10 miles from 101 ends at Arcadia. A block before the end is a public parking lot for "Squaxin Island Tribe Public Boat Ramp." Access to the beach is public but walking requires toleration, normally at a pretty high level way out here in the sticks.

Left a few feet is the light on Arcadia Point, where a palatial home and a moat-like yacht basin prevent exploration into Hammersley Inlet. But there is a busy view of many nice things: "Hammersley Point" (which see), Pickering Passage, Squaxin and Hope Islands, both appearing perfectly housefree and wild, and cute little Steamboat Island, attached to peninsula-tip Sandy Point by a bridge and totally housed.

The walk is right, southerly along Totten Inlet. In 1/3 mile are a till point pocked by bird caves and a mudflat cove; at middle tides the channel can be walked across but at high it's a swim, so watch it. Above the grassy baymouth bar are bluff houses but soon the way is wild, though at intervals the top of the 100-foot bluff is cleared, indicating unseen houses. Old, unused concrete bulkheads are passed, old unused roads to the beach, and remains of a boathouse-on-pilings overwhelmed by a clay slump. The sliding-bluff forest sometimes pushes out on the beach, making mean struggles through weedy, barnacled logs. Steamboat Island is passed. A double-trunked maple leans 40 feet over the beach. Creeklets dribble out of green-delicious gulches. Sands are tracked by deer and raccoon.

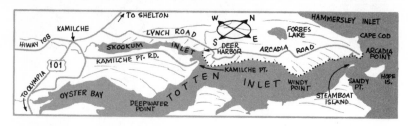

With only a couple houses encountered beside the beach in all this distance, at 2³/₄ miles is Windy Point. Views are long down Totten Inlet and to its mostly wild far shore and to the Black Hills. Though not surveyed, the way appears open and pleasant and little-inhabited another scant 4 miles to the mouth of Skookum Inlet and Deer Harbor, which surely would halt progress.

Round trip 5¹/₂ or 13 miles, allow 4 or 9 hours

The Hammersley Inlet shore of this peninsula has long wild stretches—the 2 miles from Cape Cod to Mill Cove seem totally pristine (and the opposite shore equally so, the lonesomest of all the "seas in the forest"). But there is no public access except by boat. However, a person could drive Arcadia Road to some point about ¹/₂ mile from the water, park unobtrusively, and thrash through the woods. The older surveyor cannot help you. Way out in the boondocks he was preparing to undertake such an expedition when, in a farmhouse at the limit of his vision, he spotted a pair of binoculars trained on him; as he hoisted rucksack, pickup trucks materialized from all around and began converging. He decamped, realizing that even here are defenses against vagabonds, especially those suspected of being oyster-rustlers.

Hammersley Inlet (map—page 152)

The last of the six finger seas has many claims to being the best. Virtually river-narrow most of its length, with odd little capes and secluded little coves, then opening to the big surprise of Oakland Bay and the two thundering-loud mills of Shelton, it's a stimulating mixture of industry, residence—and pure wilderness. Not to forget another element that can be exceedingly stimulating—poison oak.

Walker Park

Where US 101 veers left to bypass Shelton, go right on Highway 3 to the south part of town and turn right on Arcadia Road. In 1.5 miles turn left on Walker Park Road 0.3 mile to the (Mason County) park.

The pleasant, big-fir-shaded preserve affords a pleasing prospect westward to Eagle Point, which hides Shelton, and Munson Point, beyond which opens Oakland Bay. Tugs tow log rafts. Ships carry lumber.

Walking toward Eagle Point is made impractical by bulkheads and homes; the other direction, though populated, has an amiably high level of toleration. How far to go? In 3 miles is Skookum Point and 1 mile beyond is trip's mandatory end and trip's glory, Channel Point at the mouth of Mill Channel, the mouth of Mill Creek. After all his travels of the South Sound, this is the older surveyor's nomination for the champion of charm.

Beyond the foot-stopping channel are the greatest 2 miles of this inlet, perhaps of all the inlets. All the way to Cape Cod the shore appears pristine, and so does the facing shore, to Cape Horn. But how to get there? See Arcadia Point and "Hammersley Point."

Round trip 8 miles, allow 6 hours

Hammersley Inlet from Hammersley Point

Shorecrest Park

Farther from Shelton in commuting miles and thus only now being built on at all, and that largely with summer and retirement homes, this shore of the inlet has views equal and superior to the other.

Drive Highway 3 north from Shelton past the head of Oakland Bay. (Let it be noted that Shelton and its lumber mills are the westernmost point of Puget Sound and thus Oakland Bay is among the ends of this arm of the Whulge. For that reason an indefatigable collector of waterways may well wish to savor it. This is readily done by parking on the shoulder of Highway 3 and dropping to the beach, open and walkable much of the distance from bay-head saltgrass and mudflats to open water by the mills.) Just after crossing Deer Creek turn right on Agate Road and drive 3.8 miles to

151

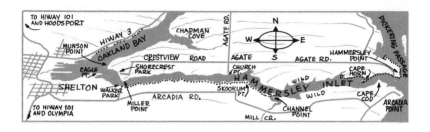

the crossroads/grocery store of Agate. Turn right on Crestview a long 2 miles and then left on East Parkway Boulevard 0.5 mile. Turn right on East Shorecrest Parkway to tiny but luscious "Jacoby Mason County Shorecrest Park."

In both directions are arrays of signs, "No Trespassing." Though the bank of iron-stained glacial drift is too low to keep houses away, most are tucked discreetly in the dry-country rainshadow woods of fir and madrona. The trees lean picturesquely over the beach. From the bank hang picturesque festoons of poison oak, shiny green (Oregon grape-like) in summer, shades of red in fall.

From the park itself is an excellent view of steaming-clunking-humming lumber mills and beautiful downtown Shelton, famed far and wide as the native land of Bob and Ira Spring. Closer, better views are east 1/2 mile from Munson Point. Continue on for expansive views up Oakland Bay to the head. Not surveyed, at 2 1/2 miles is the mouth of Chapman Cove.

In the other direction the shore quickly rounds the low gravel cliff of Miller Point, the beach easy-walking sand and pebbles under arching firs and madronas, by scattered houses. In a succession of vistas over the cozy inlet, barely 1/4 mile wide, a lake in the woods, to houses and yards and dogs barking, children playing, the beach proceeds 3 miles to Church Point light. Here is public street-end parking, an alternative start. (To get there from Agate crossroads, drive Lighthouse Road to its end.) Sad to say, the Privates are getting suddenly ferocious. One sign threatens to set killer dogs on the Publics.

Round trips 5 and 6 miles, allow 3 and 4 hours

"Hammersley Point"
Of all the undeveloped land on the inlets, "Hammersley Point" at the inlet mouth cries out the loudest to be made a state park. What a glory! But chances are that unless you hurry the "No Trespassing" signs will be up when you arrive.

Drive east on Agate Road (see Shorecrest Park) or south from Hartstene Island bridge (see Pickering Passage). At the big right-angle turn, go off on Benson Loop Road. Where the loop turns sharp right, go straight on a narrow gravel road (signed "Dead End") 0.2 mile. Four or five or more driveways go off left to shore homes. At the last one park, out of everybody's way, elevation 100 feet.

Walk the partly overgrown, undriven, log-blocked (but as of late 1987 unposted) woods road straight ahead. It curves left atop an alarmingly overhanging 40-foot shore cliff and descends to end at 1/4 mile in a field and orchard of an ancient farm. What a spot! Gnarled fruit trees compete with scotchbroom and tall grass. At just one place the formidable bank of old tills and "baked" clays dips to the beach. The views here at the mouth of the inlet are busy. Northward runs Pickering Passage, beyond which is the wilderness forest of Squaxin Island. Across the inlet mouth is Arcadia Point, with mansions and yachts, and beyond that is Hope Island (wild) and picturesque Steamboat Island at the mouth of Squaxin Passage and Totten Inlet.

North from the point (whose till cliff can only be rounded at low tide) the bluff above Pickering Passage has scattered houses atop, but the toleration is easy 1 mile for sure and an unsurveyed distance farther.

The other direction is the dazzler. Just down Hammersley are "the narrows," over which George Washington might easily hurl a silver dollar. Guarding the far shore is the formidable forest bluff of Cape Cod, and this shore the incredible bare-till cliffs of arrete-skinny Cape Horn. Needless to say, no houses anywhere near. Wild! The tip of the Cape Horn cleaver is a scant 1 mile distant. What's beyond? High tide prevented the surveyor from checking it out afoot, but evidence of maps and cross-inlet views and sideroad explorations suggests wildness pure or near it the 2½ miles to (populated) Libby Point—though an estuary 1 mile past Cape Horn might be a boot-stopper.

Even if tides prevent walking, the views are worth the trip. Poke around the old farm, amid flowers from a long-gone garden, smelling mint crushed by your boots. Clamber the till cliff of the point, admiring wall-hangings of manzanita and poison oak.

Round trips 2 and 4 miles and more, allow 1 and 3 hours and more

Pickering Passage (map—page 152)

On the other side of giant Hartstene Island is the main channel of Case Inlet. On this side, canal-narrow and woodsy-secluded, is Pickering Passage. Population is low, toleration high.

Drive Highway 3 to 8 miles northerly of Shelton, 10.5 miles southerly of Allyn, and turn east on the road signed "Harstene Island." Drive 4 miles to the bridge and park at Latimer's Landing Mason County Park, or 0.2 mile north at the former landing of the old Hartstene ferry.

Walk both ways. South ½ mile from the ferry is walk's end at the mouth of Graham Point Bay; look south along the Passage to Slalom Point at the tip of Squaxin Island, a wildwood Indian reservation. North 1½ miles is walk's end at the mouth of Jones Creek estuary.

Round trips 4 miles, allow 3 hours

Case Inlet (map—page 153)

One of the twin fishhooks-termini of Puget Sound, Case Inlet curls so far north as nearly to join the fishhook of Hood Canal and make Kitsap Peninsula an island. No pilgrim on the Whulge Trail can fail to be intrigued by the geographical significance, compelled to come pay homage. Mainly for the meditation—there's better walking elsewhere. Population is dense, meaning no wildness and requiring toleration, not always high.

North Bay

Here is the Momentous Spot—waters of the Sound reaching within 2 miles of waters of Hood Canal, Lynch Cove.

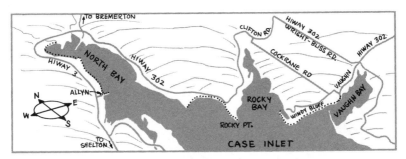

North Bay

Drive Highway 3 from Olympia or Bremerton, or Highways 16, 302, and 3 from Tacoma, to the hamlet of Allyn. Park at the Port of Allyn dock and boat-launch.

The shore south is too many-housed to interest. So, do the meditation walk north, where houses are few along the mudflats. Persisting through guck and clams and the rich reek of salt decay, in 1¹/₂ miles the holy vagabond attains the saltgrass marsh-meadows of the bay head. Turn around and start back to Bellingham.

Round trip 3 miles, allow 2 hours

Rocky Bay

On the west side of North Bay, at the mouth, is walking less momentous but also less ooky and more scenic.

On Highway 302, at 0.2 mile north of the right-angle turn at Rocky Point, park on a broad shoulder.

Drop the several feet to the beach and walk north ¹/₂ mile to a point for views to Allyn and the bay head. Then walk south ¹/₂ mile to Rocky Point for views down Case Inlet to Reach and Stretch Islands and beyond, and around the corner into cute little Rocky Bay.

Round trip 2 miles, allow 1¹/₂ hours

Vaughn Bay

Nor should the connoisseur ignore the next-door bay.

At 1.2 miles west of Key Center on Highway 302 go straight ahead on Hall Road 0.5 mile to Vaughn and park at the public boat-launch.

Vaughn Bay is another of the cozy estuaries in which the vicinity abounds. The highlight of this one is the splendid long baymouth bar. Walk west (many houses, toleration required) $1/2$ mile to within a pebble's toss of the bar tip, inaccessible across the channel but good to look at. Continue another $1/4$ mile to upthrusting naked gravels of Windy Bluff, onto another spit pushing into Rocky Bay.

Round trip 2 miles, allow 1$1/2$ hours

ISLANDS IN THE SOUTH SOUND

Psychologists have written about the "island personality" and poets the "island psyche" and publishers recognize a dependable market for the "island book." Sales around the world of Hazel Heckman's *Island in the Sound*, the Anderson story, reflect the nigh-universal longing to be an islander, safely circumscribed by guardian waters on a tight little isle. More's the pity that addled vandals ever are permitted to build de-islanding bridges.

The pedestrian yearning to seek his spiritual home on a water-surrounded shrine and not owning a boat finds most such are so far from easy as to be impossible. Still, he is by no means shut out.

Fox Island is not entirely privatized. There the walker learns to appreciate the relationship of man and glacier. Where drift bluffs lower, giving residents easy access to the water, the rascals cuddle up, invade the beach with bulkheads. But when a noble scarp of vertical (and/or slidey) till-gravel-sand-clay leaps high, they sit atop and enjoy the view and let wildness rule the waves. Most of the Fox shore is sinking under the weight of money, and the bridge has reduced it to an appendage of the Kitsap Peninsula, but ah that one fine southwest stretch of bluff peace. . .

McNeil is the future—and what a brilliant future it can be, a wildlife refuge preserving endangered populations within the heart of the megalopolis, yet in appropriate places making room for light-and-quiet-walking humans—a Blake Island writ large.

Anderson has been somewhat modified from the Heckman-portrayed past, but future will not soon destroy the pastoral-rural-wild mode, not while the ferry service is straight out of the 1920s. Long live the 1920s!

Hartstene no longer is protected by a ferry yet still has remoteness, which for now is doing the job. So large that a developer hardly knows where to start, so distant from anywhere that customers are hard to net, the interior is mostly farms scattered in second-growth wildland and the beach has more wild miles than all the other islands combined.

What's so different about islands? Not much, really. Uplands and beaches are about the same as on nearby mainland. The getting there is the most of it. Evil spirits, so wise men said of old, cannot cross water.

USGS maps: Duwamish Head, Bremerton East, Vashon, Olalla, Des Moines, Tacoma North, Gig Harbor, Fox Island, Steilacoom, McNeil Island, Nisqually, Longbranch, Squaxin Island, Vaughn, Mason Lake
Walkable all year

Fox Island (map—page 157)

A wide, clean, weather-shore beach, walkable at all but the highest tides, is securely wild for miles beneath one of the truly great naked-gravel bluffs, topped by perilously overhanging madronas. Views are continuously exciting over the water road.

Abandoned dock on Fox Island

Drive Highway 16 from Tacoma Narrows Bridge to either of the two exits to Gig Harbor and follow "Fox Island" signs intricately but infallibly some 5 miles to the bridge that in 1954 replaced the ferry over Hale Passage. On the island proceed on the main highway, Island Boulevard, some 2.2 miles to a T with 9th. Turn right 0.5 mile, then left on Kamus a short bit to a Y; go right on Mowitsh 1.5 miles. Here the public road turns right and becomes 14th; stay on it a long 0.5 mile to the end in a turn circle, elevation 40 feet.

No signs either bar or guide the way, which in fact is a public beach access, kept unmarked in hopes the public won't find it. Ignore the obvious road continuing from the circle and walk around a gravel heap blocking a wide trench dug through the glacial-till bluff; a trail descends the trench the short bit to the beach, once a boat landing, probably a public port district serving the mosquito fleet. Just left, toward Fox Point, is an elaborate but long-unused dock on massive concrete piers. Houses are beyond, nigh continuous, so don't go there.

Instead turn right, in a few steps round Toy Point, and pass a small cluster of houses. Then the splendid bluff leaps up 100, 200 feet, so formidably steep the unseen people atop have only a couple trails down. Wildness rules. Vertical jungle alternates with vertical gravel in foreset beds. In 1 mile is the glorious tip of light-marked Gibson Point. Views north to Narrows Bridge and Titlow Beach and smelter stack yield to views south to gravel mines, Chambers Bay, and Steilacoom. Tugs and fishing boats ripple the waters. Iron horses sound horns on the Whulge Trail. Army guns boom at Fort Lewis. Rainier rises high. From here the way rounds into Carr Inlet and the views extend over to the penal colony of McNeil Island and beyond to Anderson and Ketron Islands.

At 1 mile from Gibson Point is Painted Erratic, a monster hunk of granite brightened by children's spray-can art. For a short walk this is the proper turnaround; the solitude, previously total, now becomes intermittent.

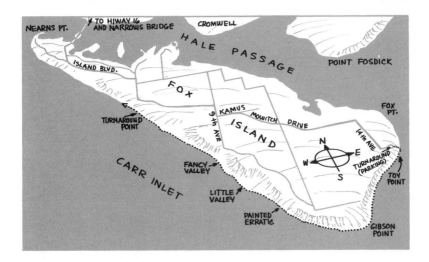

Yet still considerable. A little valley with a handful of cozy cottages is followed by a wild stretch. Beyond a bulge to which several trail-access cabins cling is Fancy Valley, a wide beach terrace crowded with houses small and enormous. Wildness resumes and views up Carr Inlet grow, reaching to the tip of Fox Island, the mouth of Hale Passage, and Green Point on the other side. Across Carr are Still Harbor, on McNeil, and tiny Gertrude Island, site of the seal rookery. Danger intrudes; on occasion hikers have been chased from the beach.

At "Turnaround Point," the bulge of an old terrace at 2 miles from Painted Erratic, the survey was terminated by deepening winter twilight and the onset of a storm that took to thrashing the beach with oceanic waves and the surveyor with sideways rain. However, the shore is lonesome ¾ mile more to another fancy valley and appeared

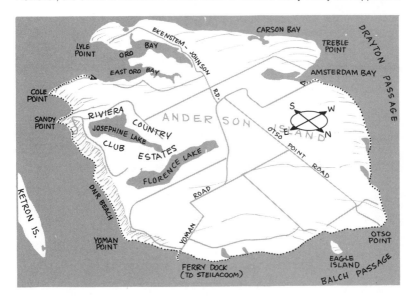

157

attractive beyond, around the bulge 1³/₄ miles to Nearns Point.—But the U.S. Navy blocks the way, and *its* guns are *really* big.

Round trip to Turnaround Point 8 miles, allow 5 hours

Anderson Island (map—page 157)

Candidly, the charm of Anderson is better savored in pages of Hazel Heckman's books than from roadside views. And the beaches are good but not exceptional. Ah, but the ferry! There's the trip!

Drive to Steilacoom (see Whulge Trail) and park as near the ferry dock as is easy. To mention those of most interest to walkers, as of 1988 there are runs to Anderson each morning at 7:40, 9:00, 10:00, and noon; returns from Anderson each afternoon at 2:30, 3:45, 5:30, and 6:30. Arrive a half-hour early to have plenty of time to park and buy a ticket at the restaurant on the dock. Passenger fare (1988) is $1.25 to get on the island, nothing to get off.

The 30-car *Steilacoom*, built in 1936 at Bath, Maine, is the proper scale for the inland sea and takes the properly sedate pace, requiring 30 minutes for the 3¹/₂ miles over Main Street—more if there are barges or log rafts to dodge. It's the happiest, old-timiest ferry ride left on the Sound. But to locals it's the new ferry, only acquired from the U.S. Navy in 1976, put in service the summer of 1977. The former ferry, now standby tied up at the Steilacoom dock, is the 18-car, wooden-hull *Islander*, even old-timier and better. Its backup was the 9-car *Tahoma*, and we're sorry we missed it.

An inch-by-inch survey of the island shore found no public access except at the ferry dock, from which a staircase leads to the beach. So, two choices:

The Old Anderson Island ferry, now on standby duty

South

Due to a beachside road the first scant ¹/₂ mile to Yoman Point, then a 200-foot wall of wildness, trespassing is rather readily tolerated to Sandy Point, 2 miles from the dock; in fact, ¹/₂ mile of tidelands is public. The bluff of gravel and carved clay and jungle is nice, and the trickle-creek waterfalls down through masses of maidenhair fern. The view is the feature: the cute ferry shuttling to McNeil Island and past cute Ketron Island to Steilacoom; barges and boats on Main Street; iron horses charging along the Whulge Trail; north to Fox Island and Narrows Bridge, south to the wilderness of Fort Lewis (boom-boom-boom) and the Weyerhaeuser chimerical superport and the Nisqually delta; over all, lofty white Rainier.

Just past the dock of Riviera Country Club is Sandy Point, from which aliens are sternly warned. On a bleary November, quiet foreigners might be tolerated the 1¹/₂ further miles around the tip into a lonesome cove with a tidal lagoon cut off by a baymouth bar, to Cole Point and its fine tall wall of sand and clay, and the next, nameless point at the mouth of East Oro Bay. From there one can view a bit of the "old island"—pastures edging the bay, farmhouses and barns from another century.

Round trip to Sandy Point 4 miles, allow 3 hours

North

Strictly for misery weather of winter weekdays is the other direction, thickly populated at the start, only gradually progressing to wildness. The beach is broken by a series of amusing estuary-gulches, and the solitary walker is likely to accumulate a pack of companions, friendly dogs who take the excuse for a jaunt, harassing gulls and herons. Directly across Balch Passage is the McNeil ferry dock and the penitentiary. Aside from that, McNeil appears mostly wild except for seameadow-like pastures and onetime farmhouses now used for penal purposes. The wildlife sanctuary of tiny Eagle Island is passed, and then at 1³/₄ miles Otso Point is rounded and the intimacy of Balch Passage yields to the wide-openness of Drayton Passage, across which are Pitt Passage, Filucy Bay, and Devils Head, the tip of Longbranch Peninsula, beyond which lies Nisqually Reach. The way now becomes wild and is embellished by the two largest and best estuaries of the route (watch those tides, folks, or be prepared to wade channels on your return). After a brief interruption by houses, wildness resumes to Amsterdam Bay, 2¹/₄ miles from Otso Point.

Round trip 8 miles, allow 6 hours

More

The island is of a size that a complete circuit might be done in an energetic day. However, Amsterdam and Oro Bays require detours via inland trails and roads. The trip would total about 15 miles, demanding steady pace, good tides, and much toleration.

The tempting morsel of Ketron Island was not surveyed, owing to a suspicion that though virtually all wilderness, it's so small that the handful of residents would be less appreciative than usual of invaders. Still, the ferry stops there on some runs and the 3¹/₂-mile shore might make several great hours, say for a lone walker on a murky February Tuesday.

McNeil Island (map—page 160)

In 1875 a federal penitentiary was established on McNeil, and in 1932 the entire 4413-acre island became federally owned, the last non-prison-connected resident expelled in 1936. The serendipitous effect of security precautions was to virtually "freeze" the island in the 19th century. The deer and the coyote and smaller mammals, the shorebirds and seabirds and waterfowls and raptors, go about their business as if glass-and-cedar ticky-tack never had been invented. Bald eagles nest. Great blue

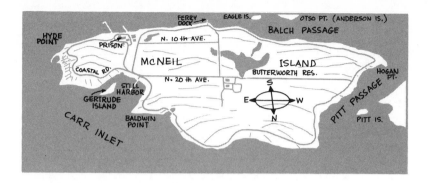

herons annually gather in a heronry to raise a new generation. The last remaining harbor seal colony in South Puget Sound sleeps easy, safe from subdividers and stinkpotters.

In 1981 the penitentiary closed and the U.S. Fish and Wildlife Service immediately moved to make the whole island a wildlife refuge. It withdrew, however, when the state of Washington obtained a lease on the prison, promising to continue the wildlife protection. Environmentalists have not been unhappy with this arrangement as an interim measure; great though the recreation potential of McNeil is, with a 16-mile beach almost totally wild, it ranks a distant second behind the importance as wildlife habitat. State plans to use the island partly for prison purposes, partly for wildlife protection under the State Wildlife Department, partly for recreation under State Parks, also might be acceptably worked out—though the U.S. Fish and Wildlife Service surely is the preferred manager.

Hartstene Island (map—page 162)

Where Puget Sound fritters away in reaches, passages, inlets, bays, and coves is one of the largest islands in the Sound and the least-known. Though virtually all beaches are private, the location is remote and as of 1988 the population is low, the mood relaxed, the toleration high. There's still a country chumminess here; residents are likely to come out not to chase a walker but to chat about the weather or give a history lecture. The canal-like waterways are intimate, the beaches varied by secret estuaries thrusting deep in wildwoods, spits sticking out in the breezes. The entire 30 miles of shore probably are walkable (for the full survey, see a future edition).

Drive Highway 3 to 8 miles northerly of Shelton, 10.5 miles southerly of Allyn, and turn east on the road signed "Harstene Island." Drive 4 miles, over the bridge that at the end of the 1960s replaced the ferry, and park on the shoulder.

Pickering and Peale Passages

The bridge footings give public access to the beach. Surveyed only by eyeball, the shore is mostly wild, with rather few interruptions by houses, south along Pickering Passage and then, beyond where Squaxin Island splits the waters, Peale Passage.

Round trip to Brisco Point 16 miles, allow 10 hours

Brisco Point-Peale Passage-Dana Passage

Drive 0.2 mile from the bridge to the T and turn right on South Island Drive. In 3.3 miles is a T with West and South Island Drives. Go right 8.5 miles down the island to the shore near the south end. Turn right at the water and drive 0.5 mile more, up the hill, where the public road seems to end in three private drives. Park here, elevation 80 feet, on a shoulder well out of everybody's way.

The righthand drive actually is an unsigned county road that drops steeply to an abrupt end—and that's why the car should be parked up the hill. The public right-of-way continues out into tidelands, so the access is public.

Here is the island's scenic climax. The spit of Brisco Point juts out in the waves; whatever traffic is headed for Olympia must funnel through narrow Dana Passage, up which can be seen the mouth of Henderson Inlet and Johnson Point at the end of Nisqually Reach. In the other direction are mouths of Budd Inlet (Olympia) and Eld Inlet, and Squaxin and Peale Passages on either side of Squaxin Island. Beyond rise Black Hills and Olympics.

Nice looking. The surveyor was out of time at day's end and so could not do much walking, but an hospitable resident praised the routes along both sides of the island, up Peale Passage to the bridge, and up Dana Passage and Case Inlet to Dougall Point.

Round trip to the bridge 16 miles, allow 10 hours
Round trip to Dougall Point 28 miles, allow days

Harstene Island

ISLANDS IN THE SOUTH SOUND

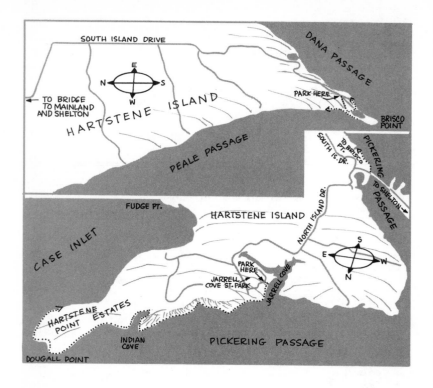

Jarrell Cove State Park

At the T 0.2 mile from the bridge, turn left on North Island Drive and faithfully follow "State Park" signs 4 miles to 43-acre Jarrell Cove State Park. Park at the beachside campground.

The estuary fingers of Jarrell Cove halt boots westerly but the other direction is open along the narrows of Pickering Passage. The bluff of iron-stained drift is high enough to guard the beach from scattered houses out of sight in trees. A wonderful mixed forest leans over the beach, making a woodland walk even as the waves lap. Cool ravines break the bluff. In 1½ miles is Indian Cove, with a boat basin and picnic shelters (private). The creek estuary pokes deep in trees, where the green-shadowed creek-aisle can be crossed on a footbridge. (The inland trail system is private; stay off.) After a scant ½ mile of cove-rounding the far tip is attained and in ¾ mile more is the north tip of the island, Dougall Point.

Here the shore rounds to Case Inlet, with views north past Stretch Island to Vaughn and Rocky Bay and North Bay—the end of Puget Sound. For an introductory tour continue ½ mile more, by the dredged basin and picnic areas and whatnot and look south along Case Inlet to Herron Island. The survey proceeded no farther but the beach appears lonesome and open and superb the 2½ miles to Fudge Point. Beyond are more great miles to Brisco Point.

Introductory round trip 6½ miles, allow 4 hours

KITSAP PENINSULA

A surprise package, a package of surprises, that's the Kitsap Peninsula. For most of Puget Sound City (saving only the Bremerton and Tacoma neighborhoods, for whom this is the backyard) the walks are well beyond the Two-Hour Circle, and even though much of the travel time can be part of the solution, via Fauntleroy-Southworth, Seattle-Bremerton, Seattle-Winslow, or Edmonds-Kingston ferry, the days grow long. Ah, but the surprises!

The Longbranch (Key) Peninsula, for example, between the twin fishhook ends of Puget Sound, Case and Carr Inlets. Thrusting out in Main Street to near views of dense-horned Tacoma-Olympia shores, and within a half-hour's drive of Narrows Bridge, it nevertheless is mostly rural, the beaches largely wild. Amazing. How come? The hiker's faithful friend, the drift bluff, helps. So does the lack of a water supply sufficient to support massive commuter subdivisions. Also soils that refuse to "perk."

The "Narrows Peninsula" and the shores north in the Tacoma-Port Orchard-Bremerton axis have water, and suburbs, and urbs. But also, thanks to noble bluffs, lonesome beaches—one veritably inside Second City.

And Hood Canal. To be sure, the fishhook from the Great Bend is house piled atop house; from Belfair State Park there is a walk to mudflats of the Canal head, a Momentous Spot but otherwise unappealing except for the peep. And granted, north of the Great Bend the Olympic shore is US 101. But the Kitsap shore has the longest most purely truly wild beaches of the inland sea. (Or so they were in 1978, though—sadly—much less so in 1983, and in 1988 . . .)

Final and least-known of Kitsap surprises is the Tahuya Peninsula, named for the long-gone Tahuyas ("oldest people"). On its north are the Green and Gold (Blue) Mountains, towering over Bremerton as their companion remnant of the "Pre-Olympic Mountains" towers over Seattle, with smashing views up, down, and across the *Footsore* world. Its south is almost entirely the Tahuya State Forest, noble in conception, flawed in the implementation, yet sure to be repaired someday, to become a car-camper's and hiker's joy.

USGS maps: Vaughn, Longbranch, Burley, McNeil Island, Fox Island, Gig Harbor, Olalla, Bremerton East, Bremerton West, Duwamish Head, Suquamish, Belfair, Lake Wooten, Holly, Wildcat Lake, Potlatch, The Brothers, Seabeck, Brinnon, Poulsbo
For the free map of Tahuya State Forest, write Department of Natural Resources, Olympia WA 98504
Walkable all year

Longbranch Peninsula

The Kitsap Peninsula is a ménage of subpeninsulas. Of these, the Longbranch Peninsula has been described by *Sunset Magazine* as "a microcosm of Puget Sound's outdoor attractions."

West Shore (map—page 164)

A host of South-Sound-typical treats—estuaries, spits, islands. Yet on this side of the peninsula there's a North-Sound-like excitement of a weather shore. Much of the distance the views are across Case Inlet to the wild shore of great long Hartstene

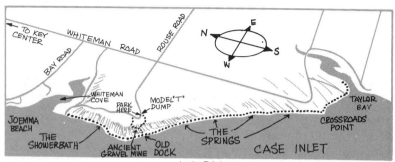

LONGBRANCH PENINSULA

Island, but farther south are over Nisqually Reach to suburbia of Tacoma-Olympia, a sight that makes the peninsula solitude the more precious. Wilderness! Barely a half-hour's drive from the Narrows Bridge, some 11 miles along Case Inlet can be walked with only a few minutes of the total journey spent passing houses. All in all, here are some of the finest beach walks on the Sound.

For how long? At the time of the first survey, in 1978, the area was so empty that toleration rarely was required; when it was needed (the beaches being mainly "private") the natives tended to be amiable. The walking was open in any season, any day of the week. By 1987, however, new people were building on the beach and, in the way new people have, were clutching their pieces of paper that mistakenly told them they "owned" the beach.

Joemma Beach to Taylor Bay

Nearly 3 miles of unbroken solitude would be merit enough but there also are an incredibly ancient gravel mine, two fine estuaries, and a unique phenomenon—The Springs.

From Highway 3 or Highway 16 drive Highway 302 to Key Center and there go south on Key Center-Longbranch Road, recognizable by the sign directing to Penrose Point State Park. In 5 miles is the village of Home, a utopian colony founded in 1896: the anarchists and nudists were run out of the country early in this century. From the bridge at Home continue south on the highway a scant 1.2 miles and turn right on Whiteman Road, signed "RF Kennedy Recreation Area." At another RFK sign in 2.2 more miles turn right on Bay Road, which leads 1 mile to the Joemma Beach parking lot of Robert F. Kennedy Education and Recreation Area, a DNR site with campground, picnic area, privies, boat ramp, public dock, and a short strip of public beach.

South from the parking area at Robert F. Kennedy Recreation Area is Whiteman Cove, a lagoon converted to a lake by raising and widening the baymouth bar. Jungled bluff commences and the beach continues purely wild for miles beneath the 200-foot guardian wall. There is a Showerbath! Water pours over a clay cliff, splashes in a green-lit forest cave hung with maidenhair fern.

At 1½ miles from Joemma Beach is an odd terrace above the beach; a person may search for the expected kitchen midden, be puzzled by heaps of cobbles, expanses of "moss meadows," and realize the terrace is not natural, this is a gravel mine dating from early in the century. So are explained the stumps of pilings on the beach—the dock. A trail climbs through the mine to a midden featuring rusting car bodies dating to Model T vintage and continues to the blufftop and a woods road from which locals dump their garbage; they also descend to the camps beside the creek under the alders among middens of beer cans and bottles.

This is the access to the beach preferred by the locals. From Key Peninsula Road drive Whiteman Road 3.2 miles. Turn right on gravel Rouse Road 0.5 mile to the bluff brink. Views over the water. No-fee garbage dump. The road turns right to a Y. Park

Springs dribbling through moss and licorice fern on the bluff near Joemma Beach

here and walk the left fork down to the beach.

A short way south from the dump access are The Springs—finest example of the type encountered anywhere by the surveyors. Some in the open, some under beach-overhanging trees, dozens of creeklets drip and splash down walls of gravel or clay, a continuous series for more than a mile. At a shore bulge where an old road-trail descends a gully to the beach is Best Waterfall; walk up the trail a bit to another showerbath, a 30-foot two-stepper down a clay precipice. The bluff becomes vertical, a garden wall colorful in summer with yellow monkeyflower around the creeks, and in fall, on drier sites, with pearly everlasting's white and goldenrod's yellow and the evil maroon of poison oak festooning cliffs and entangling the overhanging madronas.

Pause at "Crossroads Point," where the shore bends into the nook of Taylor Bay. Look down Nisqually Reach to the Nisqually delta and beyond to the Bald Hills. Look out Dana Passage past the end of Hartstene Island to the Black Hills. Look back up Case Inlet to the Olympics. As for the water vista, here is the veritable crossroads where Dana, Henderson, and Case Inlets and Nisqually Reach meet. Barges-tugs, and rarely ships, pass en route to Olympia and Shelton; most of the traffic is for pleasure.

Old piling at Burley Lagoon slowly being given a "wasp waist" by teredos

Here appear the first houses; at 3¹/₂ miles is the trip end at piling stubs of the dock of the old ferry over Nisqually Reach. This spot is reached by driving south on Whiteman Road 3 miles from the Bay Road turnoff and turning right on 182 Avenue to the dead end. However, Taylor Bay has one of the densest concentrations of "No Trespassing" signs in the Western Hemisphere—including illegal "bluff signs" on public roads!

Round trip 7 miles, allow 5 hours

East Shore (map—page 169)

The lee shore of Longbranch Peninsula is more comfortable than the weather west—not only are winds and waves usually quieter but the bluffs are mostly shorter or absent and cozy bays more numerous. Population thus is greater. Nevertheless, stretches of solitude interrupt civilization and views are superb of waterways and islands and pleasure craft cruising to and from homes and marinas. And on the south tip is one of the peninsula's two greatest walks, a real champion.

Burley Lagoon

Burley Lagoon, at the head of Henderson Bay, at the head of Carr Inlet, has almost as much right as North Bay at the head of Case Inlet to be considered the End of Puget Sound. Thus, as the barb tip on one of the twin fishhooks, it is Momentous. Aside from that it offers an easy and exceedingly popular walk.

Drive Highway 16 from Tacoma or Bremerton to Purdy and turn west on highway 302. Cross the bridge over the channel of Burley Lagoon and park anywhere on the shoulder of the 3/4-mile-long baymouth bar, augmented by riprap to be a causeway.

The lagoon head is 2 miles north; the brush-tangled mudflat shore forbids rational walking. So just look. At old pilings of old booming grounds where hundreds of gulls perch, at paraphernalia of the oyster industry.

On the south side of the causeway walk the pleasant small-pebble beach. Admire the tidal rush through the lagoon mouth. Look down Henderson Bay to the Black Hills.

The west end of the causeway is a put-in for a longer walk. After 1/2 mile of wall-to-wall bulkheads-houses from Wauna, the good bluff leaps up, man must climb high amid trees to live, and views widen south.

Minter Bay is very nearly closed off by a 1/2-mile baymouth bar. The cute little cove is the home of Minter Brook Oyster Company; should you stop there to buy fresh oysters after the walk, you can gain another perspective. The baymouth bar, "Ship Bones Spit," tells what became of the mosquito fleet. Skeletons of a dozen or more vessels form striking patterns of rib cages in the waters, the sands. Naught is left but timbers and rusted wrought-iron metalwork. Presumably the stripped hulks were beached here to provide oyster habitat. Other views: out to Raft and Cutts Islands and far south down Carr Inlet to goshamighty Rainier.

Round trip on causeway 1 1/2 miles, allow 1 hours
Round trip to Minter Bay 6 miles, allow 4 hours

Maple Hollow Picnic Area

Bless your heart, DNR! One feels ashamed for ever saying you have no soul. The nature trail on this wildwooded hillside was designed with tender loving care. Worth a trip even if one doesn't visit the beach, of which 1/3 mile is public.

(But note: In late 1987 the area was signed "Maple Hollow will be closed due to logging by trails." Will the nature trail survive? Does DNR *have* a heart?)

Drive Highway 302 to Key Center and go off on the Longbranch Road, signed "Penrose Point State Park." In 3 miles turn left on Vanbeek Road. In a long 0.2 mile turn left at a "Maple Hollow" sign; in a short bit is the parking area, elevation 150 feet.

The trail switchbacks and meanders down the steep hillside to the beach, and even with two sidetrips on loops totals a round trip of only maybe 1/2 mile. But good, but good. In mystic depths of the green are springboard-notched, monster stumps of long-ago-logged cedars and firs, mingled with old-growth wolf firs, some up to 8 feet in diameter, wow, and canopies of tall, mossy maples, and understory of sword fern and evergreen huckleberry. Stairs lead from picnic ground to beach.

The way south to Home on Von Geldern Cove is quite solidly populated, unattractive. North, though, is mostly wild the 3 miles to Thompson Spit at the mouth

Beach trail at Maple Hollow Picnic Area

of Glen Cove. Look south to Penrose Point and South Head, green pastures of McNeil Island, Fox Island, Steilacoom gravel mines. Look across to Raft Island and cupcake-like Cutts Inland.

Round trip to Glen Cove 7 miles, allow 5 hours

Penrose Point State Park

Only 146 acres? Impossible! What with inlet dips and peninsula juts, at low tide there are 2 miles of public beach. And the paths that loop around in big-tree virgin forest total golly knows how many miles. A long day is scarcely enough to sample this compact treasure trove.

Drive from Key Center on Longbranch Road, following state park signs that render unnecessary any description of the 8 miles twisting and turning through Home and Lakebay to the park entrance. In 0.2 mile, past headquarters and campgrounds (82 sites), the entrance road Ts. For the recommended complete tour turn right 0.2 mile to the picnic area parking.

First, Mayo Cove. By the privies find a trail through the mixed forest to one of the campground parking areas and down to the dock. Admire the picturesque estuary and

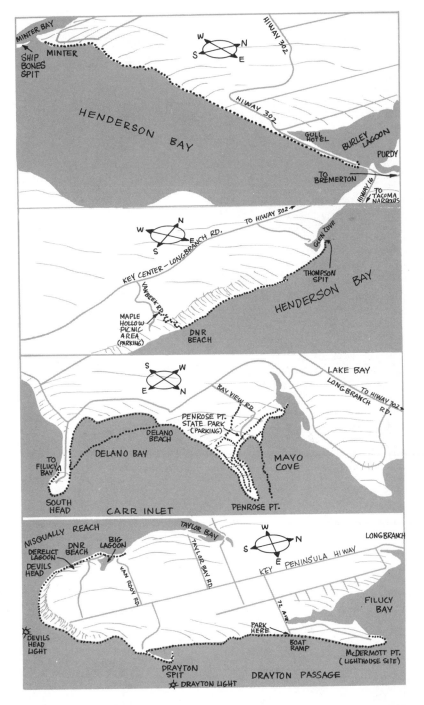

Filucy Bay

then circle back via either beach or the banktop path, returning to the start to complete a 1¼-mile loop. (At low tide a miraculous bar emerges in the middle of the cove; the sidetrip out and back amid sands and gulls, ducks and crows, adds nearly 1 mile.)

Now, the point. Round the swimming-beach cove, cross a trickle-creek at the mouth of a tiny lagoon ("ark! ark!" squawk the herons), walk the little spit to the start of low bank topped by madrona and fir—and poison oak, gaudy red in fall, a peril to pickers of the black-fruited evergreen huckleberry. In ¾ mile is the tip of Penrose Point. Look up Carr Inlet, across to Fox Island, down to McNeil Island; between Fox and McNeil see the pulpmill plume at Chambers Bay and gravel mines on the Whulge Trail. Continue a scant ¹/₂ mile from the point, past a grassy terrace with shells of a kitchen midden, and spot a trail obscurely marked with a sign, "Underground Cable."

Now, the forest primeval. A network of paths has been tunneled through the peninsula's wildwoods to make it seem enormously larger than it is. Just inland from the beach, turn left on one trail—or a bit beyond, right on another. Either way, loop around and then take the other loop. Often the way is on a bank close above the beach, trenched in head-high salal and huckleberry. Often the way is in cool-shadowed alder-maple-sword fern, or madrona groves, or old-growth Douglas fir up to 6 feet in diameter. A straight shot from the beach to the picnic parking area is only ¹/₃ mile but wiping out the whole trail system adds 2 miles. Do it.

Complete tour 6 miles, allow 4 hours

South Head

A lovely gooky bay mudflat, a peninsula thrusting far out in the water, and then miles of mostly wild beaches along Pitt Passage, with close views of McNeil Island.

From the trail south of Penrose Point (see above) continue south on the beach. Wildness yields to cottages and grand old houses of Delano Beach. At medium tides the head of Delano Bay must be rounded, crossing a trickling creek (watch for wood ducks) to the resumption of tanglewood-guarded beach; at low tide there is an elegant shortcut over the mudflats, squishing along far from land, out amid the clams and gulls and peep. Mainland is regained, and a 100-foot bluff. At 2 miles (or via shortcut 1¹/₂ miles) is South Head, with views down to Pitt Island in Pitt Passage, separating the peninsula from McNeil Island. Watch for spouting whales.

The surveyor did not proceed farther, being disconcerted by learning from shore folk, at first quite surly, that they had taken him for a convict who had just crawled out of the brush and paddled a driftwood log over Pitt Passage and squished through a mudflat. In any event, the beach appeared virtually all wild, and fascinating, the 4 miles to Mahnckes Point at the mouth of Filucy Bay.

Round trip to South Head 4¹/₂ miles, allow 3 hours
Round trip to Mahnckes Point 12¹/₂ miles, allow 8 hours

Filucy Bay

A classic spit, a lighthouse site, a charming bay, and water vistas.

From the bridge at Home (see Penrose Point State Park) continue on the highway south 4.5 miles to old Longbranch on Filucy Bay. Continue 1.2 miles on Key Peninsula Highway and turn east on 72 Avenue, which in 0.7 mile dead ends at a public boat-launch. Park on the shoulder.

Walk north under a rusty-gravel wall from whose top leans a spreading madrona. In fall the fruit of evergreen huckleberry (sweet) and bitter cherry (bitter) tempt, the wine-red leaves of poison oak warn to admire from a distance. The bluff lowers to a cluster of cottages, rises again, and drops to naught at McDermott Point. On the tip of the spit is the concrete octagon foundation of the vanished lighthouse, amid Scotch broom and grass where once grew a kempt Coast Guard lawn.

Views are smashing. Around the corner is many-armed Filucy Bay, to whose green shores cling old houses of Longbranch, whose moored boats dot the bay. Up Pitts Passage, leading to Carr Inlet, is little Pitt Island. The forests and fields and beaches of McNeil Island make the feet itch thinking of the time when the penal colony is terminated. In Balch Passage, the slot between McNeil and Anderson Islands, is tiny Eagle Island; out the slot are Main Street and the Whulge Trail.

Round trip 2 miles, allow 1¹/₂ hours

Devils Head

Close views of islands, a classic spit, a headland out in Main Street traffic, two lights, two baymouth bars with lagoons, and a charming bay. A busy walk—among the greatest of all beach walks on the Sound.

From the 72 Avenue boat-launch (see above) walk south. In the first 1 mile are trails and bulkheads and the genteel decay of the once-palatial Kraemer Estate, but only a couple small houses. Wild bluff then rises, maples arching over the beach. Chunks of bluff that have slid down on the beach require (1987) a tide below 5 feet to get easily by. The first spectacular is Drayton Spit, hooking north to enclose a lagoon. Out in Drayton Passage is Drayton Light. Across is Anderson Island, whose entire west shore is paralleled on this trip, from Otso Point past Amsterdam Bay to Treble Point. Sidetrip 1/4 mile out to the spit tip—the gulls won't like your intrusion but the exercise will do them good. A dock thrusts out on the spit and at the base of the spit are a big lawn and private picnic shelter; don't loiter.

In a scant 1/2 mile are a private-boat-launch and the bulkhead and lawns of a development, quickly passed. Now the bluff leaps to over 200 feet and the walls of vertical clay and jungle ensure solitude. In the next 1 mile Devils Head Light is passed and the shore rounds to its apex, wild and bluff-guarded Devils Head, the tip of Longbranch Peninsula.

Don't rush away. It's a Momentous Spot. Drayton Passage has been left for broad seascapes of Nisqually Reach, views extending past Anderson Island to the Nisqually delta and the green land from which come the booms of Fort Lewis war games, and to Johnson Point at the mouth of Henderson Inlet, and to Case Inlet and Hartstene Island. Here in "The Crossroads" see tugs and barges, fishing boats, pleasure boats, a few sailboats, and, if lucky, that nostalgic anachronism, a rowboat.

Now for the baymouth bars. In 1/4 mile is the first, enclosing a lagoon where two derelict houses sag into the forest beside the mud and driftwood. In 1/2 mile is the next, with an increment of human fill to make it a lake drained by a small creek. Beware of croaking herons, quacking ducks, squealing killdeer. Beware especially of the people on the shore ahead. The final 3/4 mile to Taylor Bay, whose ferry-dock pilings evoke memories of the golden age of the Water Road, is going the way of "No Trespassing."

Round trip 6 miles, allow 4 hours

Kitsap Peninsula Shores

In the surveyors' opinions, most of the best Kitsap Peninsula beachwalking is on Hood Canal (see below) and north of Port Madison (see *Footsore 3*). However, amid miles of frontyard beaches that are mainly of interest to local residents are several routes of regional appeal.

Kopachuck State Park (map—page 173)

Old forest and pretty beach and fine views over Carr Inlet.

Drive Highway 16 from Tacoma Narrows Bridge to the Gig Harbor vicinity. Take either of the two exits signed "Kopachuck State Park" and follow those infallible signs through an intricate route some 6 miles to the entrance. Pass the campground (41 sites) to the parking area, elevation 150 feet.

The 109-acre park is a maze of paths up and down and along the slope, through big firs and spruces and cedars and maples. The 1/2 mile of public beach gives views past cute Cutts Island to Raft Island and over to Penrose Point and Glen Cove. In good toleration season a person might venture south another mile on private beach into Horsehead Bay—but never on nice sunny weekends.

Cutts Island from Kopachuck State Park

Round trip 2-4 miles, allow 1-3 hours

The Narrows (map—page 174)

Incredible. In the very suburbs of Tacoma are (or were in 1988) 6 miles of beach with but a single solitary house on the shore—located at the single solitary ravine breaching the 200-300-foot cliffs that plummet to the water. And the view is across the skinniest section of Puget Sound's main channel to that jungle-bluff wildland extending from Point Defiance to Titlow Beach. Inside the city, and lonesome! Well,

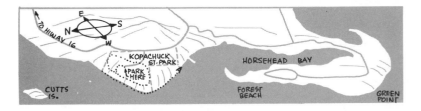

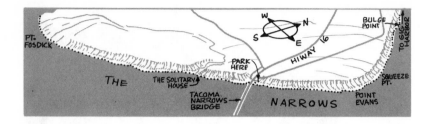

not entirely. There are close looks at pleasure boats, fishing boats, tugs and barges, occasionally a ship. And fleets of birds that grab free rides on river-swift tidal currents. Whales. The beach is narrow, yet walkable at medium tides.

Drive Highway 16 to the west side of Narrows Bridge and turn off on the road signed "Airport-Wollochet-Point Fosdick." This road loops under the bridge, permitting easy egress from the highway and easy return, from whichever direction you come. Find parking space on shoulders under the bridge or someplace in the vicinity. From the shoulder on the north side of the loop road a trail descends a forest ravine to the beach, which invites walks in both directions.

South to Point Fosdick

Yes, people live atop the bluff, but except for barking dogs and occasional paths you'll never know they're there. The only habitation on the beach is in the ravine at ½ mile. Fir and madrona lean over the beach, decorated with red-in-autumn poison oak; maple and alder arch over. "Ark! Ark!" go the herons, "Splash! Splash!" go the leaping salmon, "Hor-or-or!" go trains on the Whulge Trail, a mile across the water. In 2 miles the bluff drops to a mere bank at Point Fosdick and houses crowd the shore, including what the newspapers describe as the largest house ever built in Pierce County, valued at $411,616, not counting the 50,000-pound theater pipe organ. Enjoy views over Hale Passage to Fox Island, up to the mouth of Wollochet Bay, and turn back, enjoying the graceful arch high above the water.

Round trip 4 miles, allow 3 hours

North to Gig Harbor

Wild all the way—blufftop mansions out of sight, and the city across the way also. Just water and woods and fishing boats ambushing salmon. True, one work of man is evident, indeed dominates—the bridge—but that is in fact a chief glory of the walk.

At 1 mile is Point Evans, with a light and a woods road down the precipice; one fears this may ultimately augur ill for the beach. (In 1987 massive slides blocked the way to Point Evans; a winter or two of storms may be required to open the beach for walking at any tide higher than 3-5 feet.) For nearly 1 mile beyond the point the tidelands are public, the beach is rugged and dramatic; bare cliffs of sand and gravel form precipices and jutting ribs—at "Squeeze Point" narrowing the beach to a mere 10 or 5 feet at medium tides, nothing at high—beware! Clay and gravel ledges outcrop on the beach. And tree clumps slid from above may force brushfights. The view over the waters is distinguished by the mouth of Bennett Tunnel swallowing up and disgorging trains, the ¾-mile strip of Salmon Beach's below-the-bluff cottages, and the wilderness of Point Defiance Park.

The beach smooths, the bluff becomes less vertical, though still a steep jungle, gashed by several ravines (with creeks and trails). At 2¼ miles the protuberance of "Bulge Point" is rounded, fully opening the view to Gig Harbor and Colvos Passage and Vashon Island. Wildness continues another 1¼ miles to houses near the mouth of Gig Harbor.

Round trip 7 miles, allow 5 hours

Colvos Passage (map—page 176)

From Gig Harbor to Point Southworth the west shore of Colvos Passage extends some 15 miles around bulges and in and out of coves. The many ravines that breach the bluff permit many a shore village, large or small, fancy or modest, but much of the distance is empty, the beach wild for stretches as of much as a mile. Pleasure craft cruise the canal-like passage, and fishing boats and tugs and barges. And whales. Views are over a mile of water to Vashon Island, forest-green and mostly bluff-wild the entire length from Dalco Point to Point Vashon. The beach is largely "private" but the toleration level is high in the good trespassing season of winter and bad-weather spring and fall days. A number of put-ins permit a varied assortment of walks.

Sunrise Beach County Park

From Highway 16 drive through Gig Harbor and around its estuary to Crescent Valley Drive. Turn left 0.5 mile, then right on Drummond. In 0.7 mile is a T; turn right on

The Narrows, Tacoma on the far shore

Moller 0.2 mile, then left on Sunrise Beach Road, and descend a valley 0.5 mile to just above the water. Spot a driveway on the left and proceed to the parking area, elevation 60 feet. Formerly a private park on the old Moller homestead, it now is a county park, "Dedicated to memory of Rudolph Moller, 1868-1944, Mathilde Moller, 1880-1953, homesteaders of this property—1986."

The choice trip is south, in fine views to Point Defiance, ASARCO smelter, Simpson steam plume, and Rainier. After ½ mile of Sunrise Beach homes is ½ mile of wild bluff. Then, past a shorter row of houses, is 1 wild mile under a formidable 280-foot bluff. At the end is a baymouth bar of Gig Harbor, the most charming estuary of the region, chockablock with fishing boats and pleasure craft.

North the populated gulches and wild strips alternate the 2¼ miles to Point Richmond.

Round trip to Gig Harbor 4 miles, allow 3 hours
Round trip to Point Richmond 4½ miles, allow 3 hours

Olalla Bay

The drowned lower length of Olalla Valley, estuary snaking back into muck and trees. The place was anciently inhabited: just south of the baymouth bar are ruins of the Olalla Trading Company, offering (it did) "General Merchandise"; on the hill above is a gracious mansion with cupolas and widow's walk.

From Gig Harbor drive Crescent Valley Road north to Olalla Bay. Just north of the bridge is a large public parking area.

This is the most dependable (least toleration required) Colvos put-in. Walk south past the Trading Company and immediately onto below-the-bluff lonesome beach.

Round trip to Point Richmond 7 miles, allow 5 hours

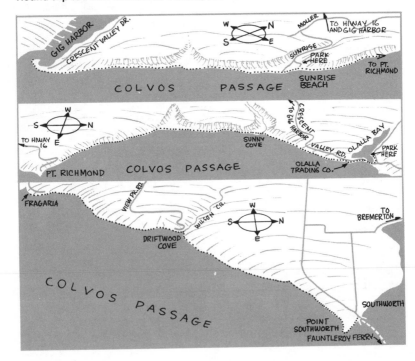

The remains of the Olalla Trading Company

Southworth Point

Now for something completely different in the way of approach. Park at Fauntleroy in West Seattle and walk on the ferry to Vashon Island and Southworth Point.

Walk off at Southworth, easily gain access from ferry dock to beach, and head south. Around the corner is a fine, grassy spit. Views are north to Blake Island, across to Point Vashon, whence appear ferries. Beyond Main Street is the densely populated Seattle shore, with the Green Mile of Lincoln Park, Alki Point, the mouth of Elliott Bay.

At 2¼ miles, mostly lonesome, is Driftwood Cove at the mouth of Wilson Creek. Houses. Several more settlements come to or near the water in the next 2 miles to Fragaria.

Round trip to Fragaria 8½ miles, allow 6 hours

Manchester State Park (map—page 178)

Nobody who has ridden the ferry through Rich Passage, close by rocky-tipped, hill-topped Middle Point, can but wish to visit.

One approach is via Seattle-Bremerton ferry, Port Orchard, Annapolis, along the extravagantly scenic shore of Sinclair Inlet and Rich Passage. Another is via

Fauntleroy-Southworth ferry, Harper, Manchester, along the extravagantly scenic shore of Yukon Harbor. Another is via Tacoma Narrows Bridge and Highway 16 to either of these approaches, both of which become Beach Drive. From the north at a long 0.5 mile from Point Glover on Rich Passage, and from the south about 2 miles from Manchester, turn east on Hilldale Road into the park and through it to the parking area.

The 111-acre park, formerly part of Fort Ward (which occupied both shores of Rich Passage) has diverse habitats—beach, grassy meadow, dry (madrona) forest, cedar stands, and, to the right of the entry gatehouse, a swamp. Frank Beyer, the 81-year-old (1987) unofficial park naturalist, says there are bear, red fox, over 105 species of birds, and over 300 species of flowers. At one time there were goats from Bikini Atoll, survivors of the first hydrogen "device," brought here to live out their irradiated lives.

The park's information boards have maps showing some 2 miles of trails, including an interpretive trail (poorly maintained) from the gatehouse. For the best walk, drive to the picnic parking area on the knoll above Building 63, a handsome brick edifice that has been placed on the National Register of Historic Places (one of three in the park) and under the name of the Torpedo Warehouse serves as a picnic shelter.

Walk down to Little Bay. Watch the waterfowl, who find a degree of refuge here, and the ferries. Then go east from the warehouse on the gated shore road, passing a road up the hill that will be walked later. The way partly rounds Middle Point, a 90-foot hillock that was an island when sea level was a dozen feet higher, to the fenced-off remains of Battery Robert B. Mitchell, mostly underground. Its guns—with those of Fort Ward on Bainbridge Island—prevented foreign navies, the swine, from bombarding Bremerton. A concrete wall on the shore anchored the south side of the anti-submarine nets that impeded ferry traffic during World War II. The sedimentary outcrops (in this area is virtually the only hard rock on Puget Sound) enclose little nook beaches, jut out in picturesque buttresses. Madronas overhang the waters—and poison oak is insidiously everywhere, beware, beware.

The special feature of the views is the big white jumbo ferry thrashing past just offshore, but there are also long looks out to Blake Island and the Green Mile of Lincoln Park in Seattle.

Return from the battery (the trail peters out beyond a rocky point) to the road up the hill and climb it to a large grass meadow (home of the hot goats, R.I.P.). The summit views through the madrona forest are out over Clam Bay and the green buildings of

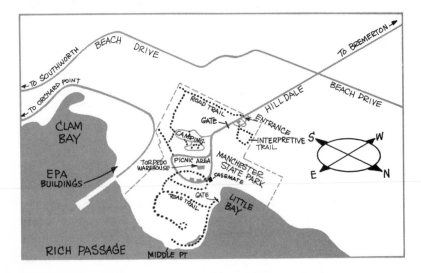

The Torpedo Warehouse (now a picnic shelter) at Manchester State Park

the Environmental Protection Agency. Beyond, on the larger, higher former island that is now Orchard Point, is the Navy's Manchester Fuel Depot—here, when time renders the war-like arrangement obsolete, will be *the* park of this scene.

Return down the road to an unsigned trail on the left, entering alder-maple forest. In a short bit is a Y, both forks descending to the parking. The right is better because it passes Mining Casemate, an historic building that served as command post for mine patrol from 1900 to 1910. There is no indication what mines were patrolled.

Loop trip 1 mile, allow 1 hour
High point 90 feet, elevation gain 90 feet

Port Orchard (map—page 181)

In the north suburbs of Bremerton are two fine walks, a short stroll in a state park combining splendid old forest and a nice beach, and a long lonesome ramble on beneath-the-bluff wild beach.

Illahee State Park

Salt shores are enhanced by big-tree forest, and vice versa. Masses throng the 75-acre park (25 campsites) on fine weekends; try it on a bright spring morning or a moody winter afternoon.

Totem pole near Port Orchard Bay

From Burwell, the new name for 6 Street (Highway 304), in Bremerton turn north on Warren Avenue (Highway 303) and follow state park signs infallibly to the entrance. Descend the loop road, passing a parking area with trailhead and a sideroad to the beach parking area. For the best walk continue on the loop to another parking area and trailhead, elevation 260 feet.

Descend a great gulch in gorgeous maples and firs a scant 1/2 mile to the beach. Lolligag south along the sands, with a sidetrip out on the dock for maximum views up and down Port Orchard, across to Bainbridge Island, and to ferries rocketing through Rich Passage. In 1/3 mile, when a fence bars the beach to public feet, climb the trail high on the precipitous bluff. What seems to be the gully of an ancient logging skidway is passed. And Douglas firs up to 5 feet in diameter, and cedars and maples and ferns—the climax is a fir snag, bark still on, 9 feet in diameter, wow. Return to beachside picnic area and parking and climb back up the great gulch.

Round trip 2 miles, allow 1 1/2 hours
High point 260 feet, elevation gain 400 feet

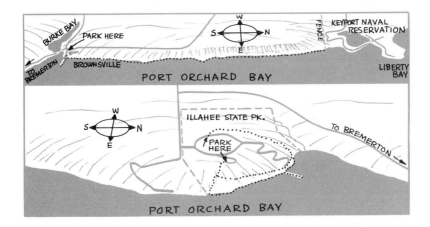

Burke Bay to Liberty Bay

Most of this vicinity lacks the standard shore-defense (against houses) system and thus the beaches are insufferably populated. Here, though a drift bluff leaps up a dandy 200 feet, giving the longest lonesome walk hereabouts; trespassing usually is amiably tolerated.

From the turnoff to Illahee State Park continue north on Illahee-Brownsville-Keyport Road 5.5 miles to the bridge over the estuary of Burke Bay. Just across, turn right to spacious parking areas of the large marina; park out of the way of the customers.

This is Brownsville, terminal of the long-ago ferry from Fletcher Bay on Bainbridge that permitted sailors on leave and Navy Yard workers to commute from the island.

A public fishing dock and float ("Use At Your Own Peril"), reached by a bluff-edge path behind an old boathouse, permit close looks at pretty yachts and long looks north to Liberty Bay, Battle Point, and Agate Pass, and south to University Point. Access is easy to the beach, alder-overhung, little molested by man at the start and less so as the bluff rises to full height. Views of Fletcher Bay yield to views of Manzanita Bay. Liberty Bay grows, and the Navy torpedo installation at Keyport. In 3 miles the fences of that reservation halt progress at the mouth of Liberty Bay, across from Point Bolin.

Round trip 6 miles, allow 4 hours

Tahuya State Forest

The Tahuya Peninsula is a plateau up to 600 feet in elevation, scarps plunging to Hood Canal south and west, something like 120 square miles of second-growth wildland. In the wake of the glaciers the rolling upland is dotted with hundreds of lakes large or small, broad-view or moody-lonesome, ever birdy, and myriad marshes and peat bogs and swamps and meadows. Also due to the glacier, the gravel soils rapidly flood off the 40-inch annual rainfall, supporting dry-site vegetation. The prevalence of pine—lodgepole, western white, even Ponderosa—is striking. So are the creekside groves of quaking aspen. Startling are the clumps of Oregon white oak. The understory also is un-Whulge-like, typically dominated by evergreen huckleberry and rhododendron and manzanita. In the meadows during the spring flowering a walker may wonder how he was magically transported to alpine elevations.

The logging that commenced with 19th-century bullteam operations at tidewater progressed via railroad over the plateau, finishing before War II, leaving only scattered "long corners" of hard-to-get-at old-growth in ravines and on ridges. The cut-and-get-out loggers let the land go for taxes—and thus the miracle of the peninsula, its last and greatest surprise, the Tahuya State Forest (formerly Multiple Use Area) of 33,000 acres (intermingled with private lands) managed by the state Department of Natural Resources (DNR) under the same statutory guidelines as Capitol Forest (which see). The land is "worked": cleanup clearcutting of old-growth continues even as commercial thinning of second-growth begins; among the charms of a visit is driving through miles and miles of Christmas trees, which grow slow and thus shrubby here on thin-soil sites poor for production of pulp or lumber; everywhere to be seen are commercial brushpickers.

But the use is genuinely multiple with due emphasis on recreation. The DNR has built interpretive signs, vista points, picnic grounds, and 13 campgrounds (good bases for visits by Puget Sounders who live a bit too far for day-tripping). A trail system of more than 50 miles is planned, permitting a continuous walk from saltwater of Hood Canal to the summit of Green Mountain. Nearly half the system already exists—come in winter for the solitude, in November to watch dog salmon spawning in rivers and creeks, in May and June for the flower show in rhododendron gardens and mountain-like meadows.

However, when is "multiple-use" *not*? When one use drives the others out. This is a domain of the DNR, which for years has had a tilt toward the motorcycle. (Tilt! This sort of lean would make a battleship turn turtle.) Nobody in DNR understands why this is; that is, they refuse to talk about it. The suspicion must therefore be that some official highly and securely placed in the hierarchy since the Cole regime just plain *likes machines*. (In fairness to DNR staff, this Machine machine may be in the Legislature, a cabal of legislators and ATV industry lobbyists.) In any event, most of the "all-purpose" trails rarely see a boot. They have been integrated into the hundreds of miles of "bootleg" trails built without permission by motorcycle clubs on old rail grades. Until the DNR retires that official, whoever he may be, and opens its eyes to reality, the walking is best on Wednesday. *Never on Sunday.*

Because of the wheels we are describing only two trails, Tahuya River and Green Mountain. The map shows the Howell Lake Trail and the Mission Creek Trail; the surveyor gazed at the wheel tracks and flinched. The suspicion arises that the reason the trail system has not been completed is that somebody up there recognizes the affair is a fiasco and had best not be bragged up.

The Overland Trail that would link the Tahuya and Green Mountain has not been completed. The Connection Trail west from Howell Lake to Aldrich Lake has not been begun.

Neither has the Aldrich Lake Trail nor the Bald Point Trail; we feel sad about that because these two, if banned to wheels, would be pedestrian joys. Aldrich Lake, a pretty pool in the forest, was a log dump in the 1920s and before. From it the logs were sluiced down a flume (its line still evidenced by a gully-like gouge) to tidewater for rafting to mills. From the scarp edge a stone's throw from the lake the forest slope plunges to Hood Canal. Across the waters are US 101, the town of Lilliwaup, the peaks of Dow and Washington and Ellinor, the valley of the Skokomish.

The 8½-mile Aldrich Lake Trail would wander the glaciated upland by marshes and lakes, crossing creeks, including the major valley of Dry (Rendsland) Creek, to Bald Point Vista. Zounds. From the tip of a spur ridge thrusting out from the upland plateau, at an elevation of 500 feet, the slope plummets to Bald (Ayres) Point, jutting into the Great Bend of Hood Canal. For the best looking, descend the slope a bit to an open grassy slope. Amid manzanita and evergreen huckleberry and rhododendron, sit and gaze. To boats stirring white wakes in blue water. To Annas Bay and the wide delta of the Skokomish. To South Mountain and the mill plumes of Shelton. North up the canal to the Tacoma City Light powerhouse at Potlatch, and to Hoodsport, and Dow. Across to Union, sufficiently settled by 1858 to have a post office, for many decades reached most easily from civilization by mosquito-fleet steamers. The original Union Cemetery was below, on Bald Point; disruption of funerals by foul weather caused relocation on

Rhododendron blooms and Hood Canal and Olympics from near Aldrich Lake

the town side of the water. The Bald Point Trail would drop 1 mile to the mouth of Dry Creek, on Hood Canal, and a trailhead park (see Hood Canal).

Tahuya State Forest has a wondrous recreational future. Once that fellow is ejected from his Olympia office and sent riding off into the sunset on his dirtbike.

A final caveat: We have not given driving directions to Aldrich Lake or Bald Point, are sketchy in some other areas, and hesitate to guarantee any directions we have given because the road and signing systems change almost yearly. Don't attempt an expedition here without the DNR map.

Tahuya River Trail (map—page 187)

Where are we? Surely not in Puget Sound country, scarcely above sea level? It feels more like a valley 8000 feet up in the wilderness of Montana. The modest river rattles in gravel meanders through meadows dotted with small pines, bright with

Hiker cooling feet in the Tahuya River

alpine-like flowers. The trail ascends from its bank to the forest plateau, passes silent ponds rimmed with reeds. No, we're not in Montana after all, but home—yet a part of our home we never suspected.

First of the trail system to be built, the Tahuya River Trail is some 12 miles long, though part of this may ultimately be attributed to an Overland Trail connecting to the Green Mountain Loop. Segments of the trail lend themselves to hikes of various lengths from a number of road accesses; these will be described south to north.

Collins Lake Road to Tahuya River Camp, 2³/₄ miles, elevation gain 300 feet

From Belfair drive Highway 300 west 3.7 miles and just past Belfair State Park turn north on a blacktop road with a bundle of sings, including "Tahuya River." In 2 miles is a major intersection with Elfendahl Pass Road going left and right; go straight on Collins Lake Road. In 3.7 miles, as the road nearly has reached a flat valley bottom, spot an obscure trail on the right, just across from a two-car parking shoulder. (If you cross the Tahuya River you've gone a tad too far.) Elevation, 200 feet.

The way climbs a bit, then goes upsy-downsy along dry-gravel drumlin ridges in rhododendrons and spindly firs and linear-pond bottoms in cool alder, partly on old logging-railroad grade. Razzer trails confuse; stay with the main track, and when there are two "mains," go left, where runs the Tahuya River, your goal.

After 1³/₄ miles, something different, something wonderful. The trail drops off the plateau scarp to alder bottom, crosses a beaver-dammed slough into copses of spirea, and emerges in broad, big-sky meadowlands dotted with young pines and huckleberry-topped stumps. Sidepaths lead to the river, where ducks swim off, herons cumbersomely flap up and away. The clear stream delights. One wants to choose a gravel bar, take off boots, and wade. In fact, one has a Great Notion of coming here in shorts and tennis shoes on a warm spring day and doing the Long Wade for miles along the Tahuya. It could be done—the stream, scarcely a "river" except in the monsoons when floodwaters roar, has plenty of bars for pausing to let feet thaw. And the Wade is truly wild, for only here and there are banks neared by trail or road. Just you and the birds, and the fish, and the deer, squirrels, and coyote, maybe a bear, even a cat.

But, back to the trail. Through fields it winds, in columbine, meadow rue, fairy bells, blue-eyed Mary, and strawberry, and by hellebore bogs and groves of cottonwood and quaking aspen, sometimes climbing the 20-50-foot valley wall, in pines and twinflower, vanilla leaf, ginger, and coolwort. After 1 enchanting mile—the best the Tahuya has to offer—the trail enters Tahuya River Camp, elevation 250 feet.

Tahuya River Camp to Kammenga Canyon Camp, 1³/₄ miles, elevation gain 100 feet

From the intersection where Collins Lake Road goes west, drive north on Elfendahl Pass Road 2.5 miles and turn west on Goat Ranch Road (commemorating an early homestead, many of whose traces remain hereabouts), signed "Spillman Camp, Tahuya River Camp." The roads past this point change from year to year, confusion to confusion. Keep the map in hand and stay alert. Drive past Oak Patch Lake Natural Area Preserve, the fascinating plant community dominated by what may be the largest stand of Oregon white oak on the peninsula. Pass a welter of signs for Camp Spillman and in 0.7 mile from Elfendahl Pass Road, or 2 miles from Elfendahl Pass, switchback down to Tahuya River Camp, largest in the Tahuya and a beauty, in lovely forest beside the delightful river.

Kammenga Canyon Camp to Toonerville Campground to Green Mountain Loop Trail

The tread north is built as far as Toonerville, 7 miles from Kammenga Canyon, but was only sketchily surveyed for this guide due to the lingering exhaust fumes, which so seriously erode ones belief in "trail."

In a scant 1 mile, after crossing Elfendahl Pass Road, is Camp Pond, ecologically amazing. The forest (with primitive camp) ringing the silent waters includes lodgepole pine and oak; unusual in second-growth, here grow calypso orchids. The little meadows of the vicinity are lush with beargrass (really!) and other plants unusual for this elevation. Note old ditches which seem unnatural—they are, having been dug by homesteaders to drain meadow-marshes to make pastures.

In another 1¹/₂ miles or so is the northern terminus of Mission Creek Trail. Ponds, marshes, creeks, forests. Another crossing of Elfendahl Pass Road, then of Tahuya River. Just before the river, pass Toonerville Camp, named for the Trolley that was famous in the funny pages of newspapers of the 1920s-30s. Here in the long ago was a logging-railroad reload, the grade later used for the "Lost Highway" that came from tidewater at Dewatto Bay and deadended here for many years, before modern county roads tied it to civilization eastward. Recross river and road. Recross road, cross Gold Creek Road, then Gold Creek. Along Gold Creek pass the falls, then up the hill to join the Green Mountain loop (which see).

Except that as of 1988 the Overland Trail has not been built north beyond Toonerville.

One-way trip from Collins Lake Road to Green Mountain loop 18¹/₂ miles

Green Mountain (map—page 186, 187)

From the mountain range nobody knows, look to the two mountain ranges everybody knows, seen from here in a novel perspective. Also look to virtually every nook of the Whulge from Admiralty Inlet south, and to cities and towns and forests, and to implements of World Wars II and III. In season, sniff the rhododendron blossoms.

Exit from the Bremerton ferry dock and go right on Washington, then left on Burwell, the new name for 6th (Highway 304), continuing on this thoroughfare as it changes name to Kitsap Way. Or, if driving from Tacoma Narrows Bridge, exit from Highway 3 onto Kitsap Way. From the Highway 3 underpass drive Kitsap Way 1.5 miles to a Y; go left, signed "Kitsap Lake, Seabeck, Holly." In 1 mile go left, signed "Wildcat Lake, Holly." In 3 more miles go left, signed "Holly Road." In 2.5 miles is False Green Mountain Road—*don't take it*. Instead, at 4 miles go left on unsigned, paved Tahuya Lake Road. In 0.8 mile the unsigned, gravel, True Green Mountain Road diverges left.

Drive Green Mountain Road, ignoring lesser sideroads and at one spot crossing the Loop Trail, 2.5 miles to a Y. The right is signed "Vista" and leads to the summit; go left, signed "Camp," and proceed a scant 1 mile, passing a trailhead signed "Green Mountain Vista 2.5 miles," to Green Mountain Horse Camp. Park at the picnic area, elevation 1150 feet.

For the most esthetic looping, walk back on the camp entry road ²/₃ mile, contouring in the forest of fir, hemlock, cedar, madrona, and pine that characterizes the route; mostly it's pretty spindly stuff. In May admire the rhododendron blossoms, in September browse black fruit of the evergreen huckleberry. At the signed trailhead leave the road and follow the upsy-downsy path ³/₄ mile to the crossing of the road, with a look up to the summit radio tower. The trail now drops gently ²/₃ mile, passing a moody stump-and-snag marsh where dragonflies patrol. For the final 1¹/₄ miles the way is steadily and often steeply up, switchbacking above the marsh bowl in larger conifers, and springs, coolwort, maidenhair fern, and (October) chanterelles. On mossy balds of metamorphosed sandstone are gardens of strawberry and alumroot and the first screened views. One feels high. At an unsigned Y of good trails, go right, uphill; the left contours ¹/₄ mile to the summit road. Soon the trail (unsigned, a matter of confusion to loopers from the other direction) emerges on the parking lot just below 1689-foot "Lookout Summit." Total distance, about 3¹/₂ miles; elevation gain, about 1000 feet.

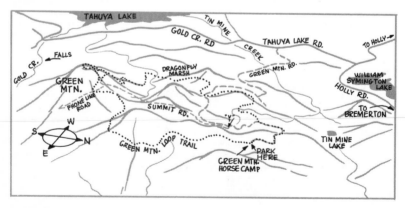

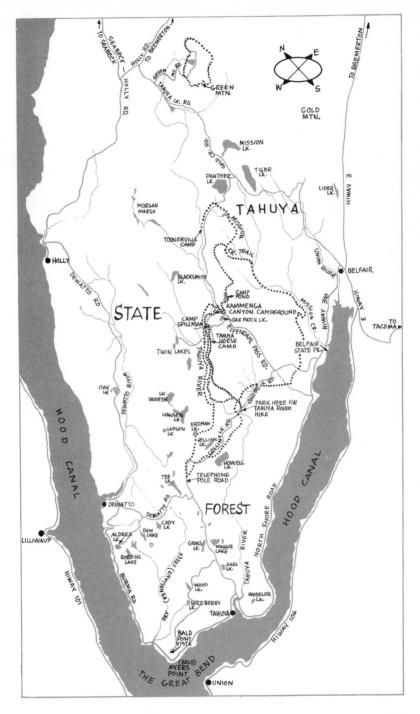

Telephoto of Seattle from Gold Mountain

Three vista points offer different panoramas. The first is a few steps north of the trailhead by a weathered wood-panel map that once identified the surroundings. Below is Tahuya Lake, west are Hood Canal, with Dabob and Quilcene Bays, and the town of Brinnon, and the peaks of Zion, Walker, Constance, Jupiter, and The Brothers, and the four major river valleys separating them. The second vista is from the rock-knob cliff-edge site of the lookout tower: south over Gold Creek to Gold; north to the end of the world at Bangor; east over waterways of Bremerton to Bainbridge and Blake and Vashon Islands, Seattle towers, and Issaquah Alps and Cascades. Now, the third. Walk from the lookout along its former service road a scant 1/4 mile south, by a radio tower, to 1700-foot "Radio Summit." Here on a rock bald amid ocean spray, manzanita, and rhododendron, look across marshy Gold Creek valley to tower-infested Gold and over green-wild, lake-dotted Tahuya Peninsula to the Great Bend of Hood Canal, mill plumes of Shelton, Black Hills and Olympics.

Now, for home. From the lookout parking area descend the main summit road. pass the old (gated) lookout service road, then a sideroad down right to a small quarry. In 1/3 mile a trail signed "Green Mountain Vista" goes off the road left (to intersect the summit trail in 1/4 mile). Here leave the road on the trail right, signed "Horse Camp." In 1/4 mile, after crossing the quarry road, the trail hits the unsigned Phone Line Road. A trail sign directs the few steps to where trail (a true one, don't confuse it with a razzer track passed first) takes off left, uphill. The final 1 1/4 miles are mainly a contour, with minor ups and downs, around the lower north summit of Green, in pleasant forest and wide-view clearcuts. After a total 2 miles from the summit, fairly consistently downhill, an alder swale leads to the trailhead by the red handpump providing well water to the campground. A short bit uphill left is the picnic area.

Loop trip from Green Mountain Camp 6 miles, allow 4 hours
High point 1700 feet, elevation gain 1200 feet

Gold Mountain (map—page 187, 190)

Though not in the Tahuya State Forest, Gold Mountain is so closely related to Green Mountain, as one of the "Blue" Mountains, it may best be described here.

The summit view encompasses Edmonds and Seattle and Tacoma and Olympia and Bremerton, and lakes and islands and saltwaterways and two mountain ranges, and that's a lot. However, the unique dazzler is a sight not to be seen from any other vantage point: spread out close below as if on a map are the "triplet fishhooks"—Hood Canal curling north from the Great Bend to its end in Lynch Cove, and the two terminal fingers of Puget Sound crooking north, Case Inlet to its end in North Bay, Carr Inlet to Burley Lagoon.

From Highway 3 just north of its junction with Highway 16 turn west on Old Belfair Valley Road 5.5 miles and turn north on Minard Road. Drive 1.7 miles, dodging myriad lesser sideroads and motorcycles and jeep tracks, the way becoming narrow, twisty, chuckholey, to a gate. Park here, elevation 800 feet.

The walk is entirely on a service road, gated so four-wheelers can't get in but harassed by millions of motorcycles on weekends. But not on Wednesday. In mixed second-growth the way climbs steadily; stick with the main road, avoiding lesser spurs. At 1 mile, 1240 feet, is a switchback; from the end a rut-trail descends to Mission Lake, whence roar multitudes of razzers on Sunday, but an interesting alternative approach (not surveyed) on Thursday. Windows begin to open, including a big one south from a short spur. Moss and flowers embellish rubbly basalt outcrops, the forest of small conifers is enhanced by rhododendron and copses of manzanita and evergreen huckleberry. At 1¾ miles, 1560 feet, the road crosses the summit ridge and winds along the north side, with windows across the gulf of Gold Creek to Green. In 1½ more miles the road bends around the east end of the ridge and goes west a final ⅓ mile, sprouting sideroads.

Gold is a blabbermouth, sporting four yap-yap facilities; one is worth visiting as the site of an old lookout tower and each of the others offers wide arcs of the round-the-compass panorama, as does the site of a second lookout on the highest summit, 1761 feet. So, there are five knobs to get, all close together; a couple are notable for glacier-polished slabs of vesicular basalt; the spring flower show is glorious. In 1980 a 700-foot TV tower was built on the summit ridge for Channel 13.

But not for towers nor flowers did ye come, but lessons in Puget Sound geography. South and southwest are the three fishhooks, and Union River, and lakes and airports and golf courses and forests, and Bald Hills and Black Hills, and the Skokomish valley and southern Olympics. Northwest and north are Hood Canal, Dabob Bay, Walker and Zion, The Brothers and Constance, and Doomsday structures at Bangor. Below, close east, are Dyes and Sinclair Inlets and Port Washington Narrows and the Bremerton Navy Yard. Trace the ferry route out Rich passage, between Bainbridge and Blake Islands—and way out there are the shining castles of Seattle. Whulge sweeps north past Kingston and Edmonds to Whidbey Island and the pulpmill plumes of Everett, and south past Alki Point and Vashon Island to the pulpmill plume and evil finger of Tacoma and on to Olympia. As a backdrop are Issaquah Alps, companion

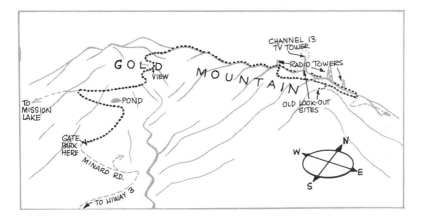

remnant of the Old Mountains, and volcanoes from Baker to Glacier to Rainier to St. Helens.

Round trip 8 miles, allow 6 hours
High point 1761 feet, elevation gain 1200 feet

Hood Canal

Old country. "Head of Canal" (Belfair, now) was settled in 1859, though not reached by overland road until 1918, despite an 1895 gold strike (fake, fake) on Mission Creek. The water road was about the only way to go in those days, and steamers from Seattle called at the major fishermen-sheltering ports of Holly and Dewatto (where, in the mid-1880s, a boat-building enterprise began) and especially Union, the metropolis. When settlers arrived in the early 1850s the Indians had more than 30 villages from "Head of Canal" to Dewatto Bay; they were moved to reservations, such as Squaxin Island, to make room for loggers—by 1876 there were 50 logging camps on the Canal, bullteam operations, logs flumed down the scarp from the plateau to the water and then rafted to mills. The walker still finds traces of Indians, loggers, mosquito fleet.

Beautiful country. The fjord-like waterway voyaged by fishing boats, pleasure craft. Olympics rising abruptly and high.

Even now, mostly lonesome country. Solid houses extend from "Head of Canal" to the Great Bend and have crept around Bald (Ayres) Point. And US 101 on the west side is continuous cars, trucks, resorts, homes. But there's a wild side, the east, where deer nibble seaweed unconcerned by the hiker, and crows harass nesting bald eagles, and little creeks ripple out of deep-forest ravines. It won't last, the end is nigh. But it's a creeping doom, the good past will linger a while. Walk now and weep later.

Or maybe not. Friends of the Earth has proposed that Congress protect the treasure by creating a Hood Canal National Scenic Area administered by the National Park Service. There may yet be time.

Dry Creek to Dewatto Bay (map—page 187)

Drive west from Belfair on Highway 300, which becomes North Shore Road. At 17.5 suburbia-slow miles round Bald Point and in 1 long mile more come to suburbia's end in the wide vale of Dry (Rendsland) Creek. Park on the south side of the creek and its splendid delta.

(This is an undeveloped DNR site. Eventually there will be a facility of some sort here and a 1-mile trail up the scarp to Bald Point Vista.

The shore north was a roaring wilderness until very recently, the only overland access by rude and crude roads, prior to illegal construction of a road from Dry Creek to Dewatto. Though a twisty, tortuous lane winding in and out of gullies along the face of the forested 600-foot cliff, the "Burma Road" has opened up the country. Year by year the realtor frontier pushes north. A gloryland is becoming just another expensive piece of real estate.

From the creek, the far south of Vancouver's 1792 voyage of discovery, walk the ½ mile to Musqueti Point and its several beachside homes. Passing these requires toleration, presently at a high level; should problems arise in future, hikers can drive the Burma Road north past the limit of thick habitation, wherever it happens to be at time of the visit, and scout for an easy and safe way 100-200 feet down one of the many ravines to the beach. (A major cause of intolerance is the slimy gold on the beaches. As the price of oysters goes higher so do feelings about rustling, virtually a hanging offense. So, leave the shellfish alone. And if chased off by oystermen posses, go away—and find a lonesome put-in from the Burma Road—which also, by the by, serves as a splendid overland return route if cut off by tides.)

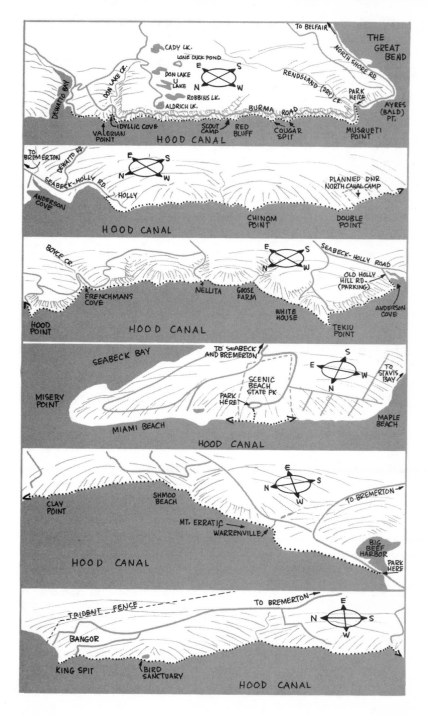

Somewhere past Musqueti Point the frontier may be reached. Much of the beach is guarded by drift bluff that always will keep the way wild. But there are pleasant deltas and terraces where Indians once camped and soon the victors will live.

Across the 1½-mile-wide Canal, plied by sailboats and motorboats and oyster dredges, is busy US 101. Hoodsport and its valley of Finch Creek stand out, and south of that, Potlatch and the Tacoma City Light Powerhouse. Dennie Ahl Hill and Dow Mountain rise above; above them, Ellinor and Washington.

A long 1 mile from Musqueti Point is charming Cougar Spit, with a pretty creek and a half-dozen cabins weathering on a terrace. In ½ mile more is another nice point with a shack bearing a sign claiming this is the veritable Cougar Spit. In a scant 1 mile more is Red Bluff, with a 120-foot naked wall of iron-stained gravel, an old Scout headquarters building, pilings of the dock where Scouts used to debark onto their Hahobas Reservation; here are the delta-point of a gorgeous creek sparkling out of the alders and a masterpiece of a forest, especially grand in May when rhododendron, madrona, dogwood, and evergreen huckleberry are in bloom.

In ½ mile of wild shore the reservation ends and the shore is crowded (by local standards)—in the next 2¼ miles a couple dozen cabins cling to the bluff. But one never would suspect the Burma Road is above. The shore bulges out, swings in, the forest and waves go on, creeks waterfall to the beach or rush from ferny-green gullies or spread over gravels of delta points. Throughout here, and all the south Canal, the beach gravels are strikingly tawny, unlike the gray gravels typical of the Whulge elsewhere, including the north Canal; the main constituents are sandstone and basalt, iron-stained, from the Skokomish Gravels washed out from the front of an Olympic glacier. This stretch culminates in the gasper of the trip, the bay and estuary-delta of "Don Lake Creek," with a creekside, mudflat-side meadow, an orchard, and an old summer house and two old cabins. Look from a distance. No touching.

In a scant ½ mile from the bay's south point is "Valerian Point," where in May the grassy wall is bright with Scouler's valerian, paintbrush, vetch, and lupine. In the final scant 1 mile are another great creek, a couple more cabins, and the rounding into Dewatto Bay, deepest indentation for miles—and presumably connected by a fault or something with Lilliwaup Bay on the opposite shore.

Admire Lilliwaup town and Washington, The Brothers, and other Olympics, and turn around to begin the 7 miles back, by beach and/or Burma Road.

Round trip 14 miles, allow 10 hours

Holly to Dewatto Bay (map—page 187)

Gone from Dewatto Bay is the boat-building industry of 1884. Gone too are the fleets of fishing boats. Old houses and moldering ruins remain—and not much of them.

Dewatto Bay presently is not a hiker's put-in (unless, like the photographer, he has a canoe). Houses block the way south. And to walk north a person would first have to wade the Dewatto River, and that would be easy, but then he'd have to thrash through estuary muck and brush to the outer beach, and that would be madness. A pity, because the beach north of the bay is the wildest on Hood Canal. It will not so remain. Aside from residential invasion, the recreationists are coming, the recreationists are coming. At the bay is a public property that will be developed in a few years either by Mason County or the DNR. Presently no public road nears the beach from Dewatto to Holly, but the DNR plans a North Canal Campground some 3 miles north of the bay.

In 1978 this stretch was surveyed from the north. From Bremerton drive west by Wildcat Lake and Symington Lake. Just west of Camp Union, at a T, go left on Seabeck-Holly Road. Drop off the plateau to water level at Anderson Cove, pass the Dewatto Road, into old Holly, originally "Happy Valley" and home port of many fishermen, now inhabited by about three dozen families. The problem is ditching the car. There's no provision for invaders—not so much as a road shoulder to park on.

This must be done wherever opportunity affords without clogging traffic—maybe 1 mile away at Anderson Cove. In any event, do not park on roadway or in driveways—not only would you mess up the good life for residents but you would bring about an end to the toleration, presently at a high level except in summer. And no toleration, no walk.

Once free of the car walk down Allan King Road, by Holly Beach Community Club, to the beach, and turn left. In a scant ½ mile a point is rounded and the last houses passed. The way now is securely wild, guarded by the steep jungle that rises to the plateau at 400-600 feet. At the start the drift bluff has much blue clay and is slidey—in the first stretch the beach may be blocked by pants-ripping tangles of seaweed-hung barnacle-encrusted tree clumps. After that the "brown beach" dotted with big erratics is easy open at tides of 8-9 feet or less, often canopied by alder and maple.

The quiet of this shore is underscored by the hum-roar of US 101 across the waters. A deer steps out of the evergreen-huckleberry thickets and calmly inspects you. Great blue herons object to your presence—the surveyor saw 20-odd, four in a single gang.

Across the Canal are villages—Mike's Beach Resort and Tree Farm, where the older surveyor's father once was resident gypo, and Eldon, Jorsted Creek, Aycock Point. The mountain backdrop shifts as the walk progresses, from Jupiter between the Dosewallips and Duckabush valleys, to The Brothers (with Webb Lookout in front) and Bretherton and the Hamma Hamma valley, to Jorsted Point in front of Pershing, Washington, and Ellinor, and at last, past the Lilliwaup valley, to Dow and Dennie Ahl and the Skokomish valley.

The beach curves in to coves, out to points, requiring many foot miles to make any heron miles. The way is enlivened by gulches, ravines, and mini-valleys, most with creeks, some with deltas. Now and then terraces of old beaches are elevated above

Hood Canal north of Dewatto Bay, Mt. Washington in distance

the tides. At 2¼ miles is the first civilization since Holly, a valley with a couple trailers parked. In another 1½ miles is Chinom Point, most prominent feature of the route, with a valley and delta-spit and filled-in lagoon and a dozen flossy summer homes. Several ancient homes/modern camps are passed in gulches the next 2 miles to "Double Point." By now the bluff has become mainly gravel, drier, with grass slopes and a forest of fir and madrona.

Poignance of a visible past. A pictograph on an enormous erratic. A lonesome apple tree bearing a lush crop of some antique species. Ironware of ancient logging rusted nearly to nothing. A huge stump grooved for a cable, at the mouth of the gully down which bull teams dragged the logs. Remnants of a waterwheel, a primitive hydroelectric plant. Stubs of old pilings, dwellings collapsed to litters of rotten lumber. More people lived here in the 1930s—the 1910s—the 1880s—than now. Met on the survey was an old settler, 77, who told how on his place, a terrace no more than 30 feet wide between beach and bluff, there was in the 1930s a chicken coop 60 feet long—the supplier of eggs and drumsticks to the entire south Canal. Until nearly War II a freight boat ran once a week, down the west side of the Canal in morning, returning up the east side in afternoon, nosing to the beach to load and unload. In earlier decades the Canal was busy with mosquito-fleet traffic and among the settlers on terraces and deltas were many who made livings cutting cordwood for wood-burning steamers.

Just past "Double Point" begin some 2 miles of public tidelands. Here the DNR is planning its North Canal Campground. The survey proceeded only ½ mile past "Double Point" to a camp in a valley, a grand spot to lunch and turn around. And so the surveyor did, 3 miles from the mouth of Dewatto Bay, suspecting this was the wildest section of the shore and wanting to save it for leisurely inspection on a walk north from the bay. A return trip in 1980, coming overland via an intricacy of gated roads to the beach, was disillusioning. The woods were gridded and flagged, the beach staked, the chance lost.

Round trip to Turnaround Camp 12½ miles, allow 8 hours
Round trip to Dewatto Bay 19 miles, allow 12 hours

Anderson Cove to Hood Point (map—page 191)

South of Holly wilderness is the rule, civilization the exception. Now, north, the balance swings the other way—the bluff relents, lessening in steepness for long stretches, more frequently breached by gully-ramps to the water. However, the mood still is dominantly lonesome, though more frequently interrupted by summer homes and a scattering of year-round residences.

There is only one easy access, at the south end. Drive toward Holly and 1 mile before that, just before crossing Anderson Creek, turn right on Old Holly Hill Road along Anderson Cove. In several hundred feet park in a wide turnout on the right.

The way curves out of the cove around a head. In the first scant 1½ miles to Tekiu Point (including ¾ mile of public tidelands) are several cabins at the start, requiring toleration, then wildwood bluff broken by tanglewood creeks, and one substantial old home. Tekiu Point is a splendid unmolested spit poking out in wind and waves, the views across to Triton Head and up to The Brothers (and Webb Lookout).

The shore turns from a northerly to easterly trend and the route can be seen all the way to the next spit, Hood Point. In a vale is a gracious two-storey two-chimney white house, and in another wide valley with a sizable creek is a comfortable old goose farm where the fowl hiss at beachwalkers. But that's the most of civilization in the 1½ miles to Nellita, a cluster of well-worn summer cottages by the beach.

Herons "grawk!" and kingfishers "ti-ti-ti" and cormorants pose on old pilings and bald eagles sail on high. Cedars and firs and madronas overhang the beach. Another cluster of quaint cottages on the hillside, and another picturesque farm—green house amid orchard, big delta of a pretty creek. Wild bluff leaps up again. At 1¾ miles from

Small inlet off Hood Canal near Holly

Nellita is the major valley of the route, Frenchmans Cove, with several houses and, inland, a fine big pasture and barn. Boyce Creek must be leapt or waded—or crossed inland on a plank bridge.

The final 1 mile is mostly inhabited. Several cottages are on a bulkhead, a couple more on a bulge, and at the base of the spit of Hood Point are a dozen fancy homes. But go out on the tip and look far south to Holly, and across to Black Point and the Duckabush valley, to Olympics from The Brothers to Jupiter, and north to Scenic Beach and Dabob Bay and the Dosewallips valley.

Though not surveyed, the next 2¹/₂ miles to Stavis Bay appear mostly wild.

Round trip 11¹/₂ miles, allow 8 hours

Scenic Beach State Park (map—page 191)

It sure is. More scenic than beach, but some strolling is to be done. And oh the looking!

Exit from the Bremerton ferry dock and go right on Washington, then left on Burwell, the new name for 6th (Highway 304), and continue on this thoroughfare as it changes name to Kitsap Way. Or, if driving from Tacoma Narrows, exit from Highway 3 onto Kitsap Way. From the Highway 3 underpass drive Kitsap Way 1.5 miles to a Y; go left, signed "Kitsap Lake, Seabeck, Holly." In 1 mile go left, signed "Wildcat Lake, Holly." Stick with this highway some 7.5 miles to Big Beef Harbor and continue 2.5 more miles to Seabeck Landing, whence once the *Lake Constance* ferried Model A's and Trapper Nelsons over the Canal to Brinnon. About 0.2 mile south of town turn right, following "Scenic Beach" and "State Park" signs here and at the Y (go left) in 1 more mile, in a final 0.7 mile entering the park and descending to parking areas near the beach.

An old farmhouse and orchard, a log cabin roofed by moss and swordferns, fine fir forest and 1/4 mile of public beach, are the standpoints for the views: across Hood Canal to Oak Head at the tip of enormous Toandos Peninsula, and into enormous Dabob Bay, within which is smaller Jackson Cove, site of Camp Parsons. Rising above are Walker, Turner, and Buck. Higher are The Brothers, Jupiter, and Constance, the mountain masses cleft by trenches of Duckabush and Dosewallips Rivers. That's scenic.

The 71-acre park is mostly devoted to spacious picnic spots and 50 campsites. In the high-toleration season of lonesome winter the beach walk might be extended in either direction: south 2 miles to Stavis Bay; north 1 mile to Misery Point at the mouth of Seabeck Bay.

Round trip 1-6 miles, allow 1-4 hours

Big Beef Harbor to Bangor (map—page 191)

The wild Canal has been left well behind, south. Now the bluffs lower, breaching gullies and valleys are numerous, highways from population centers short and fast, and people cuddling the waves many. Nevertheless, short below-the-bluff stretches are wild. And the valleys themselves, most containing coves-lagoons-marshes cut off by baymouth bars, intrigue, and littoral architecture interests. And Olympic views are continuous and stupendous.

Drive to Big Beef Harbor and park on the shoulder of the causeway that has augmented the baymouth bar. Head what seems north but is actually closer to east.

Beach population is dense at the start, then diminishes. But the time for this walk is dismal winter, not bright summer when toleration is low.

The view is from Seabeck Bay across to Brinnon at the mouth of the Dosewallips and to Dabob Bay, enclosed by the Toandos Peninsula. The mountain front extends from The Brothers (and Webb Lookout) over the Duckabush valley to Jupiter, over the Dose valley to Constance, Turner, Buck, and Walker, and over the Quilcene valley to Townsend and Zion.

Continuous bulkhead quickly ends and a bulge is rounded to the creek, valley, baymouth bar, lagoon-marsh of Warrenville. The offshore tor of "Mount Erratic" is passed, then the concretions of "Shmoo Beach" and slidey "Clay Point" leading to the cove, creek, and valley of Anderson Creek. Fancy homes of Sunset Farm are left behind at 2 miles and henceforth there is more solitude than population. Here the shore, passing the across-the-Canal tip of Toandos Peninsula, bends sharply due north.

In the next 4 miles a half-dozen gulches-valleys break the bluff, most with a few houses, though one has a wild lagoon signed "Private Bird Sanctuary." Down the 100-foot bluff come paths, even electric trams, to camps or boathouses.

At 6 miles is the trip end, on the tip of King Spit amid driftwood and gulls. Look north to the past and future. Past: Old pilings of the mosquito fleet's Bangor Landing, where Bangor Boats on a pier and the mercantile house of H.W. Goodwin on the shore have been restored. Future: The fence and the homes of Trident, and fence-patrolling troops who glower at whiskered old surveyors carrying rucksacks and umbrellas, as would be expected of fence-jumpers and/or obstructors of the White Train.

Round trip 12 miles, allow 8 hours

SOUTH OLYMPIC PENINSULA

Having driven so far from Puget Sound City, will not any sensible pedestrian proceed onward into Olympic National Forest, Olympic National Park, for trails in virgin forests along wild rivers?

Usually, yes. And therefore the survey went light on woods and waters, focused on views. Here in the last chapter of the four-book series is finished the journey along the mountain front ringing the Whulge. *Footsore 3* traces the Olympic front south from Zion. Following pages finish off the range.

USGS maps: Mt. Tebo, Potlatch, The Brothers, Brinnon, Holly, Mason Lake, Lake Wooten

Twanoh State Park (map—page 198)

Yes, you'll want to stroll the park shore and absorb the calm beauty of this quintessential sea-in-the-forest stretch of Hood Canal. But cheek-by-jowl bulkheads-houses prevent long beach tours. However, there's walking to be done—in a wild

Footpath in Twanoh State Park

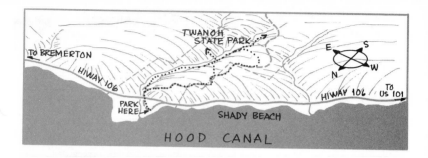

green gorge, a grand big-tree forest, on trails that climb the gorge walls and meander plateau-top woods.

Drive Highway 3 to just south of Belfair and turn south on Highway 106 to the park. Park in any of the lots, elevation 10 feet.

On the inland side of the highway, on the west bank of Twanoh Creek, find the wide trail upstream into the canyon. Ignore lesser sidepaths up the slope and walk the gorge in large firs and cedars and hemlocks, moss-swollen maples sprouting high-in-the-air ferns. In 1/2 mile a good trail switchbacks uphill right, signed "Tent Camping Area." Continue by the creek; on a winter day the dripping, hushed valley, treetops misty, has a rain-forest feel. Shortly before a major fork in the valley note a footlog over the creek, leading to a lesser trail (not surveyed) climbing the opposite wall. Past the forks the trail climbs steeper and in 1 mile from the highway switchbacks. (Off the end a meager path proceeds straight, to unsurveyed wildwoods.)

Ascending to a plateau-ridge at 400 feet, the trail enters drier woods of small firs, evergreen huckleberries, madrona, salal, and the occasional rhododendron, and Ts with an old fire road become trail. To the left the road goes an unsurveyed distance, out of the park and on and on. To the right it loops back northward past the Tent Camping Area and steeply descends to the highway.

That's a good introduction. But the 175-acre park has more trails. And there are adjoining wildwoods. A walker could keep busy all day.

In midwinter a feature of the trip is the litter of spawned-out salmon carcasses in the creek, filling the valley with a ripe aroma—and with gulls that surprise the woods walker, flying far into the green gorge seeking tasty bites.

Introductory loop 2 miles, allow 1 1/2 hours
High point 400 feet, elevation gain 400 feet
All year

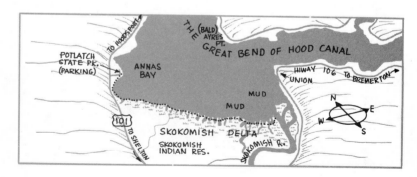

View across Hood Canal from the Skokomish Delta

Skokomish Delta (map—page 198)

The largest delta on the Hood Canal side of the Olympics also is the most scenic. It's additionally the wildest, the lonesomest—a preserve of solitude nearly 3 miles wide and up to 2 miles deep from saltwater to civilization, not counting a couple square miles of low-tide mudflats. Except for occasional cows and oysterpickers, a walker communes undisturbed with plovers and herons and clams. Beach and mudflats can be alternated with salt meadows that in spring are fields of flowers. Just be sure to pick a tide on the low side of medium or you won't get far.

Drive US 101 to Potlatch State Park, 3.2 miles south of Hoodsport, and park.

The first ¹/₂ mile is on beach close by the highway; this section can be skipped by parking at a wide turnout. Hop a nice little creek rushing over pebbles into Annas Bay and diverge from the highway into peace and quiet (except for squalling killdeer) on the delta. Views are grand over the bay to Great Bend, Bald Point jutting into the angle, and to Union, also on a jut. Close above the shores where lie Potlatch and Hoodsport rises mighty Dow, with Ellinor and Washington higher and mightier behind.

Tidal channels finger the delta; at low water the mud can be walked and trickle creeks hopped over. (Please don't step on the oysters and for golly sake don't pick them up.) Alternate by walking above the beach in fields of saltwort and sea blite and, in May, rosy-lovely masses of seablush.

Views evolve—the Tacoma City Light powerhouse grows prominent, and Dennie Ahl Hill. Cows panic at your approach and hightail for the barn. After a last mudflat squish, at 3 miles from the state park the route ends where the Skokomish River also does, rolling green waters into the bay.

Round trip 6 miles, allow 4 hours

South Mountain (map—page 200)

On the crystal-air November day of the original survey, five volcanoes were seen and one ocean, plus a Canal and a Sound and Three Fingers, Index, Phelps, Daniels, Chimney Rock, Goat Rocks, Green and Gold, Issaquah Alps, Doty and Bald and Black and Willapa Hills. Yes, and Olympics too. Rising abruptly from lowlands where the Puget Glacier petered out, South is the absolute southernmost peak of the Olympics, a unique viewpoint giving novel perspectives on the full length and width of the Puget Trough.

Drive US 101 to 0.7 mile south of the Skokomish River and turn west on Skokomish Valley Road. At a Y in 6 miles go right on road No. 23, signed "Dennie Ahl Seed Orchard." In 2.2 miles, where road No. 2202 turns right, continue straight on road No. 23, signed "Brown Creek Campground." In 0.2 mile turn left on road No. 2199. Round a promontory (look down to pastures at the upper limit of the Skokomish floodplain), drop to cross Vance Creek. In 3.3 miles from the turn onto road No. 2199, road No. 2254 (not signed) and the railroad grade join in from the right. At 4.5 miles from road No. 23 is a T at Bingham Creek; go right and stay on the main road, a wide mainline. At 2 miles from Bingham Creek is a sideroad right, perhaps inconspicuously signed "South Mountain 820." Turn up it, immediately starting to climb. In 0.5 mile is a big switchback. Park here, elevation 950 feet.

The road is perfectly drivable beyond—all the way to the summits—but the views from the near-naked slopes start almost immediately and demand constant attention. On an early-melting south slope, the route makes an excellent snowline-prober, the views richly rewarding long before the summit. Winding into valleys, out on spurs, crossing saddles, cutting through walls of rubbly basalt and harder pillow lava, the busy, entertaining way ascends in panoramas uninterrupted by the shrub plantation. Flower gardens on lava walls and in creeklets compete for attention—fields of lupine and beargrass especially striking. In 3 miles, at 2750 feet, is a saddle in the summit ridge, adding views north. Left 1/2 mile is West Peak, 3125 feet, formerly with a lookout tower, now bare and lonesome. Right an up-and-down ridgecrest 1 1/4 miles is radio-towered East Peak, 3000 feet. Both are essential.

Here on the scarp that without prelude leaps up 2500 feet are views that demand large-area maps and long hours. Close at hand, of course, are Olympics: a foreground of ridges and valleys being totally denuded of trees, one of the most surrealistic scenes of clearcutting in all the Northwest; footstool peaks, Dennie Ahl and Dow; and the rugged heights, The Brothers, Washington, Ellinor, Pershing, Cooper, and Cruiser. The East Peak (this is the one you see while driving up the Skokomish) gives the classic look down to the pastured floodplain of the valley curving around to join Hood Canal at the Great Bend. The West Peak (whose basalt surprisingly is capped with conglomerate) gives the dramatic vista to Grays Harbor. Below south is the forest plateau where the Puget Glacier terminated. Beyond this gulf where the meltwater streams flowed, including the Pretty Big River of ice-dammed rivers from the east side of the Olympics, rise the Black Hills, beyond which rolled the Really Big River from the

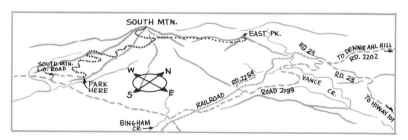

Hood Canal and Green and Gold mountains from Jorsted Point

Cascades; beyond that valley (now the Chehalis) are the Doty and Willapa Hills. Close enough below to see the house the Spring twins grew up in is Shelton, mills pluming. Then, saltwaterways, cities, Cascades. For purposes of this book Ira Spring spent the night on the summit, viewing lights from Aberdeen to Olympia to Everett, and was so knocked out he forgot to take a picture.

Round trip (both peaks) 9¹/₂ miles, allow 7 hours
High point 3125 feet, elevation gain 2800 feet
February-December

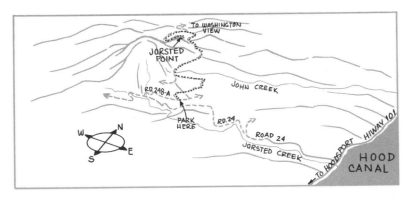

Jorsted Point (map—page 201)

Climb by flower-brilliant walls of pillow lava to a high viewpoint. Look up and down Hood Canal from the Hamma Hamma to the Lilliwaup to the Skokomish. Look east over Green and Gold (Blue) Mountains on the Kitsap Peninsula to Puget Sound and towers of downtown Seattle and volcanoes of the Cascades.

Drive US 101 north of Hoodsport to Jorsted Creek and on the north side turn west on the unsigned road, at first blacktop, then gravel, there signed "Road No. 24." At a Y in 1.1 miles keep straight left on road No. 24. In 2.2 more miles, at 700 feet, turn right on lesser and perhaps unsigned road No. 248A, which passes a gated waterworks and twists and turns up and out of the Jorsted valley. In a scant 1 mile 248A levels out at 997 feet and an obscure sideroad reverse-turns left. Park here.

The narrow, steep track is a pleasant footroad rarely molested by wheels of any kind. The way switchbacks and passes through an interesting cleft between the mountainside and a high knoll, then bends around a corner into the valley of John Creek. Now begins the rock-garden walk, vertical walls of pillow lava colorful in season with alumroot, stonecrop, Scouler's bluebells, pearly everlasting, St. John's wort, starflower, penstemon, currant. Now, too, there are windows over the John valley to saltwater.

In 1¼ miles a lesser sideroad switchbacks left; proceed straight ahead, soon crossing a lovely splash of John Creek. Now the scene shifts from deep, cool second-growth to dry woods, scrubby scrawny trees, of a burn. More basalt rubble, more windows, and more flowers—rhododendron (gorgeous in June) and beargrass. At 2¾ miles the rude track switchbacks to the ridge crest at 2100 feet.

Here is a Y. For a sidetrip take the right, contouring about 1 mile above Washington Creek to a saddle with views of Washington, Pershing, Stone, and the Skokomish valley.

For the top continue left, straight, on "Heliport" road, and in a final scant 1 mile switchback twice to the small, little-used heliport atop brushy-open Jorsted Point, 2300 feet.

Though not the highest spot around, this is the best viewpoint. Burned and cleared, the crest has only small trees amid goldenrod, fireweed, rhododendron, silverleaf, salal, and beargrass. The panorama east is grand. Boats speed and sail up and down Hood Canal. Just below north is the hamlet of Eldon on the Hamma Hamma delta. South are valleys of Jorsted and Eagle Creeks, Lilliwaup Bay and River, and, far south at the Great Bend, the wide delta of the Skokomish. The wildwood far shore of the Canal extends from Bald Point to Dewatto Bay and north to Holly, Seabeck. Dominated by Green and Gold, the Kitsap Peninsula sprawls, all the wildland of its Tahuya Peninsula near and clear. Beyond, silvery waterways of Puget Sound. Seattle, Issaquah Alps, Cascades. The mill plumes mark Shelton. Another identifies Tacoma.

Round trip (with sidetrip) 9½ miles, allow 6 hours
High point 2300 feet, elevation gain 1300 feet
All year

Webb Lookout (map—page 203)

In a straight line with Green and Gold on the Kitsap Peninsula and the Issaquah Alps east of Seattle, both prominent in its panorama, this peak can be imagined to be a companion remnant of the "Old Mountains" now incorporated in the Olympics. The view is to everywhere. In addition, here is the most intimate straight-down look-from-on-high to Hood Canal, where myriad boats draw white lines over blue waters.

Drive US 101 to 15 miles north of Lilliwaup. Just 0.2 mile north of Fulton Creek turn off west on Fulton Creek Road–Seamont Road, signed "2510-012." Stick with the obvious main road as it climbs to a T at 2 miles from US 101.

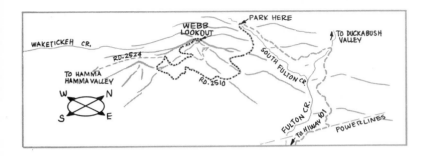

When to stop driving, start walking? The most satisfying trip is from beach to summit, the nearly unique opportunity presented by this route. For a shorter day, through, turn left at the T and drive 2.5 more miles, crossing Fulton Creek (pretty), to the crossing of South Fork Fulton Creek (also). The suggested compromise starts here, elevation 1250 feet.

Beyond the T the route is an old logging railroad grade sliced in the steep Olympic scarp; watch for ghosts of old trestles. It's a lovely footroad tunneling in spindly trees, a 1938 Forest Service plantation after a forest fire whose silver snags are everywhere still. Traffic is rare, walkers practically never bothered by razzers. Woods pleasures are sweet, the more so in the season of forest flowers. But views are the feature and at 1³/₄ miles, 1700 feet, the first window gives promise of what awaits on high. More windows maintain the interest, as do rhododendrons, and gardens on rubbly basalt walls. At 3¹/₄ miles, just after the road (No. 2510) passes through a 2000-foot saddle in a spur ridge, is a junction with better road No. 2524 (a bore to walk) up from the Hamma Hamma. Switchback right on it and swing around the corner into nearly continuous whoopee views. In ³/₄ miles, at 2400 feet, this good new (logging) road continues straight; switchback left on a little old road.

Mt. Washington from Webb Lookout

SOUTH OLYMPIC PENINSULA

In the final $^1/_2$ mile to the summit a sideroad left a short bit gives the best look down Waketickeh Creek to the Hamma Hamma, and to Washington and Pershing. Above looms the bald knob of East Rock, 4269 feet, blocking the view of nearby The Brothers.

And then the 2775-foot summit. Here came the older surveyor late in the fall of 1978, nearly 2 years to the day since the start of his *Footsore* journeys. He looked up and down the Olympic front from South to Jupiter. And up and down the Canal from the Great Bend to Dewatto Bay, Holly, and Bangor. And over the Kitsap Peninsula to peaks ringing the Puget Trough from Black Hills to Rainier to his home-base Issaquah Alps to Index to Glacier to Baker. Behold, it was very good.

Round trip 9$^1/_2$ miles, allow 7 hours
High point 2775 feet, elevation gain 1600 feet
February-December

INDEX

INDEX